THE CLASS OF FOOTBALL

THE CLASS OF FOOTBALL

WORDS OF HARD-EARNED WISDOM FROM LEGENDS OF THE GRIDIRON

EDITED BY

ADAM SCHEFTER

WILLIAM MORROW

An Imprint of HarperCollinsPublishers

All photographs courtesy of the Pro Football Hall of Fame.

HarperCollins books may be purchased for educational, business, or sales promotional use. For information please write: Special Markets Department, HarperCollins Publishers, 10 East 53rd Street, New York, NY 10022.

FIRST EDITION

Designed by Lovedog Studio

Library of Congress Cataloging-in-Publication Data has been applied for.

ISBN 978-0-06-166253-9

09 10 11 12 13 OV/RRD 10 9 8 7 6 5 4 3 2 1

To my Hall-of-Fame family, Sharri, Devon, and Dylan—there should be bronze busts of you for putting up with me. I love you.

We thank thee for this great sport of football, not only for the pleasure we derive as spectators, but also for the invaluable training that young men across America in high schools, colleges, and the professional rank derive as they participate. There are lessons in sportsmanship, fair play, and teamwork.

We ask that it may always be so and that the many who lead and coach, these who are to be enshrined here today, the stars of yesterday, as well as those who are the stars of today, might be aware of the tremendous influence they exert on American youth. May that influence always be in the right direction. Help them to be aware that to whom much is given much shall be required.

We pray also for those many young men who've exchanged the football uniform for that of a solider, and who now serve this nation in the armed forces around the world. We ask thy protection upon them and pray for the day when they can be returned to this land.

—REVEREND HAROLD HENNIGER,
PASTOR OF THE CANTON BAPTIST TEMPLE,
1966 INDUCTION CEREMONIES

Check out exclusive audio and video clips
of these speeches and more at
www.classoffootball.com

CONTENTS

FOREWORD

THINK BACK TO GRADE SCHOOL, TO HIGH SCHOOL, TO your favorite teacher. Mine was football.

The tackle football games we used to have at Macomb Street playground, right up the block from where we lived in Washington, D.C., taught me a great deal. My brothers, my friends, whoever was around, we'd take off our jackets, our sweatshirts, whatever layers of clothes we could. Those layers would form the outlines of the sidelines and end zones, an instant football field. Everyone played. Everyone tried. Everyone battled. We'd play every day, as long as we could. Right then, I started to get a taste of what was unique about football. There was nothing like the physical challenges, the collective goals, and the multiple sacrifices of it in teaching us what it took to be successful.

Lessons came in other ways, too. One time, when I was eight years old, in the second grade at John Eaton Elementary School in Washington, our class was told that two Redskins, Brig Owens and Mike Bass, were coming in to talk to our class. You remember Mike Bass. He was the Redskins safety that intercepted Dolphins kicker Garo Yepremian's failed field goal with two minutes left in the fourth quarter of Super Bowl VII and returned it forty-nine yards for a touchdown. It's still replayed, even now. Mr. Owens and Mr. Bass came to our school and delivered a message I still remember today. It was all about what it took to be successful. In their case, it was all about hard work, determination, sacrifice. What was true then is still true now.

As powerful as that moment was, the turning point of my childhood came in high school, in the fall of 1976, after another football practice. At the time, I was a tight end. We were running laps and the moment was so memorable, I can still tell you the exact spot I was standing on the track when the thought hit me. Right then, I realized other players might be better and faster, but none would work any harder. I could outrun them simply by outworking them. Right then I learned if you worked harder, you could achieve. So I just kept going.

I kept going whenever any goal was important. Right after college, I kicked off my NFL letter-writing campaign, mailing about forty letters to NFL teams, NFL Properties, and the NFL Management Council, and one I still have to NFL commissioner Pete Rozelle.

July 2, 1981

Dear Mr. Rozelle:

I am writing to you in reference to any job openings you may have in your offices.

Having just finished my undergraduate education at Washington and Jefferson College this past May, I am presently looking for a position in the management of professional sports. Being an avid football fan, I have always desired a career in the NFL. Consequently, as a great admirer of you, it would be both an honor and a pleasure to work for you in any position that may be available.

Thank you for your consideration. I look forward to hearing from you.

Respectfully,
Roger S. Goodell

I received a big pile of rejection letters, including many from the NFL owners that eventually hired me as their commissioner. But Commissioner Rozelle did have one of his top aides, Don Weiss, interview me. And after our interview, I sent him handwritten letters almost every week, not taking no for an answer, until finally he realized that this kid must really want this job. In 1982, Weiss offered me a three-month internship—probably just to get me to stop writing him. His offer allowed me to combine my undergraduate degree from Washington and Jefferson with the masters I went on to earn from Rozelle and Tagliabue. Those men—my mentors—shaped my knowledge and beliefs about the NFL.

Some of them: Change before you're forced to change. Address issues directly. Look around corners. Challenge assumptions. Don't assume you know the answers; be a good listener. Never be satisfied with results. Find a better solution. Always look for a better way. Hire a great team with strong skills. Set the bar high and raise it continually. Make people accountable. Have integrity. I always tell our team here at the NFL, "It's not just results, it's how you achieve those results that counts. There can be no compromise between results and integrity."

Football has taught me that teamwork is critical. We see NFL teams prove it each season. We see Hall-of-Fame players accentuate it during their enshrinement speeches each summer. Just listen to what they say. Listen closely. Read the passages in this book. Notice how Hall of Famers don't reflect on their talents; they reflect on their coaches, their teammates, their family and friends. They do not make it about what they accomplished individually; they make it about what they accomplished collectively. They recognize everything and, more important, everyone it took to make them successful. It is vital that the players of today connect themselves to the league's rich history. The players of today need to recognize the contributions of the many that came before them.

The priority of teamwork is one of the concepts that makes football so unique. Of course there are many. People ask me all the time, as much as any other question I get, "What makes football special?" Plenty. It's all in the pages of this book, all the lessons there are to be learned. It's the camaraderie and the contact, the competition and the passion, the strategy and the energy, the elements and the emotion. It's so much. There's nothing better than walking into Lambeau Field on a snowy day in January, with close to seventy-three thousand screaming fans, and two teams battling the way they would if they were on any playground in the country.

But maybe my favorite part of football is that every game, like every day, brings a different challenge. Every game, like every day, brings a different opponent. Games, like days, have unexpected changes and challenges. Every time there is a chance to rise up and win. I learned this back at Macomb Street playground in Washington and in the commissioner's office at 280 Park Avenue in New York.

Football keeps inspiring me. Football keeps teaching me.

—Roger Goodell

INTRODUCTION

ANNUALLY AND INEVITABLY, NO PLACE COMBINES TOUGH
guys and teardrops quite like Canton.

As the most famous figures in football history stand at a podium
in Fawcett Stadium, in the shadows of the Pro Football Hall of Fame,
at the entrance to immortality, their lives and accomplishments flash
before them. These men pause to reflect on a day that links past
achievement with present glory.

Some inductees stay strong. They manage to make it through their
speech seemingly unaffected. Like they did throughout their football careers, they hold up and don't break down. This is what Hall of
Famers do.

But many do not. They succumb to the moment, just as they were
warned they would by the men who have been in the same position
in previous years. This also is what Hall of Famers do. They cry for
what it means to come from random playgrounds to football's most
hallowed ground. They cry for the obstacles they have overcome, the
odds they have beaten, the challenges they have conquered. They cry
for all the people—parents, siblings, coaches, teammates—who stood
by them, supported them, and lifted them. And they cry for all those
who did not live to see this momentous occasion.

On one August night, in one window of time, with thousands of fans sitting in front of them and living Hall of Famers seated behind them, their lives come full circle, and they are hit with the realization that they have made a team from which they never can be cut. The power of the moment arouses heartfelt and profound thoughts.

Gone are the clichés that they may have fed to sportswriters over the seasons; the words are boxed up and packed away. In their place come real words, pulled from deep within each Hall of Famer, philosophies that helped propel these men to the type of greatness to which we all aspire.

Each man gets his turn, one final performance in a football stadium. Only this time, the helmet is off, and the player appears as himself—not in a number or at a position, but as a man, a son, a husband, a father, a friend, a person whom fans rarely got to see during his great career. Now people hang on his words instead of his play. Childhoods are recalled, parents are praised, history is retraced, mentors are thanked, lessons are taught, guidance is given, hope is granted, and faith is restored.

Every one of these speeches comes in midsummer, on the same stage, at the same podium, in the same high school stadium, in the same northeastern Ohio city, twenty-four miles south of Akron and sixty miles south of Cleveland. For years, the enshrinement ceremonies were performed on the steps of the Pro Football Hall of Fame. But the ceremony, like the sport itself, blossomed in ways our football forefathers could not imagine. Speeches have evolved into events. The ceremony now has moved to a stadium. It now is broadcast on two networks, NFL Network and ESPN. Canton is the warm and welcoming host to it all.

But Canton prides itself on more than just football. Our twenty-fifth president, William McKinley, lived there and is interred there. The musician Marilyn Manson came from Canton, as did the R&B group the O'Jays and R&B singer Macy Gray. New York Yankees catcher Thurman Munson grew up in Canton and was killed in a plane crash there as well. And three Hall-of-Fame football players—Dan Dierdorf, Marion Motley, and Alan Page—all hail from Canton, where they were taught the Hall-of-Fame principles they later espoused in their induction speeches.

Canton's most notable contributions come from the men whose bronze busts reside there. Yet, as memorable as their words were on the day of induction, they were forgotten, not unlike the careers of some of the Hall of Fame's first inductees. But now their words, as well as their legacies, can be recalled.

Their words have been dug up, delved into, sifted through, edited down, and brought together on these pages. It is a book filled with wit and wisdom, football and faith, that has been in the making almost fifty years, since 1963, the year the Pro Football Hall of Fame opened.

When former Washington Redskins head coach Joe Gibbs—Class of 1996—was told in December 2007, hours before his team battled the Chicago Bears, that the most memorable words of every Hall of Famer were being gathered for publication, he was stunned.

"I didn't even know they existed," Gibbs said as he stood outside his team's locker room in FedEx Field.

Then his tone went from surprise to excited. "How do I get to see them?" he asked.

Simple, coach. Just turn the page.

—*Adam Schefter, February 2009*

THE CLASS OF FOOTBALL

CHAPTER 1

CHILDHOOD

MIKE SINGLETARY

ONLY THE CHOSEN GET TO WEAR THE FAMILIAR GOLD jackets presented to each Pro Football Hall-of-Fame inductee. But anyone can grow up playing, watching, or following football.

Every child remembers the touch football games he used to play in the street or the tackle ones at the neighborhood school. Every child had a favorite player whom he used to imitate in those games, be it Joe Namath throwing another laser, Earl Campbell bowling over a defender, or Lynn Swann making an acrobatic catch. Every child remembers the famous football plays from his youth—"The Catch" or the "The Drive."

As a child, almost all dreams are attainable. Yet the one that out-distances most everyone is advancing to Canton, Ohio, and the Pro Football Hall of Fame.

Only the fortunate make it. Only the very best do.

■ ■ ■ ■

Mike Singletary
Chicago Bears Linebacker
Class of 1998

An All-Pro selection nine times,
Singletary also played in ten Pro Bowls.

Presented by His Wife, Kim Singletary

It's only fitting that we honor the character of this football player. For that truly belongs in a Hall of Fame. The countless hours of film he watched is legendary. It was imperative to him to be able to anticipate any play before it happened. But few knew that he took it upon himself to learn the responsibility of each member of that defense on each play. And in his later years, he stayed after practice to develop his backup linebacker and fine-tune his skills. I asked Mike once if he didn't get nervous about helping the player and putting himself out of a job. And he assured me that it would only make himself and the team better.

But the quality that I most admire is his ability to listen. Whether it's a meeting with a coach, a player in need, his Sunday telephone conversations with his mom, or even on a porch swing with my grandfather, he is never too busy to give you his undivided attention.

When you walk through the halls of this building, you get a sense of the history of those who loved this game and helped form the foundation of what it is today. It's only fitting that a young boy from Houston, Texas, who dreamed of an opportunity to have the privilege to play this game that he loved, be enshrined today with those who have dedicated themselves to being not only great football players but great human beings. Men like George Halas, Vince Lombardi, Tom Landry, and Roger Staubach all helped Mike form some of his intensity and work ethic.

This is an age when professional athletes sometimes run away from their responsibility as role models. Well, this is one man who not only embraces that responsibility but finds greater joy in training men and women to be their own children's role model.

Mike Singletary

This story began a long way back—Houston, Texas—when I was twelve years old because there were a lot of things happening at that particular time in my family. We were going through a lot. We were trying to go to the next level. And I am the last of ten kids and when you have ten kids, sometimes it's a little bit of a struggle to make it work.

That year when I was twelve, Mom and Dad went through a divorce. When I was five years old, my brother, Dale, passed away and my second brother would pass away when I was twelve. That was a tough year. I had no confidence, had no self-esteem. I was just a young ghetto boy in Houston, Texas, trying to figure out who he was and where he was going to go from there.

And I want to tell you today, my mom sat me down one day when I was moping around and feeling sorry for myself, close to giving up. I had begun listening to everybody else in the neighborhood who said, "No one gets out of here. No one has ever made it out of here and you won't, either. Besides, you don't have the ability, you don't have the skill, you don't have anything."

My mom sat me down that day and she let me know something that I always knew, but man, I needed to hear it. Mom said, "Son, I want you to know something. I want you to know that there is greatness in you, there's something special about you. I prayed for you before you were born and every day since. It's in there! You've got to go find it yourself. I'm going to do everything I can as a mother to get it out of there but you've got to find it."

She put her hands on my forearm and she asked me if I could become the man around the house. I said, "Mom, I can do that." That day I went to my room and I wrote down my goals. And at twelve years old, it went something like this: find a way to get a scholarship to go to college, become an All-American in college, get my degree, go to the NFL, and buy my mom a house and take care of her for the rest of my life.

When I think back on that time, I think how important it is that we need to let people know, let our kids know, let our spouses know, how important they are to us. Don't keep it a secret. Because that day, my life began.

■ ■ ■ ■

Chuck Bednarik
Philadelphia Eagles Center/Linebacker
Class of 1967

Bednarik was selected to eight Pro Bowls. He missed three games in fourteen years, and was named the NFL's all-time center in 1969.
When you're a kid just coming up, I guess you look forward to being a high school football player. And then you go to your next stepping stone, you want to become a college All-American. And when you achieve that, you want to go into the pro ranks. And then, of course, the pinnacle or highlight of your entire career comes on this particular day—entering the Hall of Fame.

■ ■ ■ ■

Andy Robustelli
Los Angeles Rams and New York Giants Defensive End
Class of 1971

Robustelli anchored defenses in eight championship games and was named the NFL's top player in 1962.
This is a long way from that little kid that used to love to go to the store for his mother because when she needed Italian bread, it looked

like a football, and he could take it and toss it up into the air and then run from the store to his home yelling, "Robustelli's on the goal line! He's home!"

Well, it was a long way from the offensive days of a little kid to the defensive days of today.

As I look upon this place at the Hall of Fame, I try to be very realistic because I think that, in life, one learns to become realistic when he uses the tools that have been available to him. In my life, football has been a tremendous tool. Looking at myself, I know that no one does anything alone. There's a great family, a wife, hardworking parents, and a lot of good defensive people.

I look at the days and I think about the days that I looked at all those films and, like our society, I think I was looking for what is right. And I hope that these young kids today that participate in sports are looking for what is right, because until you can look at yourself as an athlete on film or wherever and say, "Yes, it's me, it's my fault, I was a little lazy, I wasn't dedicated, I expected my teammates to do what I was supposed to do," or "I took the easy route, I really didn't try," and until we as athletes can look at ourselves and admit failure, then do we start to grow.

And as I look at our country, some people say we are divided. Well, maybe this is the start, ladies and gentlemen. Because in being divided, you know where to start. So, as we do in sports, let's look at ourselves and let's start to put all of the pieces together like so many men that are here have done over the years in their pro football lives. They've taken failures and made them successes.

■　■　■　■

Ollie Matson
Chicago Cardinals, Los Angeles Rams, Detroit Lions,
and Philadelphia Eagles Halfback
Class of 1972

Matson scored nine touchdowns on kickoff and punt returns and, in 1959, was traded for nine players.

When I was a youngster, I didn't have the money and my family didn't have the money to buy a football. We had to take a can and wrap it up, and we played with it. So in playing with this can, I used to tell my mother, "I'm going to be a football player." My mother had a different opinion. She said, "No, son, you're going to be a doctor." I said, "No, I can't be. I want to be a football player." So we went on and proved to her that I was a football player.

I think the most significant thing in my life is that there were many people that I have met that had the faith and courage that I could do a lot of things. And I would like to talk now about making the 1952 Olympics. I know many of you know or remember a man by the name of Dink Templeton, the late Dink Templeton [a track-and-field athlete and coach].

Dink told me, "Ollie Matson, you will never make the '52 Olympics because you have been playing football for four years. Those fellows have been training for four years, their legs are trained to run and your legs are not."

I looked at Dink and I said, "You know, Dink, if the boat sails, I'll be on it." I made up my mind then that Ollie Matson was going to make the '52 Olympics, and I did. And when I did, I walked up to Dink and I gave him my medal and I said, "You know, Dink, there is one thing in life that I guess that you must have forgotten and that was this: When a man wants to do something and he has worked diligently, honestly, and sincerely, as I did, you can't beat him. There has to be a way."

And as I look through the stadium today and at a number of young people, I would like to say to you, "Don't quit." Don't always ask for something without working for it. Because this life is not that way. You only get out of life what you put into it. And I put a lot into it. And now I'm receiving a lot.

Another thing I would like to say at this moment as I look at my wife is that we have four youngsters. We are pushing them to know that you can make it if you try. And as I close today, I would like to say I have many youngsters in a Los Angeles high school and I tell my young people this: "Don't come to me unless you want to work."

Football will enable you to do many things. And I had a football player tell me when I was voted to the Hall of Fame, he said, "Mr. Matson, you may be in the Hall of Fame this year, but I'm going to make it next year." And I looked at this young man who didn't know what he was saying and I said, "Son, look, I hope that you can make it next year. But remember, it took me twenty-six years."

■ ■ ■ ■

Raymond Berry
Baltimore Colts Wide Receiver
Class of 1973

Berry caught 631 passes for 9,275 yards and sixty-eight touchdowns. He set the NFL title game mark in 1958 with twelve catches for 178 yards.

Presented by Colts and Jets Coach Weeb Ewbank

According to our scouts and criteria used in picking ends, Raymond had none of the characteristics you normally attribute to a great pass receiver. As a matter of fact, we used to build up Raymond's shoe because he had a back condition and also wore a brace for that back. The doctors here gave him his first set of contact lenses, which made him see better, and then he had special rib pads.

It is true also that he wasn't possessed with blinding speed, he wasn't physically overpowering, and he didn't stand several inches taller than the defenders trying to stop him. However, Raymond's pass patterns were so minutely perfected that he was almost unstoppable. Raymond had many other things going for him—unusual jumping ability, a pair of fantastic hands, and a dogged sense of purpose that allowed him to become nothing less than the very best.

As one newspaperman in Baltimore said, "It wasn't the great passes always thrown by Johnny Unitas that made this a great Baltimore team but rather it was the great passes that Raymond caught." There may be pass receivers blessed with more natural ability than Raymond but few have ever approached the standards of proficiency that became a weekly habit for Raymond. And it should be emphasized that Raymond, and Raymond alone, made himself into the superstar he was.

Raymond Berry

When I came into professional football with Baltimore, I can assure you that the furthest thing from my mind was making the Hall of Fame. I was hoping that I would make the first thirty-three players for just a couple of years.

I don't know if you've ever considered how long the odds are for a young Texan high school football player to end up in this spot today. The odds are unbelievable, and the reason how it happens is it depends on a whole lot of folks and a whole lot of things going for you.

I'd like to start with my parents because I came from a home that gave me background and stability that a football player needs to play the game. I was born in the state of Texas and they take great pride in their high school athletic programs in that state. I benefited from the work that many men have put into that athletic program because I had the opportunity that a program provides for a youngster to grow.

In every level, an athlete is dependent upon coaches seeing something in him, encouraging him, and giving him a chance. When I was in elementary school, high school where I played under my dad, when I went to Southern Methodist University, and then when I went to the pros, I always had coaches who believed in me and gave me a chance and encouraged me along the way. And if it had not been for the men who made pro football possible, I would have gone into some other profession.

■　■　■　■

Ray Nitschke
Green Bay Packers Linebacker
Class of 1978

Nitschke was the MVP of the 1962 title game and was named the NFL's all-time linebacker in 1969.

Presented by Packers Assistant and Head Coach Phil Bengston

Ray's enthusiasm was, of course, always obvious on the field, both in games and in practice. But he was also a very enthusiastic student of the game and was very attentive in squad meetings and shoptalks.

I remember one week we were preparing for an opponent and, in the film study, I asked Bill Forester to keep track of the first-down plays, I asked Dan Currie to keep a chart of the second-down plays, I asked Willie Wood if he would watch the third-down plays, and I asked Willie Davis if he would keep the short yardage plays.

And before I had a chance to assign a category to Ray, he said, "What do you want me to keep? Quiet?"

Ray Nitschke

Football is a game that I enjoyed and a game that I tried to play as hard as I could, never dreaming, never thinking, that someday I would have the honor of being enshrined and immortalized here in this wonderful city of Canton, Ohio. . . .

The Green Bay Packers organization is here and boy, I am so proud to have played here for fifteen years. I do want to say how important the game of football was in my life.

When I was a child, I lost my mother when I was thirteen and I lost my father when I was three years old. My brother, Bob, became my guardian, and he more or less adopted me and gave me direction, and he put me on the right direction of sports.

And I played sports, and I played football, and football gave me a chance to express myself, to get recognition, and to do something well. I was committed to the game of football, and I will never forget the great game that it is, and that it gave Ray Nitschke a chance for an education, to better himself, and be a better human being.

Looking back at it all in a nutshell, looking back being a quarterback in high school outside of Chicago, being a fullback at the University of Illinois, being a linebacker with the Green Bay Packers, I just wish I could go back twenty years—more than twenty years—and do it all over again.

■ ■ ■ ■

Jim Otto
Oakland Raiders Center
Class of 1980

Named the AFL's all-time center, Otto played in 308
games, twelve AFL All-Star games or Pro Bowls, and six
AFL/AFC title games.

Presented by Raiders Owner Al Davis

For two memorable decades in the last twenty years, the Oakland Raiders have had the greatest players, the greatest coaches, the greatest plays, and performed in the greatest games ever played in the annals of sports. During the period of 1960 to 1974, the Oakland Raiders had the best record in professional football. Among the greatest players, the quarterbacks during these years, were names like Flores, Lamonica, the legendary Blanda, Stabler. But there was one constant, one center, one captain, one original Raider who started in each of the 210 consecutive regular-season games during those fifteen years. His name was Jim Otto, his number was 00.

For more than a decade he was the standard of excellence by which centers were judged in professional football. He was the most honored offensive lineman in the history of professional football. But statistics are just a measure of accomplishment, not really the measure of a man.

If it is true that great men inspire in others the will to be great, that alone qualifies Jim to be a great man. He had towering courage in spite of his first injuries. His loyalty, devotion, dedication still carry on in Oakland and reach the rewards of victory. While the word "company man" has a bad and good connotation, Jim Otto was an organization man. He played football for the organization, he wanted to win for the organization. Plain old-fashioned wholesomeness was not passé. He was an organizational dream.

The enshrinement here in Canton of Jim Otto is like a reaffirmation of the values and the virtues of what is still the American way of life. Religion, family, and country, as he preferred them in that order. The fires that burn brightest in him are for the great love and enthusiasm he had and has for the game of football and everyone and everything in life.

Jim Otto, the seasons have stopped rolling, the cannons are still, the playing field is quiet, the crowd no longer roars, that silver-and-black uniform is retired. But I can still faintly hear the National Anthem and those of us who saw the Raiders battle to the top during the last decades will never forget you and now, no one else will forget you, either. Because the name of Jim Otto will ring down the corridors of remembered times as long as this Hall of Fame immortalizes the greatest warriors of the greatest game. My friend, someone that I will always love, someone who has been a vital part of my life, and I will always hope I have been a vital part of his, my friend, Jim Otto, Hall of Famer.

Jim Otto

It started with a dream and it wasn't an unconscious dream. It was a daydream. It started when I was about eleven years old and part of that dream is coming to an end today, but the rest of the dream will go on.

Daydreams are the best because you can always remember them and you can work on a daydream to make it come true. My favorite daydream was that I was going to be a professional football player someday, and it was at the age of eleven while listening to a football game on the radio that I told my grandfather that someday I was going to be a professional football player. And it wasn't long until that day began. Not all dreams come true, it takes a lot of dedication, a lot of pride, and, above all, a lot of faith and prayer.

My minister, Pastor E. H. Bertermann, back in Wallsall, Wisconsin, was a big help in getting me going as a youngster. Back in those days things were hard. There wasn't too much money and at one time I started getting cards from the YMCA giving me a membership. Then when I was thirty-four years old, I went home to Wallsall for a visit to speak at the high school dinner and Pastor E. H. Bertermann was there to give the invocation. It was at that time, he told me, "James, when you went to school, there was a little bit of shyster in you and it had to come out and I knew the only way to get it out was to send you to the YMCA." He was the one who gave me the membership to the YMCA all those years.

So you can see God put these people out there for me so I could be guided properly. The dream must go on now, but only to my other plans and that is to help my fellow man in some way and to save my own soul.

■ ■ ■ ■

George Blanda
Chicago Bears, Houston Oilers, and
Oakland Raiders Quarterback/Kicker
Class of 1981

In a twenty-six-season, 340-game career with the Bears, Colts, Oilers, and Raiders that turned out to be the longest career in NFL history, Blanda scored 2,002 points.

Presented by Raiders Owner Al Davis

It is true that great men inspire in others the will to be great. George Blanda inspired a whole nation. I used to think that the fires that burn brightest in George was the will to win. It was more important than any single event.

But George Blanda, a fierce competitor, had a God-given killer instinct to make it happen when everything was on the line. He knew how to lead. He knew how to win. I really believe that George was the greatest clutch player that I have ever seen in the history of professional football.

George Blanda, I can hear the roar of the crowd, the clock is ticking down and in a few moments, number 16, you will be here at this microphone and it will be the most important play of your life, your enshrinement in the Pro Football Hall of Fame.

George Blanda

If I had one word to describe how I feel, it is proud. Being proud to be here, being enshrined with the other athletes who had the good fortune to make it to the Pro Football Hall of Fame.

I'm also proud of the fact that I grew up in a very, very small town with a great mom and dad who raised eleven kids in that tradition of playing football in Western Pennsylvania. Proud I grew up in a little town called Youngwood, which was in the heart of football in Western Pennsylvania. I was very proud of my heritage and I developed a lot of character in the early days and learned that with hard work, dedication, discipline, tenacity, and never giving up, you can succeed in improving your life.

I never aspired to be a professional football player. All I wanted was to go to college, get an education, and better my life.

■ ■ ■ ■

Mel Blount
Pittsburgh Steelers Cornerback
Class of 1989

A five-time Pro Bowl selection, Blount intercepted fifty-seven passes that he returned for 736 yards and was named the NFL's Defensive MVP in 1975.

Presented by Steelers Owner Dan Rooney

You've all heard of Amos Alonzo Stagg—he was the great coach that the rules were written to stop. Well, Mel changed the rules in the NFL. He was so big and tough that they changed the bump-and-run rule to stop Mel from dominating wide receivers.

His appearance is dominating, as you can see. But even with the new rules, he continued to defend his position like no one else. Scouts say they don't even look for corners like him anymore because you don't get corners with his size or his speed or who can jump like him.

One time my brother was working on a hot-shot prospect that had a great vertical jump and as Mel wandered through the stadium hall, the prospect touched a mark so high that he bragged it was the top mark. Mel, in his street clothes, then jumped, touched a higher spot, and when he landed, said to the kid, "That is the Steeler mark." And he has made many Steeler marks.

Mel Blount

It is an awful long way from the cotton and tobacco fields of Vidalia, Georgia, to the Hall of Fame here in Canton, Ohio.

It is a great opportunity for my family and young people through-out the country to see exactly what can happen when you are willing to pay the price and when you are willing to make a commitment and when you are willing to give it all you can.

If the odds were against anybody, they were against me. Being the youngest of eleven kids, brought up on a farm in Georgia, a family who lived and prayed and hoped it would feed eleven kids off the land. Out of eleven kids, seven of us were able to go to college because we had the kind of parents that America is thirsty for today, parents who are committed, parents who want to see and will instill in their kids that they strive to be the best.

We have too many young people in this country that are drug addicts. We have too many young people who are too lazy to work. If there is anything we could do as professional athletes, we must give our time. We must give our service to our youngest people and let them understand that they can make it and we need them because they are the greatest resources that this country has, our young people.

A lot of my colleagues said, "Mel, you'll get up here and you'll break down." But I've cried enough. There is a struggle you will pay for anything that you will accomplish. For me, this is an opportunity to get up and say exactly what we represent in the country as athletes.

What we've done on the football field is history. What we will do from this stage on is yet to be seen. . . . I came from a beautiful family, a family that struggled in the Deep South and instilled in its kids that you can do anything if you are willing to pay a price. It doesn't matter where you come from; it matters where you are going. That is what makes the difference between success and failure.

■　■　■　■

Bob St. Clair
San Francisco 49ers Tackle
Class of 1990

An exceptional offensive lineman who also played in goal-line defenses, St. Clair blocked ten field goals in 1956.

This all started when I was nine years old. I was a Cub Scout and a flag bearer in the East-West game out in San Francisco in Kezar Stadium and I can remember looking up and seeing these giant football players and saying to myself, "Oh boy, someday, would I love to be able to play football and be like these giant athletes." Well, needless to say, I played 188 games in that stadium and hold the record today.

I can remember when I was in high school, I got the best advice from my football coach. He told me, "Bob, you are five-foot-nine, you weigh 160 pounds, you're fifteen years old, you're not big enough to make this high school football team. My advice to you is go home and grow a little." Damn it, I did exactly what he said. I grew six inches in one year and put on 60 pounds.

My twelve years with the 49ers were so great. They weren't great in the sense we won championships, but they were great because of the fact that I was able to play with such great football players, my teammates who I dearly love and respect today.

The satisfaction we had when we played as an offensive line is to watch a back like Hugh McElhenny lead you around the end and flatten that DB and get up and watch Hugh go all the way for a touchdown. Or Joe Perry slashing through the line after you flatten the middle linebacker. Or John Henry Johnson, who was very difficult to block for because every time you knocked someone down, he wanted a piece of the action and he would hit into you, too. That's what an offensive lineman gets out of the game.

■ ■ ■ ■

Earl Campbell
Houston Oilers and New Orleans Saints
Running Back
Class of 1991

With four games of two-hundred-plus rushing yards in 1980, Campbell finished his career with 9,407 rushing yards and seventy-four touchdowns.

Presented by Oilers and Saints Coach Bum Phillips

When you draft a guy, first pick in the whole country, you better know something about him besides his height, weight, and speed. The way it worked out with Earl, we didn't know we were going to get to trade for his rights, so I didn't take a whole lot of time studying Earl Campbell. I knew he was the number one pick. I knew he was the best back in the country. But I really didn't study him very much.

It may have been about a week before the draft when we got a chance to trade for him. Just before we made it, I said I better find out just how good a kid he is, too. So I called a guy sitting right here in the audience, who I think a lot of, a good amount of, Darrell Royal. I said, "Coach, what kind of kid is Earl Campbell?"

And his exact words, and I will never forget them, he said, "Bum, he ain't got a hole in him nowhere." And believe me, Darrell Royal, you were right.

He ain't got no holes in him nowhere.

Earl Campbell

Every team I've played on, I've always tried to share with the guys that I played with. And I think if any of them ever had anything to say about Earl Campbell, they would say he is a giver, not a taker.

And there goes my mother, Mrs. Ann Campbell. I was listening to her coming back from the Hall the other day going to the hotel. She has seven boys and four girls, and I am number six in the family. I said, "Everything is great; it's amazing how God blesses you."

She said: "I remember one Sunday morning when I was getting dressed for church and I told your daddy, 'I will never get to go anywhere. I will never get a chance to see anything.' He said, 'Darling, you ought to be careful because you never know what God has in store for you.'"

Well, she said to me, "Who thought I would be here in Canton, Ohio?" I never thought I would be here, Mama, but I am happy you are here.

The other morning I was jogging and I got to thinking what I really wanted to write down and what I really wanted to say, and I might as well be honest. I said, "Earl, stop fooling yourself, you were a speech major in college, but you never really wrote a speech. Just get up there and talk it off the tilt."

But the more and more I tried to write a speech, the one thing about this day beyond football is that my daddy, B. C. Campbell, is up there in heaven with his buddies and he is telling them what a great son he had.

And every day is not a great day in my life. I mean, I am like everybody else. I work hard and that is all I ever do. I got a lady that has been with me twenty-four years. You stay with them so long you kind of forget it. If it was me, some days I would have said, "Earl, I am through with you, son." But she reminds me of a song that Willie Nelson and Merle Haggard wrote called "Tougher Than Leather." That is my wife, Reuna. . . .

I just want to let all you people in America know that there is no place like this. I've never been no place else, but I have heard people talk about it. But I am so proud to be an American. I am so proud of being in the Hall of Fame with the Jim Browns, the Franco Harrises, and someday I'm sure the Walter Paytons and the Tony Dorsetts. But when they say Campbell, I want you all to remember this: the old boy gave it his all.

Walter Payton
Chicago Bears Running Back
Class of 1993

When he retired after thirteen seasons, Payton was the NFL's all-time leading rusher with 16,726 yards and combined net yardage with 21,803.

When you stand up here and you give talks and you give your acceptance speech, there are humorous things that come to mind. One of them is my brother, Eddie Payton, and my sister, Pamela. Because when I was growing up I was the baby and when they had to clean the house on Saturdays and do things when Mom went to work and said, "I want this house clean when I get back," I thought, "Hey, I was the baby, I didn't have to do this." So these guys beat me up.

That's the reason why I had the moves that I did because when you have an angry sister and angry brother chasing you with a broom and a wet dishrag, you tend to pick up moves you never had before. . . .

There was a guy who was supposed to be here today to cointroduce me with my son. But Mr. Jim Finks is having a bout with lung cancer and I want him to know that our prayers are with him because he was the guy who gave me my start. He was the one who called me when I was at Jackson State University the day before the draft and asked me a question. He said, "Walter, how would you like to play for the Chicago Bears?" My answer to him was, "Jim, I will play for anybody."

And that was the way I felt at that particular time, and I think if I would have answered that question any different than the way I did, I probably would have been playing for someone else, maybe even Pittsburgh. But blessings come and blessings go.

The thing I am most proud of and the thing I am most ashamed of coincide with each other. You saw my son up here a few minutes ago and believe me, I had a lump in my throat that was so big it was unbelievable.

I also have a little daughter, Brittney Jeannette Payton. And I think about her also because their mom was with me for those thirteen years I played and believe me, they were not good because I was not the easiest person to get along with. And because of my wanting to give to so many other people, sometimes you tend to neglect the people you truly love the most.

And I want to stand up here and say that in this point of my life, that Jarrett, Brittney, and your mom, you guys will not have to worry about anything in your life, no matter what the situation or how it ends.

I am going to close by saying, life is short, it is oh so sweet. There are a lot of people that we meet as we walk through these hallowed halls, but the things that mean the most are the friendships that you make and take along with you.

■ ■ ■ ■

Tony Dorsett
Dallas Cowboys and Denver Broncos Running Back
Class of 1994

During his career in Dallas and Denver, Dorsett ran for 12,739 yards, caught 398 passes, and scored ninety-one touchdowns.

Presented by Cowboys Coach Tom Landry

Tony holds the all-time record of a ninety-nine-yard run versus Minnesota in January 1983. The only thing that was surprising at that time was, we only had ten men on the field. That shows you how much coaching has to do with running.

Tony Dorsett

I come from a blue-collar background, my hometown of Aliquippa, Pennsylvania, and when I was growing up, I pretty much grew up in two different worlds. Played ball and studied in Hopewell Township and went home to Aliquippa. It was like school was one environment and the streets were another. But looking back on it, I just want to say that it was probably the best thing that ever happened to me, not going to school with all my buddies, because it gave me a different perspective on learning and on life.

You know, when we were growing up, I didn't know if we were rich or poor. We were growing up in government housing in the projects, but I didn't know if that meant that we were poor. And the truth is, I had everything that I wanted and everything that I needed. And that is a tribute to my parents.

I can remember very distinctly the first time I tried out for football in Hopewell Township, my buddy Michael Kimbrough and myself. We stuffed rocks in our pockets to try to make the weight limit. And we were still too light. When I did start playing football, I was scared. I remember the first time I ever touched a football I was so afraid of getting hit, I took off like a little rabbit and ran seventy-five yards for a touchdown. . . .

Coming out of high school, everyone said I was too small to be a major college running back. There was one guy that didn't think so. His name was Johnny Majors. I still use today that advice that Coach Majors gave us. Coach Majors would say the little things make big things happen. It is the little things you do—the extra studying in the classroom, running a little farther, envisioning what might happen in a ball game and planning your reactions—that make the big things.

There was another coach at Pitt, Coach Jackie Sherrill. Jackie Sherrill recruited me to the University of Pittsburgh and gave me a chance. He gave me hope. And he also told me with my size, he said, "Tony, to play major college football, you will probably get knocked around playing the Penn States and Notre Dames of the world."

He was right; I did get knocked around. And I remember that sometimes, sometimes coming through the sidelines so beat and bruised up, I didn't want to go back out there and Coach Sherrill would be there to meet me at the sidelines and say, "Oh, come on, this team needs you. We need you to get back out there for us." Coach, I just want to tell you, you helped toughen me up. You helped me deal with pain, pain I took for being so small. You also helped me understand that if I wanted to succeed, I had to put the pain behind me and keep going. . . .

Before I leave, I would just like to say a big word to all those people that are out there trying to make something of themselves. And that is, I am good testimony that you can accomplish just about anything you want to in life. What I'm trying to say is, "Don't listen to other kids when they tell you that you cannot achieve your dreams. Go out and set some goals for yourself and try to accomplish them. It is what you think of yourself that will make the biggest difference in yourself. And just remember these words: you can, you can, you can."

■　■　■　■

Dan Dierdorf
St. Louis Cardinals Offensive Tackle
Class of 1996

Named the NFL's best blocker three times, Dierdorf was voted to six Pro Bowls and All-Pro five times.

Presented by Cardinals Coach Jim Hanifan

It is my pleasure, and indeed it is an honor, to introduce Dan Dierdorf today. It's a well-deserved honor of debt for Dan, but it's also unique, and so many of you out there know that.

Think of the odds, a young man, from Canton, born and raised right here, started his football career here, goes off to college, becomes an All-American, drafted in the National Football League, played thirteen years, and then comes back today to his hometown, to Canton, and be enshrined into the Hall of Fame. Unbelievable, the odds.

I'd like to tell you how he did it. I spent ten years with Dan Dierdorf, and I know him extremely well as a player and a person. He is one of those unique persons who has all the qualities to attain greatness in whatever field he would have chosen. And he's done rather well, I'd say, in both fields that he has taken on.

As a player, he had that rare combination of size and speed, quickness, strength, and balance. And yet more than that, and what really kind of separated him apart from so many of the others, he had intelligence. Believe me, as his personal coach for years and years, he truly never made a mental mistake. Never did. The attitude, the persistence, the tremendous will, he had a toughness of spirit and a tenacity to excel, and that he did.

I would have former players—and this is an unbelievable compliment to a player—I would have other players in his era, after they retired, come to me and say: "Dan Dierdorf made me a better player because when we played, he embarrassed me. He embarrassed me and because of that, I told myself that was not going to happen to me again, ever again, and I became a better player."

As a coach, the greatest compliment one can give to a player is really truly use their play as an example to younger players. And I have for many years used Dan's film footage, of him in action and, yes, in practice, and I've kept those reels over the years to show my young ones, "Hey, this is how you can do it."

Some of them wouldn't believe me and then they'd see Mr. Dierdorf execute what I was asking for and they'd go, "My goodness gracious, you actually can do it like that. That's unbelievable." And he truly was.

Dan Dierdorf

I was here in 1962 to watch the groundbreaking when Pete Rozelle turned over a spade full of dirt to start the construction of this building.

I used to walk down here from my house right there. If you just go under the bridge, and up Harrison Avenue, to Thirty-sixth Street and make a right turn, about two-thirds down the block on the left side, it's about a mile from here and I could walk it in about fifteen minutes.

And I used to walk down here and I used to look at that steel over the rotunda here that was making that football, and I was thinking to myself, "What the heck is that?" And then I went to every enshrinement ceremony, every Hall of Fame game until I went into the National Football League in 1971. Then, of course, I've been here for the last ten years as part of the broadcast crew that does the Hall of Fame game.

And you think back to what are some of the things that you remember, and I'll never forget, as long as I live, the teams used to dress originally over in the Field House. And I remember I was probably fourteen years or so of age, and I was standing outside that locker room, and I was distracted. I was looking the other way. And all of a sudden the locker-room door burst open and out of this locker-room door—and you guys will know who I'm talking about—out came Bob Brown, the old tackle for the Philadelphia Eagles and the Rams and the Raiders.

Bob Brown was about six-foot-six, three hundred pounds, and he had on those old nasty grass spikes that we used to wear, those things about an inch and a half long with steel on the bottom of them. When you're walking on the asphalt, sparks come off those things. And Bob Brown walked by me and I thought it was an eclipse. The sun was blotted from my vision and I thought to myself: these men, these men are God. These men are things that I could never be. And there is no way on God's green earth that I would ever be able to stand here long enough, talk loud enough, or be eloquent enough to ever possibly explain to you what it would be like to go to the side of that locker-room door, to have Bob Brown go past me, to make the quarter-mile trip down here to stand on these steps. It's truly beyond my comprehension and I'm overwhelmed by it all. . . .

My election is a validation, not just for myself, but for an awful lot of people who are in the same position I was in. And that is simply this: For a long time it appeared that the only way you could get in the Hall of Fame is if you played on a Super Bowl champion team. . . . There are an awful lot of good football players in this league that never had the good fortune to be drafted by Pittsburgh, or by Dallas, or by Miami, or by the Raiders. We just happened to go to another team. It doesn't mean we worked any less, it didn't mean we weren't as good. We just weren't as fortunate in where we had the opportunity to play.

And let me tell you something. I can only assume that it's a whole lot easier to get up in the morning and go down to the stadium for practice that first week of December, when you're 10-2, than it is when you're 2-10. Cause I know what it feels like to go down there when you're 2-10, and you try to screw that baby down tight, to play for some pride and to play for the respect of your fellow players around the league. . . .

And lastly, I know I have spoken too long, but I only get to be here once. I just have one last thing to say. It was my father who brought me here in 1962 to watch this building being dedicated. It was my father that brought me to every Hall of Fame game. It was my dad who went to every one of my high school games, and it was my father who stood with me and watched me grow. And my dad died fifteen years ago and all I can think about is how much he would enjoy this, how much he would enjoy seeing his baby boy go into the Professional Football Hall of Fame.

And Dad, all I can tell you is that I hope I honor you by being here today.

■　■　■　■

Mike Munchak
Houston Oilers Guard
Class of 2001

A devastating blocker, Munchak was selected to nine Pro Bowls.

Presented by Oilers and Titans Offensive Lineman
Bruce Matthews

I met Mike in 1983 at training camp in San Angelo, Texas, when the Houston Oilers had drafted me. My first impression of "Munch" was that he was quiet, and more important, he could lay out a lot of pain on the football field.

The guy was impressive in his uniform, to say the least. He had these big ol' guns, and it looked like the good Lord just slapped flesh on his shoulders and triceps where it wasn't on other people.

I think the fortunate thing that for me as a player was that I had the type of player that I wanted to be like playing on the same line as me. When we watched film, I would first watch to see how I did on the play, then I would watch Mike to see the way that it was supposed to be done. Playing alongside Mike and following his example is a huge part of what has made me the player that I am.

He set a standard of excellence that myself and every offensive lineman who played with him has tried to emulate. The hits that he put on linebackers were legendary and they were frequently the topics of many mealtime conversations with the Oilers.

One play that comes to mind was a shot that he put on a Browns defender whom I hold in high regard—because it's my brother, Clay. On a screen pass in 1992, Mike ran out in the flat and the defender, he saw him coming for about five yards. Mike hit him, the guy gyrated through the air five yards back, and it was one of the most awesome hits I've ever seen. Our free-spirited punter Greg Montgomery later commented that it looked like a cat getting hit by a pickup truck.

After Mike retired, he stayed on as a coach, an offensive line coach—my coach. And we've never had a problem balancing our friendship and the player-coach relationship. I believe that I'm one of the very few players, if ever, who has shared the kind of relationship that I have with Mike right now. It's something that has kept me playing and helped me be the player I am.

Mike believes that there are a few basic fundamentals that if you can master as an offensive lineman, you can be successful on every play, and he hammers them into us daily, almost too often. I sometimes have to chuckle, though, when the rookies come in and they are

"Yes, sirring" and "No, sirring" Coach Munchak and they're shaking in their boots at his every beck and call.

Mike doesn't scream much, he doesn't raise his voice much, but when he speaks, there's an authority in it because we recognize that there isn't anyone who has ever done it better than him. So we better darn well listen to what he's saying.

Mike Munchak

I've been sitting up here the past hour, nervous as heck because I've been envisioning that any moment someone from NFL security is going to show up and say, "Hey, Munchak, what are you doing up here? Get off that stage. It's for the Hall of Famers. You're just some blue-collar guy from Scranton, Pennsylvania."

I say this because that was my initial thought when I was told of my election. "How could I be a part of this elite group here?" Heck, I was thrilled when I was a kid just to have their football cards. We'd even fight over them in the neighborhood, flip over them, just try to fight for them.

I have always loved pro football. From as far back as I can remember, I spent Sundays watching the NFL on TV with my dad. My favorite part was watching that sixty-minute highlight show of the past week's action narrated by John Facenda—his famous voice describing the hard-hitting action, the slow-motion replays, and that great NFL Films music that went perfectly with the game action and gave me the chills. In fact, it still does as I watched some of the highlights last night. I still get that same feeling inside me, like I was ten years old all over again.

It made me wish that someday I could be one of those great warriors. After the games, we'd go outside with my friends and pretend to be those guys. We'd pretend to be Bart Starr throwing a touchdown pass to Lynn Swann making the acrobatic catch or Jack Youngblood sacking the quarterback. And Nick Buoniconti leading the "No-Name" defense. I never pretended to be an offensive lineman. I guess now I know who the important guys truly are.

■ ■ ■ ■

Elvin Bethea
Houston Oilers Defensive End
Class of 2003

An eight-time Pro Bowl selection, Bethea led the Oilers in sacks
six times. He played sixteen years and 210 games.

I must begin with my high school coach, back in 1960-whatever. His name was Coach Clements. Clements was a very small man, and I still remember him today. He started the foundation on which others have built upon for my journey here today. He inspired me from the very first day, I remember.

I was on the junior varsity squad, never knew what football was. I went out with a friend of mine; we said that we're going to go out for football. Had never played football, always played soccer up until my ninth year. That first day, I went out for the team. The next day, the coach says, "You're on the varsity squad." And I'm saying, "How did I make it onto the varsity squad after one day?" His answer was to me that he liked the way I hustled, he liked the way I moved around the field, and he liked my tenacity and toughness.

So, I think that has gotten me here today. That's from a long time ago. What my coach would always say was, "What you put into practice is what you get out of it." And that's what has gotten me here from that day on to today.

He also would say, "You always practice and push for perfection." And, I guess that's the reason why I'm here today, because every time I went out to practice or whatever I did as far as my sports—whether it was track or football—I wanted to be perfect. And I think that has given me the strength in everything that I needed to get here today.

■ ■ ■ ■

Dan Marino
Miami Dolphins Quarterback
Class of 2005

When he retired, Marino held the NFL records for passing yardage (61,361), completions (4,967), attempts (8,358), and touchdowns (420). He was voted to nine Pro Bowls.

Presented by His Son, Daniel Marino

I've always felt that I was truly blessed in so many ways. But, most importantly, in the way that no one could ask for better examples of people than my parents. There's never been a situation that they didn't know how to approach or how to act in. They've always treated people with so much compassion and are so grateful for everything in their lives. I think that all five of my brothers and sisters would agree that we were all so lucky to be raised by such wonderful people.

My father has made a lot of smart decisions on the field but I believe his smartest decision he's ever made was one he made off the field. He chose my mom. Together, they have shaped me and my family in such a meaningful and positive way. And, so rarely do you find parents so willing to give you everything in return only for their children's happiness. My parents will belong in my and my siblings' personal Hall of Fame always for that.

I'm often asked the question, "Are you a football player?" or "Does your dad want you to play football or sports?" It may seem to many people that that would be appropriate, but my father has always supported me in whatever I chose to do. Whether I was performing, whether Joey was golfing, whether Allie was horse riding, whether Michael was deejaying, and, I'm sure, he'll support Niki and Lia in whatever passion they choose to pursue.

My father's friends have always said to me repeatedly how proud he is of his children. They tell me that he can't seem to stop talking about us. My father only asks us to work hard at what we do. It seems odd to me that such a modest request can make my father so happy. But our passion for something seems to make him as eager and as happy as if he was waiting to go on the field. For this, me and my siblings are all so very fortunate.

Perhaps this can shed some light on the man off the field—the family man who has always been a loving father. My father played quarterback for the Miami Dolphins from the years 1983 to 1999. I don't claim to be the biggest football fan in my household. Aside from my dad, my brothers Joey and Michael have that honor. Growing up watching my dad was difficult with a preteen attention span and even tougher with a preschool attention span. However, from that time I will never forget the scars on my arms from my mom's fingernails when she squeezed them for dear life watching my dad on the field. But now that I'm older I can appreciate more what my father did.

And I sometimes watch my father's old games on tape and I can't put into words the experience of watching your father, when he was young, win a game: when he yells, when he skips off the field, hugs his teammates and his coach, a look of competitive accomplishment on his face. That look always made him stand out for me a little on the field. I don't think my father was ever out of the game. If you watch him from the sideline, he watches every play with intensity. And if the Dolphins had a bad play, the cameras would have to cut away for the family audiences.

In the same way that my grandfather is my father's hero, my father has always been my hero, and in the same way, I hope my children will look up to me one day. But it would be selfish of me to say that I'm the only one who looks upon my father as a hero. My father has given so much to the community he lives in. The time he has spent with the sick and terminally ill children; the Dan Marino Children's Hospital, founded for children with neurological disorders; the Dan Marino Foundation that has worked with children's charities in South Florida have, I'm sure, all earned him the status of hero with many other people. Both my parents have given so much time to helping the community in which they live. And my father's hand reaches far beyond the community he lives in as well.

My father was always committed to his team and his teammates. Even if my father scored four touchdowns and failed to win, it was always, to him, a lost game. The Miami Dolphins were and still are my dad's team. More than that, they are, in a way, his extended family. My father's seventeen years were spent with one franchise, the franchise he loved. And that seems to be so rare in professional sports today, I thought it was worth mentioning.

I always felt that talent if nothing else is something that you don't have control over. My father was very lucky in that department. But it's what you do with your talent that counts. My father, when he played, worked his hardest and always played to the best of his abilities. I think that's all a coach could ask of a player and, furthermore, all you could ask of a person.

When I started writing this speech, I realized that you have to start thinking very hard about how you feel about your father. And I realized how completely unselfish my father's life has been. His induction into the Hall of Fame is recognition of his abilities and career on the field. But, I personally feel, it is also in recognition of father's life in many ways—a life that was never about him but about his team, his fans, his community, his friends, and his family.

Dan Marino

As a young man, God blessed me with a special talent to throw a football and I was very fortunate to grow up in an environment like the city of Pittsburgh in the neighborhood of Oakland, an area that was full of football tradition. My dream started right there on Parkview Avenue in Oakland and it stayed there for twenty-one years.

There's not many players who can say they went to grade school, high school, college all in the same neighborhood, all within a short walk from the home that I grew up in. It was literally a ten-minute walk from my home to the fifty-yard line of old Pitt Stadium. I lived right across the street from a church when I was a kid and I still have vivid memories of playing football for St. Regis.

On the morning of games, going to church in full dress uniform, we'd have cleats, pads, helmets, everything. We were wearing everything and the coaches would lead us in prayer. We would say Hail Marys and Our Fathers in praying for victory and then we'd march down the street, cheerleaders, band playing, to play our game. And it didn't get much better than that. And you know what? We never lost. I'd like to think that God was on my side, but then again it was a Catholic Church League and He was on everybody's side.

Football is the ultimate team game and, as you know, no one gets to the Hall of Fame alone. And right from the start my teammates helped me.

I remember my first start going back to 1983. It was against Buffalo and I was a rookie. To be honest, I was a little nervous. And as I stood on the sidelines, I remember a veteran, a veteran safety, Lyle Blackwood, coming up to me. He came up to me with a serious look and he shook my hand and he said, "Dan, good luck today. And I don't want you to feel any pressure, but remember this one thing: If you play bad, we'll lose." Now that's pressure on a rookie.

To my mother and dad, we've come a long way from Parkview Avenue. Mom and Dad, I still can't figure out why they called it Parkview Avenue because there wasn't a park and there wasn't any view. But I can tell you that a son couldn't ask for better parents. And, Mom, thank you for your dedication to Cindi, Debbie, and me. We were lucky we got to be raised in such a healthy and loving environment. You're the best and I love you.

My dad, you're my hero. Dad, you're my role model, you're the best coach I've ever had. You taught me how to throw a football, you taught me about hard work and how to be positive. I'll always remember the times that we'd just sit and talk about football and about life. You taught me how to treat people the way you want to be treated. You would always say that you didn't deserve anything in life; you only deserve what you earn. My only hope is that Claire and I could pass on those important values to our children.

My dad would always tell me that no one does it better. Well, let me say that no one is better than you.

Looking back on my career I've accomplished many things. But what I cherish more than any record that I hold, any fourth-quarter comeback, any win that I was involved in, what I cherish more are the relationships that I've made, the people I've worked with, the team-mates I've lined up beside, the opponents that I've competed against. The friends and family, that's what I cherish most.

My son and I talked about what I was going to talk about in my speech and we went back and forth. He said, "Dad, you need to tell everyone what you miss most about the game." To tell you all what I miss most is for seventeen years, running out of the tunnel knowing I was the starting quarterback for the Miami Dolphins, and playing in front of the greatest fans in the world. That's what I miss most.

■ ■ ■ ■

Rayfield Wright
Dallas Cowboys Offensive Tackle
Class of 2006

Wright played in six NFC championship games and five Super Bowls. He was named to the NFL's All-Decade Team of the 1970s.

Presented by Fort Valley State Coach Stan Lomax

Rayfield's belief is where we are born, where we grow up, must never determine how high we rise. Could it be that professional football games are played primarily on Sunday afternoons for reasons other than the convenience of scheduling, of viewer preference? Today I have the temerity to believe there is a spiritual quality about football. The rules of the game suggest it. The history of the game supports it. Lombardi, Brown, Landry all would have divested themselves were that not so.

Someone once said, "I would rather see a sermon than hear one any day." For more than twelve years, Rayfield Wright, with displays of commitment and determination, delivered his message clearly and emphatically each Sunday afternoon. Primarily he had two admonitions.

One, Thou shalt not touch Roger Staubach. The second was, Thou must not impede the forward progress of Calvin Hill or Tony Dorsett.

Rayfield Wright

I learned a poem in the eighth grade entitled "The Road Not Taken." It's about two roads. One was well traveled, the other was grassy and wanted wear. Through this poem, I discovered that life would give me choices. It was recognizing those choices that proved to be the greatest challenge.

Looking back, my instinct was to always take the easy road. But the easy road never came my way. You see, I grew up in Griffin, Georgia. My mother and my grandmother raised me, my brothers, and my sister. We didn't have much money or any luxuries to speak of. Times were tough, and I recognized at an early age the struggles that we faced.

I remember getting on my knees when I was ten years old beside my grandmother, and I simply asked God something. I asked him if He would just give me the ability that I could do something, that I could help my mother and my grandmother, and I could help other people. My grandmother taught me the power of prayer and what that prayer meant to me. And it's still in front of me today. . . .

My career started as a tight end. Don Meredith was our quarterback at the time. Recently I asked Don. I said, "Don, you remember throwing me a touchdown pass against the Eagles?" He laughed and said, "Rayfield, I wasn't throwing the ball to you. You was just so tall, you got in the way."

Two years later, Coach Landry called me into his office and said, "Rayfield, I'm going to move you to offensive tackle." I looked at him and I said, "Coach, I never played that position before in my life." He said, "I know, but you're quick, you learn fast. Besides, we got a young quarterback coming to the team this year, and his name was Roger Staubach, and he don't stay in the pocket. He runs around a lot, and he needs a little bit more protection." But I was never one to question the authorities of elders. Coach Landry, I believed in his decision, and that was good enough for me. . . .

And to my mother, Mrs. Opel Wright, from the day I was born, you watched me take the road less traveled. Mom, you are my rose garden, you watered each day with your love, with your faith, and with your prayers. Your roots are deeply instilled in me, and your soul is so beautiful, in spite of all the painful thorns that life has put in your way.

Now, parents, teach your children well. Encourage them with your faith and leadership. Remember that you are the windows through which your children see this world. Take notice of yourself and the things that you do in hopes that your example will stir their hearts and souls.

To every young athlete within the sound of my voice, it takes courage to dream your dream. Don't let them sit in the locker room. Take a leap of faith. Listen to your parents and respect your elders. Learn from your successes and your losses. Defeat is possible and is a challenge to do better next time. Be satisfied you gave the game everything that you had and remember this: Don't be afraid to travel the road less traveled because Larry Rayfield Wright did, and you can, too.

■ ■ ■ ■

Fred Dean
San Diego Chargers and San Francisco 49ers
Defensive End
Class of 2008

After seven seasons in San Diego, Dean helped San Francisco win two Super Bowls, posting a career-best seventeen sacks in 1983.

Presented by 49ers Owner Eddie DeBartolo Jr.

While it cannot be said that Fred Dean's greatness as an NFL player began when he came to the 49ers in 1981, I can say, as the owner of the team, that the greatness of the 49ers began with Fred Dean's arrival in San Francisco.

The 49ers won just eight games in Bill Walsh's first two seasons as our head coach. But going into 1981, there was a fresh sense of hope. On offense, our young quarterback Joe Montana had taken charge. On defense, a spectacular rookie, Ronnie Lott, anchored our secondary. But we had yet to get the quality wins that give a team confidence to believe that it can be a champion. And we lacked that explosive pass-rusher who could blow up offenses in those critical moments that determine the outcome of games.

Enter Fred Dean. When Bill Walsh learned that the Chargers were willing to trade Fred, he came to me like a kid with his eye on the niftiest possible Christmas present. You see, Bill had something different in mind for Fred, something downright revolutionary.

He would take this every-down Pro Bowl defensive end and turn him into a dynamic situational pass-rusher. Nothing like this has ever been done before. "Wait until you see what we do with Fred tomorrow," Bill told me the night before Fred's first game with us. Tomorrow we were playing the dominant Dallas Cowboys at home.

The funny thing was while Bill was telling me how significant Fred would be against Dallas, in that wonderful manipulative way of his, he put out the word that Fred would be a nonfactor. In fact, he told John Madden, who was doing the game, that Fred wouldn't play much, if at all. Oh, did he play. He sacked Danny White three times.

And we won 45–14.

Two weeks later, we played the NFC West powerhouse Rams at home. Fred sacked Pat Haden five times, and we also won that game. Now you didn't have to be a rocket scientist to figure out that something different was going on down on that field with Fred Dean in a 49er uniform. We finished the season 13-3. We beat the Cowboys in the NFC championship game.

And we went on to win our first Super Bowl. The amazing thing is Fred was this destructive force on sheer quickness, technique, and pure talent. He didn't even lift weights. Fred Dean was truly the natural. You know, Fred never said much. He was a quiet giant. But when the defense needed him to make a big play, we looked to Fred, and he never let us down. Never. No matter what the situation was.

Every player on our second Super Bowl team recognizes that he gave us the shot in the arm we needed to win that championship. Fred was the leader in the way it counted most, with his play. The National Football League has been the great love of my professional life. I was blessed to have had the magnificent good fortune to be represented by an organization of players, coaches, and executives that won five Super Bowls. We wouldn't have won five if we hadn't won the first two. I assure you we would not have won the first two if it weren't for Fred Dean.

We look back today, and it comes time to put Fred Dean's spectacular career in historical perspective. First off, he was a pioneer. He was the forefather of the great hybrid jet pass-rushers. He led the way for players like Derrick Thomas, our own Charles Haley, and the great Andre Tippett, who is being inducted today with Fred. Also, this era's Dwight Freeney and Jason Taylor.

Most importantly, Fred now joins my very dear friend Reggie White and Deacon Jones and Lawrence Taylor on that Mount Rushmore of pass-rushers who have earned immortality on this, our sport's sacred ground.

Fred Dean

God puts people in your life that have an impact on it, both spiritually and physically. For me, Mom and Dad were two of those people. See, I was a little boy, I was born in Arcadia, Louisiana, but I grew up in Ruston, Louisiana—a time during the change in our country.

Lincoln High School, an all-black school, was my first attendance. And, you know, I was small in size. And being small in size, I know that there are a lot of you got bullies around you sometimes. And they want to take advantage of a situation. But I'm here to tell you now, even though I was small, I got into a few incidents. And one day, a coach walked up to me. And his name happened to be Coach Robert Smith. And he said to me, "Why don't you take some of that energy to the field?" And I proceeded to take the energy to the field, as he had asked.

Later I went to Louisiana Tech, and at Louisiana Tech, Coach Lambright allowed me to have a twinkle in my eye at that time. And I want to set the record straight, finally. I was a defensive end then, and I wanted to be a defensive end now. So I wasn't a linebacker then—I was a defensive end. You know, when you get used to getting down in the dirt, getting your clothes dirty and wallowing a little bit, it makes everything come out right when you can stand up out of the mud or sod and feel comfortable. So, I said to myself, "Hmm, I like the dirt. And if I can beat somebody in this dirt, it's going to be a good thing." And another thing that I knew is that when you tried to talk about me, when I was coming up, I was small in size, but I tell you dirt can't talk about dirt.

So we need to understand that out of all of that I ended up with the San Francisco 49ers. And to me, that was a dream come true. I could consider it being born by the Chargers but having a renewal of life with the 49ers. And being with the 49ers, I found that on the other side of that bridge, on the other side was my rainbow, the true ending of a rainbow. Not financially, but with all the people there. You see, my richness came from my father, who is in heaven, and it was with you all. I loved it all. I loved the game of football.

I said to myself, I didn't dream about playing football. I didn't dream about being in the Hall of Fame. But I always heard, and we always talked, about the great vintage players that were in the Hall. And it was really an eye-opening thing for me. But yet and still, I didn't plan it. You see, what I found is, sometimes in our lives we can sit down and write out our aims and goals, but whether we know it or not, God already has the aim and goal set for you. And in that direction is the direction in which you will end up going.

You probably ask me why do I say that and how do I know? It's because I got a connection with the Father. You see, I look at myself as being the prodigal son. I went astray for a while because Mom and Dad always raised us up to love and appreciate the things that we had and the people surrounding us. I always wondered why, when I'd go out and pick a whole thing of peas and shell them, Mom and Dad would give half of them away. I'd kind of be upset. But it was a lesson to be learned. It was the giving, because I learned about the rich man who didn't make it.

My father, he was with my brother one day—and you know this is the way he is—and he was going down the road, and he was walking off the curb, and he fell. You see, my father is eighty-eight years old. And being that age, you know, you kind of get a little frail. My father, he fell, and he said we sat there and I said, "Are you all right, Father?" He said yes. I asked him, "Are you hurt?" He said no. But he said, "You know what? When I fell, I fell so hard it shook like thunder." And you know I couldn't help but think about the things he used to say to me, the old clichés. It's like, boy, if you ever want to make it on the road to success, get off that dirt road to failure. And my father, with that pavement of success, I feel that I finally got there, Dad.

■ ■ ■ ■

Darrell Green
Washington Redskins Cornerback
Class of 2008

Nicknamed the "Ageless Wonder," Green spent a record twenty seasons in Washington, going to seven Pro Bowls and winning two Super Bowls.

Deacon Jones said I would cry. You bet your life I'm going to cry.

A lot of people have traveled this with me. It's been a long time. The most special of them all is my parents. Both of my parents are deceased. They're the most special of them all, because I'm not here if they weren't here first. Everybody said, "You're too little, you can't do it." My dad, Leonard Green Sr., said, "Boy, you can run that ball."

They said no. And he said go. The most encouragement you can ever get in life is when a dad encourages his son. Encourage your son, that's what he did for us. I'd sure like to have a drumroll right now because I'm going to talk about the greatest mother in the world.

Am I going to cry? You gotta be kidding me. You don't know my momma and daddy. Gloria Green, baby, Gloria Green. She told me a story one day. I was about ten years old. She said, "You know, the day you were born, I was in the room there, and they had me up on these things and nothing was happening. You weren't doing anything, and everybody left out of the room, maybe twenty, thirty minutes." And all of a sudden she heard a scream. Somebody said, "Catch that baby!" She said, "You were about to hit the ground."

When I got into football, she said, "Don't let them big boys hurt you now." My parents were the best. They were the best.

CHAPTER 2

FAMILY

MICHAEL IRVIN

COACHES COME AND GO, AS DO TEAMMATES. OFTEN THEY change from one season to the next. But family is teammates for life.

Family is the support system that never leaves. It is there in the beginning and at the end. It is there for the wins and the losses. It is there for the ups and the downs.

As strong as this group of Hall of Famers is, so many draw their strength from a parent, a sibling, a spouse, or a child. Their words and support often mean more than any coach's or teammate's. They provide the inspiration that even Hall of Famers need.

Hall of Famers often provide for their families, but they know it also goes the other way. Family never boos. Family never leaves a game early. Family is always there.

■　■　■　■

Michael Irvin
Dallas Cowboys Wide Receiver
Class of 2007

Irvin caught 750 passes for 11,904 yards and sixty-five touchdowns. He had an NFL record eleven 100-yard receiving games in 1995.

Presented by Cowboys Owner Jerry Jones

A championship team can have a catalyst. They can have a spark, someone that can put a fire in another person's heart. The Dallas Cowboys of the 1990s were champions. They were in three Super Bowls and won them in four years' time. Ladies and gentlemen, I'm here to tell you tonight that the heartbeat, the heart and the soul of those championship teams, was Michael Irvin.

Michael came to Dallas with a self-proclaimed nickname, "The Playmaker." Now, at first many people didn't understand why this young guy would brand himself with such a bold nickname. But we began to figure it out real, real soon.

When it was third and long, opposition coaches knew exactly where Troy Aikman was throwing the ball. The defensive backs knew exactly where Aikman was going with the ball. Everybody in the stadium knew where the ball was going, but they couldn't stop it.

Troy Aikman often said the greatest thing about Michael Irvin is you could throw him the ball when he was covered, or you could throw him the ball when he was open, and the results were usually the same almost all the time. It was a completion, and most of the time it was for a first down.

Now, when you've got a quarterback that has that kind of confidence in your receiver, you can have some offense. That's how you earn the name "Playmaker," and that's how you keep it.

His performance always improved as the level of competition increased. He routinely had his best games against [cornerbacks] Deion Sanders, Darrell Green, Rod Woodson, Aeneas Williams. And his numbers increased as that long season went along and we got closer to the playoffs. From the regular season to the playoffs, from the playoffs to the Super Bowl, that was Michael Irvin's best days.

At the pinnacle of his career in 1995, he had eleven 100-yard receiving games, a mark that is still an NFL record today. But the Dallas Cowboys' offenses really weren't designed for the receiver to get big stats. They really weren't designed for Troy, the quarterback, to really rack 'em up in statistics.

The teams were designed to win championships, and what that meant was take what the defense gave you. Now, with the backdrop of all of that, the fact that one team could produce the NFL's greatest all-time rushing leader in Emmitt Smith, the fact that last year the first opportunity that he had a chance to be honored with these men, Troy Aikman came into the NFL Hall of Fame.

And the fact tonight that Michael Irvin is going to go in the Hall of Fame, it just shows you the team concept and shows you the balance that was there. The player that epitomized it more than anyone on the team, the player that taught it, the player that embellished it, that was Michael Irvin and his leadership.

You can't get to Canton, Ohio, without exceptional talent. But athletic ability alone was only a part of Michael's gifts. His hard work is legendary. In two days, the grind of all of it, you'd be on the field in the morning and in the afternoon, and someone would look around and ask, "Where is Michael?" He'd be down on the field with pads on in the hot sun, getting some more in.

His passion, his competitiveness were really possibly his greatest gifts. He shared them with his teammates on a daily basis. He practiced every day with the determination of a rookie that was hanging by a thread to make the team, and that's the way this great player approached it.

Aikman told me yesterday that Michael would never let the team have a bad practice. If there was a lull, he would create something between the defense and the offense. He'd get some stuff going just so that team could practice and get better for what they had to face Sunday.

Maybe that's the quality that separates the good players from the great players, the Hall-of-Fame players. Or maybe it's just the natural instinct of a man who had sixteen brothers and sisters, and knew that nothing in life was going to be given to him.

In the locker room, he was a teammate first, a competitor second, and a superstar third. His leadership style not only transcended the cliques in the locker room but his leadership style on our team and our organization went from the locker room and the equipment room all the way to the boardroom. It permeated it.

I don't know that we'll see again a professional football player with a combination of his strength and his skills as an athlete on the field and his unbelievable people skills. Smart, resourceful, communicative, charm, the kind of charisma and tremendous will with the strength to get the respect of the team. He had his faults—but in a unique way that only Michael Irvin could pull off.

His fallibility by the people who followed him—by the people who were looking at him—his fallibility gave them strength because they knew, too, how fallible they were, and they wanted to see somebody that could go down and come up stronger and try to get better when they got on their feet. That's what Michael Irvin brought to the Dallas Cowboys and his locker room.

He learned his game from his older brothers in Fort Lauderdale. He had a great high school he played for, St. Thomas High School. He became a star at the University of Miami, drafted by Gil Brandt and Tex Schramm. He was nurtured by Coach Tom Landry. He was coached in college and embellished when he got to pro football by one of the greatest coaches, Jimmy Johnson.

He spent his entire career in the loving embrace of the Dallas Cowboys. His journey reaches a destination tonight here in Canton, and it was a longer journey than most, with a lot of bumps in the road. He got knocked down for the last time at Veterans Stadium in Philadelphia. But tonight he'll get up again and he'll take his place among the immortals of this great game.

Michael Irvin, he's a friend. If you're in my shoes, you feel like he's a son. He's an inspirational and natural born leader. He's a loving father and husband. He's a wonderful brother and son. He's a Dallas Cowboy. And tonight, forever more, he's a member of the professional football Hall of Fame.

Michael Irvin

Jerry, those were kind words, thank you. You know, when I first met Jerry he had just purchased the Dallas Cowboys. He had a bit of a concerned look on his face. I said to him, I said, "We will have fun and we will win Super Bowls." You see, I knew Jerry had put all he had into purchasing the Cowboys. That's the way I see Jerry. He's a man that's willing to give all he has, and all he wants is to bring the Cowboy family Super Bowls.

Jerry, I appreciate your commitment to family, the Dallas Cowboy family and your own family. He has a beautiful wife, Gene. I tell her this. I just love her to death. Her spirit exudes beauty. Her mannerisms exude class. She's one of a kind. Gene, I do love you.

These [Hall-of-Fame] gentlemen behind me, these men, they inspired me to become the player that I became. As I spent this week with these gentlemen that I've admired growing up, I kept thinking about how gifted they are. Man, they're gifted to run and cut, gifted to throw and catch, gifted to run through blocks and make great tackles.

And then I met their wives and their families, and I realized that it's not only about the gift God gave us but equally important is the help that God gave us. It's the people that God put in place to support us on our journey. So I will try to put the credit in the right place tonight and share with you my help and my journey.

I thank God for the help of my father, Walter Irvin, whom I lost at the age of seventeen. He was my hero and he loved, I'm telling you, he loved the Dallas Cowboys. I woke up this morning smiling, knowing that my father would not be here in the flesh but that he is in heaven watching and celebrating with his all-time favorite coach, Coach Tom Landry.

Before my father made his journey to heaven, I sat with him. His final words to me were, "Promise me you will take care of your mother. She's a good woman."

As you've heard, my mother raised seventeen children, most of who are here tonight. There were challenges. But she would never complain. She always walked around the house and said, "God has promised me that my latter days will be better than my former days."

My mom and my aunt Fannie, her oldest sister, they are part of my travel squad now. As we travel, all they want is a nice room and an open tab on room service. When my workday is done I get to come by their room and we tell stories and we laugh and we have fun. We always end the night with them telling me, "Baby, this is what God meant when he said, 'Our latter days will be better than our former days.'"

I can't tell you how it makes me feel to know that God uses me to deliver His promise. I love you, Mom.

You know the Bible speaks of a healing place. It's called a threshing floor. The threshing floor is where you take your greatest fear and you pray for help from your great God. I want to share something with you today. I have two sons. Michael, he's ten, and Elijah, he's eight. Michael and Elijah—could you guys stand up for me? That's my heart right there. That's my heart. When I am on that threshing floor, I pray. I say, "God, I have my struggles and I made some bad decisions, but whatever you do, whatever you do, don't let me mess this up."

I say, "Please, help me raise them for some young lady so that they can be a better husband than I. Help me raise them for their kids so that they could be a better father than I." And I tell you guys to always do the right thing so you can be a better role model than Dad. I sat right here where you are last year and I watched the Class of 2006: Troy Aikman, Warren Moon, Harry Carson, Rayfield Wright, John Madden, and the late great Reggie White represented by his wife, Sara White. And I said, "Wow, that's what a Hall of Famer is."

Certainly I am not that. I doubted I would ever have the chance to stand before you today. So when I returned home, I spoke with Michael and Elijah. I said, "That's how you do it, son. You do it like they did it." Michael asked, he said, "Dad, do you ever think we will be there?" And I didn't know how to answer that. And it returned me to that threshing floor. This time I was voiceless, but my heart cried out. "God, why must I go through so many peaks and valleys?"

I wanted to stand in front of my boys and say, "Do it like your dad, like any proud dad would want to. Why must I go through so much?" At that moment a voice came over me and said, "Look up, get up, and don't ever give up."

You tell everyone or anyone that has ever doubted, thought they did not measure up or wanted to quit, you tell them to look up, get up, and don't ever give up.

■　■　■　■

Roger Staubach
Dallas Cowboys Quarterback
Class of 1985

Staubach led the Cowboys to four NFC titles and victories in Super Bowls VI and XII. When he retired, his 83.4 quarterback rating was the league's all-time best.

Presented by Cowboys Coach Tom Landry

In any profession, there are two ways to make a winner—how he performs his job and, more important, how he performs as a human being. Roger Staubach is an All-Pro in both categories.

Roger Staubach

One of the sportswriters at the press conference today mentioned the fact that Joe [Namath] was about ready to have a little one, and O. J. [Simpson] was going to have a little one, and I had a grandchild, and he said, "You are really a competitor, Roger, what are you and your wife going to do about that?" I said, "I'm not a competitor with you guys anymore. I'm in the Hall of Fame with you guys now. That's as far as my wife and I are going."

It was a pretty neat deal when I got married. I married a nurse. I didn't know I was going to be a professional football player at the time, but it sure came in handy. She was a good one. She was a good nurse, but more than that, she was a loving wife, and it's tough.

It's tough to leave a home and go out and play professional football when things aren't right at home. Boy, it's extra tough. Well, I never had that problem. I had someone who loved me and I loved her very much. She is up here, too, with my teammates and with my coaches.

■　■　■　■

Fran Tarkenton
New York Giants and Minnesota Vikings
Quarterback
Class of 1986

At retirement, Tarkenton held the NFL records for attempts (6,467), completions (3,686), yards (47,003), and touchdowns (342). In his first NFL game, Tarkenton threw for four touchdowns.

Presented by Vikings President Max Winter

The great thing he did was, he was an innovator. A new concept was born as he became the quarterback. He was a fellow that showed the quarterbacks who stayed in the pocket behind the center, and either passed to a running back or threw a pass from the pocket, how to scramble, how to score, how to win. He was the greatest scrambler and emulators galore now come from all teams that want to emulate Tarkenton's ability and record.

Fran Tarkenton

Mr. Winter mentioned something about scrambling. I did a little bit of that during my day. I really didn't want to do that, but if you look up here at some of the past enshrines, you see Doug Atkins, Deacon Jones, and Ray Nitschke, and they were trying to kill me, ladies and gentlemen. That pocket got crowded and I wanted to get out and I did, and I turned into a very elusive fast man because of that.

When I look back over eighteen years of professional football, four years of college football, four years of high school football, which I believe comes to twenty-six years and a lot of losses, a lot of wins, a lot of disappointments, a lot of high points, and you think you will never get over the losses and the wins that take you to the highest point. And you think, "Boy am I pretty good," and finally you overcome all that, too. And you see what came out of twenty-six years of playing.

What comes out are the most important things—not the wins, not the losses, not the awards, not the publicity, and not the money, Lord knows wherever that went. What lives are the experiences of the people you played with, the Jim Marshalls, the Mick Tingelhoffs, the Carl Ellers, the Bob Tuckers, the Spider Lockharts. Those are the things that live in your heart and stir your soul and move you on. Those are the things that live in your heart and those are the important things.

My little mother of seventy-three years young, who is stronger than all of us on this stage, who what little competitive fire I've got, I got it all from her because she is a fighter. Every year I didn't get into the Hall, she would always say, "I hope I can live to see the day when you do." Mom, you did.

To one who is not here—and I'm going to try to get through this gang without crying, but I'm not sure I can, so please bear with me. A little five-foot-six man who happened to be a preacher man, who wasn't a man of great stature, he wasn't on television, and he didn't make a lot of money, he didn't own any businesses. But that man was a great man and a great father, because when I fell down and disappointed him, instead of kicking me around and telling me I was a no-good so-and-so who wasn't like they used to be, he pulled me up through my deepest sorrows and disappointments and hugged me and told me he loved me and let me understand what love is all about.

That little five-foot-six man, who didn't know whether the football was blown or stuffed, loved to watch his son play football, and he died watching me play football when we played in the famous "Hail Mary" game against the Dallas Cowboys in a playoff game. He had just finished his sermon in Savannah, Georgia. That little man is not with us here today in person, but I know he is looking on, and I know he is proud.

■　■　■　■

Jack Lambert
Pittsburgh Steelers Linebacker
Class of 1990

Lambert was considered the leader of Pittsburgh's vaunted "Steel Curtain" defense. He was the NFL Defensive Player of the Year in 1976 and was voted to nine Pro Bowls.

It goes without saying that one does not come to stand on these steps without the guidance, the direction, and the support of others.

In the short time I'm allotted today, I would like to start with my mother, Joyce. When I was growing up, she was undoubtedly my biggest fan and supporter. I can't ever remember playing in an athletic event that my mother did not attend.

I can still see my mom late at night after a football game, scrubbing and soaking the grass stains out of my pretty white football pants. Mom thought it was very important that her son have the whitest pants on the field.

My father, Jack, I get my athletic ability and temperament from my father's side of the family. Most of the time we spent together was throwing the baseball back and forth or playing tackle football.

Back before the days of NFL Properties, my dad had enjoyed buying football helmets and painting them the colors of NFL teams. The helmet he chose to paint for his son at that time was the Pittsburgh Steelers.

■　■　■　■

Bud Grant
Minnesota Vikings Coach
Class of 1994

Grant led the Vikings to eleven division championships, four Super Bowls, and a 168-108-5 coaching record.

My dad always referred to me as "The Kid." My father was very important in my life, and was interested in sports, and got me interested in sports.

I remember the night Joe Louis knocked off Max Schmeling, my dad and I jumped up and down as we listened to the radio; it was great. But something really changed in Superior [Wisconsin] in 1939. The New York Giants came to Superior to train.

They trained in 1939, 1940, and 1941. As a kid, I hung around the Giants, and my dad had a concession stand at the ballpark, got to know Steve Owen. My dad kept saying, "Hey, my kid is going to play for you someday."

Every year Steve Owen would come back and measure me a little bit bigger. My dad would say, "The kid is going to make it; he is going to play for the Giants." Steve would say, "Keep working on him, keep feeding him, and I am sure he will."

Well, the war came, and a couple of years we prepared to go to war, but the Giants came back in 1948. Now the kid was a little bigger, and Steve was looking at me a little more convinced that someday I would play in the National Football League. And my dad said, "The kid is going to make it."

My dad used to tell me stories about the NFL because two players born in Superior that played in the NFL are presently in the Hall of Fame. Tuffy Leemans came from Superior and played with the New York Giants, and Ernie Nevers, one of the original Hall of Famers, came from Superior.

So there was a background even in a town of thirty thousand way up in Northern Wisconsin, way up in Lake Superior. The radio didn't carry the games, and we would get the Chicago paper once in a while. My dad would tell me the stories of [Hall of Famers] Red Grange, Johnny "Blood" McNally.

I asked him where did Johnny "Blood" get a name like that. He said he was a tough guy; he broke his nose every game, and the blood would stream down his face. John "Blood" McNally is here today. [Hall of Famer] George Trafton, great center—always these guys were the toughest guys in football.

George had a finger missing. I asked, "How did he lose that finger?" My dad said they bit it off in the bottom of a pile. I didn't believe that so I asked George that one day, how he lost his finger. He said he stuck it in a .45 in Chicago and they blew it off, so I didn't know what to believe.

Bronko Nagurski from Minnesota—my dad would tell me stories about Bronk. Of course living close to Green Bay, Curly Lambeau was a legend. Don Hutson was the greatest receiver of all time, my dad would tell me. If you ever want to be a receiver, do what Don Hutson did.

Of course we didn't have any film so we didn't know what Don Hutson did; we just read about it. Sammy Baugh, many stories about him. Raised on all that. Those were my dad's heroes.

And I am here with my dad's heroes. So I go back a long way, back to the 1930s, following NFL players. And I am here with Tuffy and Red, Johnny Blood, Bronko, Curly, Crazy Legs, Night Train, Bulldog. You can't imagine what an honor it is and if my mother were here today—she is ninety-three years old, she couldn't make it—I would look at her face and see the pride she would have that only a mother could have.

And if my father were here—he was different than I was, a very gregarious guy—he would stand up and he would say, "The kid made it, he finally made it!"

And one other thing my father told me a long time ago: if you are ever asked to speak at such an auspicious occasion, with so many great speakers, make sure you stand up good and tall so they can see you; and talk good and loud so they all can hear you; make a short speech so they all will listen to you; and then sit down so they all will like you.

■ ■ ■ ■

Randy White
Dallas Cowboys Defensive Tackle
Class of 1994

White missed only one game in fourteen seasons. He was co-MVP of Super Bowl XII and a nine-time Pro Bowl selection.

Presented by Steelers Defensive Tackle and Cowboys Assistant Coach Ernie Stautner

Through all my career, all I heard was I was too small. All you had to do was draw a line in front of me and tell me I couldn't cross it. Years later when I was coaching the Dallas Cowboys, onto the field walks this kid. Draw a line in front of Randy White and you were in real trouble. Nobody could stop him from crossing.

Randy was a blue-collar worker on a country-club team. He didn't read the *Wall Street Journal*. All he wanted to do was play football and to be the best at what he was doing. Even his own teammates didn't want to practice in front of Randy because he didn't know what practice speed was. Everyone on the field was his enemy.

[Cowboys defensive back] Charlie Waters nicknamed Randy "The Manster" because, as Charlie put it, anybody that can play the way Randy does has got to be half man, half monster.

Randy also had a great sense of humor. One day after a very tough and grueling road trip, I came into the locker room and there was Randy looking terrible. I asked him what was wrong and he said, "God, I really feel bad. That was a tough road trip. I'm constipated."

So I told Randy to go see the trainer. The next day I came in and Randy was there and he looked even worse. I asked him if he'd seen the trainer and he said, "Yeah, I saw him and he gave me a suppository, but I don't think it really helped me at all. Besides, I had the darndest time swallowing it."

Randy White

The guy that just introduced me, Ernie Stautner, is in the Hall of Fame. I tell you, he's the guy that showed me how to get into the Hall of Fame.

Ernie used to tell me, "Randy, as a player, when you're out there on the field and you feel something and you know there is a play that's going to happen, you go ahead and go for it." But he also told me, "Randy, you better be right a lot more times than you're wrong or we'll both be in trouble with Coach Landry."

Ernie really taught me how to do it, he really did. And I appreciate the fact that a lot of times he gave me a lot of freedom out there on the field to use the knowledge and what I had and my ability on the field. But besides everything that Ernie did for me on the field, I also wanted to tell you that Ernie Stautner is one of the best friends that I've had my whole life.

And I'm pretty proud of my daughter, Jordan. When I retired from football, Jordan was ten years old. And the media guys came in there and they were doing an interview. Well, they asked Jordan a question. They said, "Jordan, what do you feel about your dad retiring from football?"

And Jordan said, "Well, I never really watched the games anyway. I just sat there and drank Cokes and ate popcorn. But you know, that's my dad. And I love him whether he plays football or doesn't play football."

And I'll tell you what. To me, that's what it is all about right there.

Lee Roy Selmon
Tampa Bay Buccaneers Defensive End
Class of 1995

A six-time Pro Bowl selection, Selmon posted 78.5 sacks, 380 quarterback pressures, and forced twenty-eight fumbles.

Presented by His Brother, Buccaneers Teammate Dewey Selmon

For me, it goes back to 11-19-53, the day I was born. As I was born, my parents probably said to themselves, "Dewey will be lonely, he needs a playmate." Eleven months later I had one. They are a devoted, loving, Christian family that takes care of their sons.

I grew up with Lee Roy. For thirty-one years, he was my celibate wife. We would do everything together. In fact, on the night of his senior prom, it was I who took him there. At that point, his good looks had not developed and I was his best date. But as time went on, good looks would come and he would rule at Oklahoma University.

Lee Roy Selmon

People have said that I know your parents must be proud of you, but I want you to understand that I am more proud of them. Everything that I have been taught in football and in life came from them—those words about commitment and determination and hard work, never quitting, sharing, and caring. Those types of characteristics were born in a household of Lucious and Jessie Selmon. Those characteristics were not only taught to me but to all nine of their children.

And they had nine good reasons to leave, but they didn't. They were committed and they hung in there with us. This is a lesson that we can all take with us. It's a lesson that we have all taken with us from that household.

I was very fortunate as Dewey mentioned. I'm the youngest of all nine, and I often wondered with Dewey being the eighth child and only being eleven months younger than him if I was a planned child. I never asked Mom and Dad, but I'm glad I'm here. I'm glad they did what they did that got me here.

You wonder as I've gotten older how they really stuck to that situation because I know it was difficult. I know they wanted the nicer things in life, but they couldn't have them because they committed to all their children to make sure all their needs were met.

But in their commitment there was a lot of love, caring, and understanding. They may not have been able to provide us with the material things that we as children might have wanted, but they provided us with the most valuable things that life can offer: respect, caring, understanding. Things that will last a lifetime and the things that we grew up on.

In closing, I would like to share a story with you that talks about children and how important they are. This story is about a man and his son.

During the middle of the week, they were home resting and the son came up in the evening with two gloves and a baseball and he said, "Dad, can we go out and play catch?" The dad was a little tired and said, "Son, why don't you come back on Saturday and I will play catch with you."

Well, Saturday came and the father was relaxing in the easy chair, reading the morning paper. The son came back on the weekend with two gloves and a baseball and said, "Dad, will you play catch?" The father said, "Well, son, I'm reading the morning paper. Can you come back a few minutes later and I will be ready to play?"

A few minutes later he came back. "Dad, can we go out and play catch now?" The father was getting a little disturbed at all the interruptions. He came upon an ad in the paper that had a full-page picture of the world on it. So he showed it to his son and tore it into small pieces and said, "Take this to your room, and when you put it together, come back and I will be ready to go out and play catch with you."

The son took those pieces of paper, went to his room, and came back in a short period of time. He took the paper, and it was put back together perfectly, and his father was amazed. He asked his son how he did it so quickly. "Dad, on the other side of the paper there was the face of a little boy, and I knew if I put the little boy back together, the world would take care of itself."

I feel that way about our youth, and that is the challenge we all have. If we can put our youth together one at a time, this world would be a much better place to live and they would have the chances I did.

■ ■ ■ ■

Joe Gibbs
Washington Redskins Coach
Class of 1996

Before he retired the first time, Gibbs led the Redskins to three Super Bowl titles with three different starting quarterbacks and also compiled a 124-60 regular-season record. He finished his coaching career with a 154-94 record.

For the last six months I've been asking myself something: How did I get into the Hall of Fame? And I tell you, I think I have discovered the answer to that, and I want to share it with you.

As we look down through history we find out that God at certain points picks very average men and women. And what He does is, He gives them a life, gives them some talent, surrounds them with great people, and guides them to some achievement. I figured out that I am one of those average people God looked down on and touched.

The first thing He did for me was give me a great family. My mother is here today. About three months ago we were worried; I wasn't sure if my mom was going to make it. It is one of the great thrills of my life to have my mom here. I want to say to my mom, thank you for all the times that you and Dad sacrificed for me and Jim. Thank you, Mom. We lost my dad about five years ago, but you know God tells us in His Word that those that have gone on before us are in heaven cheering us on. . . .

As I took off in life, I learned that I loved to play games. And I loved to win. And I discovered that life was a game. And let me tell you, it's the greatest game of all time. I know, like you guys, that I wanted to win. As I made my travels along as I started to have my dreams, as I started to grow up, God put a special person in my life and that was Pat, my high school sweetheart. And Pat and I made the same discovery in life and we decided that we wanted to play the game of life together. Any of you that knows my family, we took a vote. And we voted Pat the captain of our family. I play on her team. It's one of the greatest teams that God could put together. We decided that Pat would run the home and I would coach. . . .

As we moved and coached, all of a sudden there were a couple of additions to our team. That was J.D. and Coy. The best way I can describe this is that Pat and I changed our priorities. It kind of goes with this little story. In 1983 we had one of the greatest football teams I think that has ever been put together. Everybody remembers that. We had just won a big game at RFK and I can remember that I woke up the next morning, we were going down to play Dallas for the division championship. I got up that morning, strutting around, thinking how great I was. Isn't it amazing how God gives us great wives to put us in our place? About halfway through that morning, Pat said to me, "Do you mind picking up your socks and bathrobe?" I thought, the nerve of her talking to such an important man that way!

As the morning went along she started sharing some things about Coy and J.D., and again I thought, why would she be bothering me when she knows I have such an important week coming up? Why would she start bothering me with these problems with J.D. and Coy? So I kind of stormed out of the house, slammed the door, and as I climbed in the car, I have always made a promise that I would pray on the way to work. As I prayed on the way to work that morning, I made a discovery. When I got to work, I called Pat and this is what I told her: "Pat, what you are taking care of at home is more important than what I am taking care of at work." The football games and the Super Bowls and all the fun we had, the fans, and everything, are some of the greatest memories anybody can ever have. But Pat and I came to the conclusion, the greatest thing we will ever leave on this earth is our two boys.

I have to say thanks to all the players. Some of those guys are out here in the audience. One of the favorite questions that people ask me is who was the greatest player that you ever coached? And every time they say that, I can't list the greatest player I ever coached, there are too many of them. If I started to list the players, it would go something like this: Reggie Branch, Pete Cronan, Otis Wonsley. And those guys would all say whose that? Those guys were not some of the heralded guys; those were some of the special teamers. I know Joe Jacoby and some of the guys out there will agree with me. Some of the greatest players on our football team were free agents. They were guys that gave their guts and covered those kickoffs and made all the rest of us look good. . . .

I think I'm one of the most blessed guys in the world. And one of the final notes I took this morning and I'm going to share with you is that I realized that I have five families. I have been blessed to be in five different families. I am in God's spiritual family. I want to thank Him for that. I have an earthly family: my mother, my dad, and my brother. I have my family that Pat and I have put together: Pat, J.D., Coy, and now Melissa. I have a Redskins family that I will always be a part of. And I now have a Hall of Fame family. Guys, I want to thank you for paving the way. I want to say thanks to everybody because I got everything.

■ ■ ■ ■

Nick Buoniconti
Boston Patriots and Miami Dolphins Linebacker
Class of 2001

Selected to the AFL's All-Time Team, Buoniconti also was All-AFL/AFC eight times.

Presented by His Son, Marc Buoniconti

This great game of football has given our family its brightest moments and its darkest days. Dad, eighty-five was your lucky number. But 1985 brought some tough times for the Buoniconti family.

Early that year, you lost your own dad to cancer, and then in October, I had my paralyzing injury playing linebacker for the Citadel. Looking into your eyes, I saw a mask of pain and fear transform into that familiar look of determination. I knew you were getting ready for our biggest challenge.

So when they started usinvg labels for me and telling you all the medical clichés that I'd never walk again, that I'd need a machine to breathe for me, that paralysis can't be cured, once again you didn't listen. You made a bedside promise to do everything and anything to help me walk again.

Your promise that October day sixteen years ago became the Miami Project to Cure Paralysis, the world's largest, most comprehensive spinal cord research center. It is a symbol of hope for hundreds of thousands of Americans who are waiting for a cure.

Dad, you never believed the labels and the limitations others described to you. Instead, you faced each challenge head on and made believers out of them. So in closing, I've got a label for you that I've never heard mentioned. Dad, as I look at all the things they say you couldn't do it seems to me that you're just not a very good listener.

Who would have thought that the son of an Italian baker from the south end of Springfield, Massachusetts, would go on to run a Fortune 500 company? Or that a guy with a degree in economics would be helping to make medical history? Or that a thirteenth-round pick of the fledgling AFL would today be inducted into the Pro Football Hall of Fame?

Dad, you've always been by my side and have been more of a father to me than I could have ever imagined. The best father one could hope for. Whatever it is you've got inside you, we see it, we feel it, and it gives each of us a little bit more reason to believe.

Nick Buoniconti

Well, it looks like the final chapter in my professional life has been written. It was a challenge. I took the challenge head on. It was a mountain and I climbed the mountain. But as I close that book on my professional career, as my son Marc says, the biggest challenge and the highest mountain is yet to be climbed.

You know, I wear this Super Bowl ring, which is the only ring ever produced that says the Miami Dolphins were undefeated and were perfect. I would trade this ring in and all my individual accomplishments if one thing could happen in my lifetime. My son, Marc, dreams that he walks. And as a father, I would like nothing more than to walk by his side.

■　■　■　■

Jim Kelly
Buffalo Bills Quarterback
Class of 2002

Kelly mastered the no-huddle offense that propelled the Bills to four consecutive Super Bowls. He passed for more than three thousand yards in eight seasons.

Presented by Bills Coach Marv Levy

Never mind his eye-popping statistics, he never cared about them anyway. He cared about winning, and he was a winner. He cared about his team and about his teammates. He cared about his wonderful family, and about our loyal and enthusiastic Buffalo Bills fans. He cared about his community, and he showed it.

Never mind about his arm—it was great—but what was really noteworthy about Jim was his heart. Jim Kelly's heart was as stout as a nose tackle's butt.

His qualities, he had them all. Toughness—coaching legend Joe Paterno tried to recruit Jim to come to Penn State to play linebacker. Leadership—was he good in the locker room? Heck no, his locker was a mess! Our equipment managers were good in the locker room. Jim led by his actions on the field.

Jim Kelly

Then there is my only son, Hunter, born on February 14, Valentine's Day, my birthday—the son I've always wanted. I've dreamt what every father dreams about, playing catch in the backyard, going fishing, camping, everything that fathers and sons do.

But within four months, my son was diagnosed with a fatal disease called Krabbe's Leukodystrophy. They told us to take him home and make him comfortable. And from that day, my wife and I decided to fight this disease.

And so, we made it our lifelong commitment to make sure that kids all over the world don't suffer like my son does. Since the day I was selected, I prayed to God that my son would be here with me today. God has granted me that blessing.

It has been written throughout my career that toughness is my trademark. Well, the toughest person I've ever met in my life is my hero, my soldier, my son, Hunter. I love you, buddy.

Editor's note: Hunter Kelly, whose battle with the fatal nervous system disease inspired the charitable works of his Hall-of-Fame father, died on August 5, 2005. He was eight years old.

■ ■ ■ ■

Joe DeLamielleure
Buffalo Bills and Cleveland Browns Guard
Class of 2003

A six-time Pro Bowl selection, DeLamielleure played thirteen years and 185 games.

I'm going to go into this quick. I'm going to talk about my mom and dad. Ten kids—my dad had a bar, I think it was forty-three years that he worked it—from seven in the morning to 2:30 at night, open seven days a week except Thanksgiving, Christmas, and Easter. He taught me the meaning of work and what it meant. He was a dedicated dad who cared about his kids. And, the ten kids were a beautiful family—we had a ball every day. I know my mom and dad didn't enjoy it but we sure did.

My mother taught me two things. My mother taught me teamwork and how to pray—two very important things. Teamwork came from this—one bathroom, no lock, ten kids. We learned to share early, and I appreciate her. I know they're up there. I thought they were crying they were so happy. Those were tears of joy from all of our parents that are all passed away.

I was Bo Schembechler's first recruit. I got recruited by lots of schools but I was Bo Schembechler's first recruit. I really wanted to go to Michigan bad. I wanted to go so badly, they put me with Paul Seymour when I got recruited. That was a pretty tough experience, but he still didn't deter me from wanting to go to Michigan.

But, I went to my dad and I said, "Dad, I want to go to the University of Michigan." And he said, "Joey," which he always called me, "I don't want you going there." I said, "Why?" He said: "Two reasons. Duffy's Catholic and I can't say Schembechler." So I said, "DeLamielleure, and you can't say 'Schembechler'? Good God."

But I always did what my dad told me. I took his advice. I went to Michigan State and it was the best decision I ever made. I'll never forget our first meeting and this is very important. Duffy Dougherty gathered us together as freshman and he said, "Guys, to be a great football player you need three bones—a backbone, a wishbone, and a funny bone." And I took that advice my whole life. My kids will tell you, the biggest bone I got is a funny bone.

And I am glad for Coach Dougherty and the guys I played with. I'm going to mention two who I roomed with because those guys set the bar high for me. They made Hall of Fames of their own.

My college roommate Bryce Bowron—he hurt his knee, three surgeries, eighteen months. I never forget this, at one hospital, I said, "What are you going to do now?" because our dream was to play in the National Football League, all three of ours. He said, "I think I'm going to give the Secret Service a shot." Man, did he give it a shot. He was director at age forty-three—the director under Bill Clinton. Right now, he just got named Director of Security here at the Cleveland Clinic. I've always looked up to him because he's a tough guy—three surgeries, career cut short, he didn't whine about it, he moved on with life and became a winner himself.

My other roommate, John Shinsky, from Cleveland St. Joe's. He was in an orphanage, came to Michigan State with a very bad SAT, or low, whatever. John was just an amazing guy. He used to read hard. He didn't practice hard, he read hard. Now he's a doctor, a PhD, and John lived in an orphanage. He always impressed me, so I go, "John, what are you going to do when you're older?" He said, "Joe, I'm going to open an orphanage." John didn't open one orphanage; he opened two. He had the interest; he got two orphanages going in Mount Morris, Mexico. . . .

When I was a boy—I'm going to end with this—I was ten years old, I think it was 1962, the Green Bay Packers played the Detroit Lions on Thanksgiving Day. They call it the "Thanksgiving Day Massacre." I went with my dad and my four brothers to that game. I don't know if you guys remember this but you guys got the bad seats, me and Dad got to sit on the fifty. I held Dad's hand and I said, "Dad, someday I'm going to play in this game." He didn't doubt me for a minute. He said, "When you do, I'm going to be there."

1978—time passed—we played that game. But my father had a heart attack maybe three or four weeks before. In the game, O. J. Simpson got 273 yards. Jim Ringo told me, "I've never seen you play a game that hard." I played it because my dad's not going to be there. I then walk out of the locker room, and there he is. I go, "Dad, what are doing here? Man, you shouldn't even be here. What are you crazy?"

He said, "Don't you remember 1962? I'm not going to miss this for the world." And that's a true story.

■　■　■　■

John Elway
Denver Broncos Quarterback
Class of 2004

The King of the Comeback, Elway passed for 51,475 yards and three hundred touchdowns. He was a nine-time Pro Bowl selection and MVP in 1987 and Super Bowl XXXIII.

Presented by His Daughter, Jessica Elway

As you might suspect, growing up with the last name Elway made for some pretty interesting questions. The most common one we get is, "What's the coolest part of having John Elway as a dad?"

"That's easy," we'd always respond. "We're too young to remember the first three Super Bowls."

Some of our most vivid memories came from Mile High Stadium. But they didn't have anything to do with football. We spent more time watching my dad on the sideline, waiting for him to wave up at us, than we did watching the game. And sure enough, he always did. Looking back, those are some of my most treasured moments.

As proud as we are of my dad, we'd be just as proud if he had not made the Hall of Fame. I can't tell you how much he has taught us about life. He has taught us to be leaders, to set goals, to dream, and to never, ever, ever make excuses. Above all, he has taught us to be tough. No one knows more than his children how tough my dad is, how competitive he is, how badly he wanted to win those Super Bowls.

We saw the black-and-blue marks at the kitchen table. We saw the bruises on his arms, the cuts on his fingers, and the scrapes on his elbows. Whenever one of us kids would ask him about it, he'd just smile and say, "Oh, it's okay."

He had twelve surgeries during his career. With all those aches and pains, he didn't exactly have a lot of sympathy when one of us kids came crying. I remember one time, I stubbed my toe, and he said sarcastically, "Uh-oh, better go call 911." It was a funny moment—until my little sister, Juju, called 911.

As long as I'm telling you family secrets, let me tell you another one. After the Broncos won their first Super Bowl, I asked my dad to quit. I told him I wanted him to be happy, to go out on top. But he wouldn't do it. Dad, let me tell you something I've never told you before, and I'll probably never tell you again. Thanks for not listening to me.

John Elway

Someone asked me the other day if I had any regrets about my career. There's only one, and that's that my father, Jack, and my sister, Jana, couldn't be here.

My dad wasn't just my best friend, he was my hero, my mentor, and my inspiration. He was the keeper of my reality checklist, and the compass that guided my life and my career. And he taught me the number one lesson of my life—always make your family proud. Now that he's gone, I thank God every day for letting him see the Broncos win two Super Bowls.

My dad didn't so much teach me how to play football, but why to play it. He taught me to compete, to never give up, to play every down like it's your last. He taught me to appreciate the game, to respect it, to play it like it was meant to be played. He taught me to enjoy my successes and learn from my failures. And above all, he told me, "Make sure when you go out with your offensive linemen, you pick up the tab."

My dad isn't here today, but my other hero is. But then, you've always been there for me, Mom. Thank you. I hope I've made you proud today and every other day. You think going ninety-eight yards in the fourth quarter against the Browns was tough? Try cooking breakfast and dinner every day and raising three kids while your husband is off coaching. Try driving your son all over town so he could chase his dreams. And try doing it in your spare time after working forty hours a week.

I'm going to tell a little secret that my mom and I had. It was when we were going to Super Bowl XXXII against the Packers. My mom was over and sat in my house and offered these heartfelt words of encouragement, words only a mother could say to her son—"Do we really have to go back to the Super Bowl?" I knew right then that we'd better win that one or she'd never go back. Thanks, Mom. I love you.

I'd also like to thank my many teammates—Granada Hills, Stanford University, and the Denver Broncos. I'd like to name every one of you here today, but time won't allow. Just know that I'm proud to have called you my friends and my teammates. This bust here would not be here, and neither would I, if it weren't for you guys.

People sometimes don't realize how dependent the quarterback is on his teammates to do their jobs. For every guy that ever stepped onto a field with me, I accept this honor today on behalf of all of you. Thanks for protecting me, catching my passes, defending our goal line, for sharing my highs and lows. And more than anything, thanks for not losing confidence in me when I lined up for a snap as a rookie behind the left guard.

■ ■ ■ ■

Reggie White
Philadelphia Eagles, Green Bay Packers, and
Carolina Panthers Defensive Lineman
Class of 2006

White retired as the NFL's all-time sack leader with 198. He was named All-Pro thirteen of his fifteen seasons, including ten as a first-team selection. He was voted to thirteen straight Pro Bowls.

Presented by His Son, Jeremy White

Reggie was an honest, humble, honorable, dedicated, determined, passionate, and caring man. He is inducted today not only because of his athletic achievements, but because he was a great player on the field in accordance with being a great person throughout life.

If life were to have a Hall of Fame for people who were important in society, I would be so bold as to say that my dad would be in the life Hall of Fame. His passion for God, his love for his family and community, and his dedication toward making the world a better place would at least get him nominated.

He always used to say that after he passed away, he wanted people to remember what he did away from the football field rather than being remembered for the records he broke, the games he won, the quarterbacks he sacked. Reggie will always be remembered as the man he was. He was a compassionate father, a loving husband, a selfless friend, and a loyal teammate. I know that he will be an inspiration to countless people who want to make their dream a reality, whatever their dream might be.

Even though Reggie is not here to receive this great honor the NFL has allowed him to receive, I know he is with us. He is with us in spirit, but most of all he is with us in our memories. As long as we continue to remember anyone we have lost, they are never completely gone. They are with us. The legacy that he leaves behind is what he taught everyone he met. He will live on through everything he taught. And if what we have learned and our memories of him live on, then in essence, Reggie and his legacy will continue to live on.

If people can remember that about anyone they have lost, they will realize that memories should bring joy, not sadness.

Accepting on Behalf of Reggie White, His Wife, Sara White

When I met Reggie White twenty-five years ago as a friend, I never dreamed that I would be here, let alone make this speech, let alone have the NFL career that we had together as a family. I praise the Father that I had kids who understood that their father gave of himself to so many people. Some may look at it as neglect, but we look at it as a way to reach out to people. We look at it as compassionate. We look at it as it lifts us up. The more people we help, the more people we influence, the better we are.

And just to let you know, Reggie was no phony. He stood for what he believed in. That's the thing I want to encourage you. Whatever you believe in, you stand on your principles. Do not let anyone sway you.

Often people ask: "How have you made it? How are you so strong? How do you mourn?" Everybody mourns differently, and we can't judge those who mourn outside or inside. And everybody treats death differently. But praise the Father, I know that this is not the last stop for any of us. I know where Reggie is, because I understand what he's doing and his purpose. He lived forty-three years. He's done so many things that people have not done at seventy years old.

But they ask me, "How can you be so happy? How do you survive?" Well, first of all, I have to be. You just can't lay down. But my motto is: Forgive, live, love, laugh, and pray. And that's how I've been holding my strength together for my family.

One last thing. We're talking about history. We knew Reggie, Reggie's history in football. Just like Jeremy said, "Reggie's legacy will live on through you. If you continue to do what you need to do, and your family first, your community, your school, at your work job, your legacy, you would take Reggie's spirit and legacy with you because that's what he would want you to do."

Remember, it's not how you die—it wasn't about Reggie's death—it's how he lived. I encourage you to live like Reggie lived.

■   ■   ■   ■

Thurman Thomas
Buffalo Bills and Miami Dolphins Running Back
Class of 2007

Thomas amassed 16,532 total yards, including 12,074 rushing yards. He scored eighty-eight touchdowns. He is the only player in history to lead the league in yards from scrimmage in four straight seasons.

Presented by Chiefs and Bills Coach Marv Levy

Twenty years ago today, neither I nor hardly anybody else in Buffalo knew who that fella sitting over there was. And several months later, on draft day 1988 when our Buffalo Bills were in dire need of an outstanding running back, we found ourselves in the forlorn position of not having a first-round draft choice.

Well, when our turn to pick finally came, seven running backs had already been selected. Well, I'll tell you, I was disheartened. But our running backs coach, the always astute Elijah Pitts, was elated. The one he had hoped for all along was still available.

Well, that prospect that Elijah coveted so much was about five feet nine inches tall, weighed less than 200 pounds, and was still laboring to recover from a very severe knee injury. Elijah was ardently persuasive, however, stressing not only this fella's abilities, but he assured me as well that the man was a team player, a person of high character.

"Well, what the heck," I said, "let's take a long shot chance on this guy. What did you say his name was again, Eli?" Well, it didn't take me or anyone else who loves NFL football very long to learn that his name was Thurman Thomas.

How lucky could a coach get? How lucky could his teammates get? I must admit, however, that just two weeks after the beginning of training camp that rookie year, I did seek a clarification from Elijah.

"Eli," I asked, "did you say this guy has character or that he is a character?"

Our coaches and players soon learned that both descriptions applied. Yeah, this man could really play, and he was fun, too—unless, of course, you had to play defense against him. Then he wasn't.

Most of all he contributed immensely to that fantastic team mentally that was so representative of the Buffalo Bills during Thurman's playing days there. Possessing a bubbling and extroverted personality, he was one of the most unselfish players I have ever known. On a team with many stars, never did I hear a complaint from him about not getting the ball enough, or about being taken out of the game even down at the goal line.

I also don't believe there has ever been a more complete player at his position than Thurman.

Thurman Thomas

For real, Marv [Levy], you are my inspiration. I wanted to play my best because I never wanted to disappoint you. You made me feel like every extra effort I made for the Bills was appreciated.

Marv, I remember my first game against the Houston Oilers, I spiked the ball. When I came over to the sideline, you had this look in your eye like you were very upset at me. You grabbed me by my jersey and said, "Why did you spike the ball?"

I said, "Coach, every little kid that ever watches football at least wants to do that at least one time in his career." He said, "Well, that's great, don't ever do it again. Act like you've been there before." After that, I never spiked the ball again.

Someone once told me I needed to enjoy every minute of my football career because when it ended I would miss it. I look at all of you today and every memory comes back. The memories are amazing, of a time when teammates were like brothers—regardless of race, religion, or politics—we all got in trouble just because how close we were. The wives didn't completely understand our camaraderie, which I think at least now most of them do.

To feel that rush again, I just walk through the front doors of my house and see Olivia, my oldest daughter. When she comes home from school, my little University of Florida Gator, with her amazing heart and sense of responsibility, I'm sure her little brother and two sisters know that they couldn't have been blessed with a more loving and outstanding role model.

To Angel, my free-spirited, beautiful, kindhearted comedian. If Angel can't brighten your day, make you smile, then you have to be a pretty tough cookie. I can be madder than a junkyard dog and she can make me laugh.

My ten-year-old sweet little Annika Lee. We wanted a boy so bad that we were blessed again with another girl. All I can say is thank you, God, for giving us that little girl. She is growing up to be just as lovely and beautiful as her sister.

Last but not least we decided to give it one more try. We prayed hard and we finally got our little man, Thurman III. He is everything that we had dreamed for, a blend of all five of us. Little Thurman, Daddy loves you.

To my wife, Patti, what a design only God could have planned. I was a senior at Oklahoma State when I met a freshman golfer from Buffalo, New York. We dated my senior year. I got drafted to her hometown of Buffalo, New York. That's been almost twenty years. I sit here today and I say thank you, Patti, my friend, my wife, mother of my kids. It's been twenty years since we've been together, and I would like to take this time and this opportunity to let it be another twenty years we can spend together, but also with the plan of asking you, "Will you marry me again?"

■ ■ ■ ■

Bruce Matthews
Houston Oilers and Tennessee Titans
Offensive Lineman
Class of 2007

Named to a record-tying fourteen straight Pro Bowls, Matthews played in 296 games, the most by a positional player at the time of his retirement.

Presented by Oilers and Titans Guard Mike Munchak

I don't know if there's ever been another player like Bruce Matthews in the NFL, and I don't know if there will ever be another one again.

Bruce and I have a unique relationship. I was his teammate for eleven years, his coach for eight years, but, more importantly, he has been like family to me for the past twenty-four years.

We played together on the offensive line for the Houston Oilers for more than a decade. I played left guard, he played everywhere else. His work ethic, his competitiveness, his passion for the game were contagious. I know that he motivated me to become a better player. Many of his former teammates, several who are here today, would say the same. He raised the standard for all of us.

Competitive is the word that best describes Bruce. His desire to be the best is unmatched. He wants to win at everything he does: a sport, a video game, even an argument. He can claim an opinion he doesn't even believe in just to see if he can still win the argument.

Classic Bruce, though, is when you're in a car with him and a song comes on the radio. He immediately yells out the name of the song and the artist. He would say, "Springsteen, 'Glory Days'—bam!" Even though no one else is playing this game, he's still competing.

Bruce's competitive spirit was his secret weapon and a reason why he played nineteen seasons. It kept him young at heart. He always found a way to make it fun, and it showed on the field every Sunday.

Bruce and I have followed parallel paths during our days in the NFL. We were drafted a year apart by the Houston Oilers in the first round. As offensive linemen, we had similar successes on the field. We shared sweet victories and unfortunately some tough losses.

We have been business partners. We were married two weeks apart. Our wives, Marci and Carrie, of twenty-four years became best of friends, and our children are like brothers and sisters. Because of our similar experiences, we developed a special bond that goes way beyond the football field. There were many nights after we put our kids to bed that we'd get together and talk for hours. Sometimes we would just sit outside on Bruce's ranch and have a beer, other times we'd go bowling or play some one-on-one basketball, which I guess I'll admit he usually won.

But during this time together, we'd have great discussions about our careers, our families, and our Christian walks. We were always there to encourage or challenge each other as we worked our ways through life's ups and downs.

Now that Bruce is retired from the NFL, these talks have continued over the phone lines. Bruce, I just want you to know I've always appreciated your advice and honesty over the years. You've been a great example to me of what it takes to be a good husband, father, and Christian. I'm blessed to know you.

Bruce Matthews

Many people never had anyone that they looked up to while they were growing up, but I was blessed to have two people in my house who were my role models. The first was my father, Clay Sr. He is, without a doubt, the man I most admire and respect in this world.

He played in the early 1950s for the San Francisco 49ers. Although I never saw him play, I can only imagine he would have been a handful to play against. My dad taught me about doing what was right no matter what the cost, never quitting, and what it meant to be a man of integrity.

One of my finest memories of the day the Hall-of-Fame results were announced was three or four hours later after the phone lines had cleared and I finally had a chance to talk to my dad. I said, "Dad, did you hear the news?" My dad jokingly said, "Yeah, I didn't make it in again. I guess I'm no longer eligible."

Obviously we had a great laugh, and I just want to say, Pop, I love you very much. I still respect and admire you.

My next role model was my older brother, Clay. Cleveland Brown. He is five years older than me. So as I grew up, he was the one I wanted to be like. He was and still is my favorite player of all time. I love to brag to teammates about him.

He played linebacker for the Cleveland Browns for sixteen years and the Atlanta Falcons for three years. Since the Browns were a division rival of the Oilers, I got to play against him twenty-three times. Getting to play against your idol twice a year was one of the highlights of my career, and it was always something I looked forward to. I especially loved to play in Cleveland and check out all the banners and number 57 jerseys in the crowd, see how much they loved him and still do.

I always felt as though I was witnessing something special, something that nobody else had had the opportunity to do in the history of the game. My favorite part of game week was Wednesday morning when our offensive coordinator would give an overview of the Browns' defense. I would beam with pride as he talked about how we would deal with my brother. I had to learn to watch every play on film twice: First time I watched my brother, and then the second time I had to watch the guy who I was supposed to block.

My hope was that my brother would have a great game individually, but we would win the game. Although it ended up pretty even. One of us won 12 and one of us won 11. As many times as I counted, I can't remember who won the most.

Those games proved challenging and I would find my mind wandering, wondering how my brother was doing. It took me a couple of years to learn how to prepare and play against him.

In 1986, he beat me for a sack. Although I hated giving up sacks, I didn't mind because it was to him, although I swore not to let it happen again, and it didn't.

I want to go on the record as saying that my brother Clay Matthews was without a doubt the best all around linebacker I've ever played with or against. There were some who may have been better at one discipline of linebacking, but none better all around. He played outside, inside, played the run well, covered backs, wide receivers, tight ends, rushed the passer, and excelled at all of them.

In an era of specialization, he was on the field every play and holds the record for most games played by a linebacker. The only negative surrounding my induction into the Hall of Fame is that my brother isn't already in here.

All I can say is I look forward to the day when he's standing up here getting inducted because he's very deserving. He taught me about hard work, discipline, dedication, and the mind-set necessary to excel. He was not only a role model, a big brother, but a best friend, and I thank God for him. I love you, my brother.

■ ■ ■ ■

Charlie Sanders
Detroit Lions Tight End
Class of 2007

Sanders finished with 336 career receptions for 4,817 yards and thirty-one touchdowns. He was selected to seven Pro Bowls and named to the NFL's All-Decade Team of the 1970s.

Coach McKee was my first junior high school coach. He inspired me the most. It wasn't so much what he did but what he said.

I was preparing to attend Dudley High School, our senior high school, and Coach McKee calmly walked up to me and asked me, "Are you going to try out for the football team?" Without hesitation, I responded, "Yes." He looked at me with a gleam in his eye, smile on his face, and he said, "I don't think you're tough enough."

As I look back, I don't think he doubted me; I think he wanted to see if I doubted myself. I have since learned that growth is a mental obstacle you overcome and not just a physical accomplishment you attain.

I am not that self-proclaimed Hall of Famer who desired to be in sports. I am a guy that liked a challenge and challenged myself with the understanding that winning is finishing. To my fellow brothers in the NFL, pre-, during, and some post players, that I have put the nails in the house that I had the opportunity to play in, I thank you for your sacrifice.

I wrote a poem in 1976 that I think is fitting for my brothers. I realized that I was mentally preparing for a season that my body did not want to cooperate with. The poem is called "The NFL: Just Passing Through."

Here today, gone tomorrow.
If you don't accept it, it's a life of sorrow.
Trying to use our God-given talent,
Being brave like a knight, bold and gallant.
Those who can make it feel lucky indeed.
It's God's own way of letting you succeed.
Our efforts we extend in hopes to win.
Some play their hearts, others just pretend.
So give your all and nothing less.
Today we win, tomorrow we rest.
You're not just my teammate, but my very best friend.
Let's play together until the end.
Today we hang together, just you and me.
For tomorrow is a day we may never see.

My life was written by the one I hold the highest. Like most, I question the bad and I take in the good. There have been times that I have looked back at my life and asked, What if? What if I could change one, two, maybe three things without disturbing the whole picture? What would that be?

You haven't heard me mention anything about the one person who was very important in my life: my mom. My daughter, Charese, came up to me in Cleveland as we prepared to go to a fight by my daughter, Mary Jo [a professional boxer]. She said, "Dad, thanks for being my dad, because if you were not, we wouldn't be able to go to places we go and do the things we do."

Without hesitation I looked at her and I said, "Don't thank me, thank your grandmother." She said, "But, Dad, I don't know my grandmother, I never have." My response: "That's just my point."

You see, my brothers and I lost my mother when I was only two. Of all the things I've done in football, and there have been a lot, there's one thing that I really, really regretted. Many times I've seen athletes, college, professional, often look into a television camera and say, "Hi,

Mom." I always thought that was special and always something I'd want to do but couldn't.

So I take this time right here, right now in Canton, Ohio, at the Pro Football Hall of Fame to say, "Hi, Mom. Thank you for the ultimate sacrifice. This day belongs to you, for it was written." I want to thank everyone for helping me enjoy the best day of my life and may God bless you.

■ ■ ■ ■

Emmitt Thomas
Kansas City Chiefs Cornerback
Class of 2008

Kansas City's all-time interception leader with fifty-eight, Thomas had a single-season career best twelve in 1974. He went on to become a successful assistant coach.

My personal road to Canton is very simple. I love playing football. I never wanted to cheat the fans, my organization, my teammates, or my coaches by not giving my best at all times. It wasn't a complex program; it boiled down to desire, preparation, and effort—how I played the game, and that's now how I teach it. Respect for the opponent, respect for my coaches and teammates, and respect for what it took not to just be average but to be the best football player I could be. I owed it to the fans. I owed it to Mr. Lamar Hunt, and, finally, I owed it to myself.

Every member of the Pro Football Hall of Fame has a special story how his career began. Some began in a dramatic fashion. Others spawned from a very humble beginning—much like the story I'm about to tell you. I lost my mother when I was eight years old. I could tell you that the situation shaped and molded and had a significant influence on a young man who was desperately trying to find his way.

I learned early on that the good Lord always has a plan. His plan for my sisters, my brother, and for me during those trying days was my grandparents, who became the Teflon protecting guardian angels to all of us. My late grandfather, Lewis Fyles Sr., is still my hero. I remember those long hot summer nights sitting on the porch listening to baseball games and prizefights and other sporting events. It was during these times that he taught me life's greatest lesson. He taught me about honor, commitment, love, religion, hard work, and respect.

Growing up, I was resentful and angry at other families around us because they seemed fully intact. I'd often lay awake at night wondering why our family had to be different. But I came to the stark realization that the good Lord wanted us to be reared and raised under the guiding hands of my grandfather, who in his own right was a giant of a man.

He's the big reason I'm standing here today at this summit of pro football's biggest shrine, and as a tribute to him, I asked the Pro Football Hall of Fame to let me enter the hallowed halls of Canton as Emmitt Earl Fyles Thomas.

They were kind enough to accommodate my request. Thank you, Pro Football Hall of Fame. As every member of the Hall of Fame can attest, no one gets here without a lot of help and support. I've learned some valuable lessons in my life. And one of them is in every relationship that you have, there are opportunities to learn, get better, and grow.

To all the mothers and fathers out there who are raising children, I offer you this: You're looking at a man that has a lot of blemishes, abrasions, and scars dealt to him by life's highs and lows, but you're also looking at a man who stood tall in the arena, never quit even though it looked like the game was over on many, many occasions.

And the last forty-three years of my life involved with the NFL have taught me through faith, hard work, determination, and a willingness to help someone else somewhere lead a better life, we all have a chance to rise from the most modest circumstances and become a Hall of Famer—just like this old undrafted free agent country boy from Angleton, Texas.

As I go to my seat, I'd like to leave you with these final thoughts. Our talent is God's gift to us. How we use that talent is our gift to Him. My sincere hope and prayer that God finds my gift back to Him a worthy one. May God bless you and keep you. Continue the good fight of faith.

CHAPTER 3

HISTORY

GEORGE HALAS

SOMEHOW, A SELECT GROUP OF MEN BUILT TEAMS, A league, and the public's trust, all at once. Through time and work, they invented the new national pastime.

George Halas, Paul Brown, Curly Lambeau, many others—these are now considered football's founding fathers, as important to the sport's history as George Washington and Thomas Jefferson are to American history.

They saw what others didn't. They envisioned what others couldn't. They took a game played in Ohio, and grew it into an across-the-country sensation. Yet were they alive today, even they likely would be dumbfounded at their creation.

They created a sport. They created history.

■　■　■　■

George Halas
Chicago Bears Owner
Class of 1963

A charter enshrinee, Halas led the Staleys and Bears to 324 wins. He was the only person associated with the NFL throughout the league's first fifty years. He coached the Bears for forty seasons, winning six NFL titles.

A few weeks ago, a few of our grandchildren visited the Bears' training camp and I was talking to them about this trip to Canton to participate in the dedication of pro football's Hall of Fame. Somehow the conversation got around to an earlier trip that I made to Canton some forty-three years ago when we met in Ralph Hay's showroom, his automobile showroom, and founded the National Football League.

I told them some of the informal aspects of that meeting and among them being that there was a lack of chairs, and also that we had to sit on the running board of the car. That prompted my nine-year-old grandson to say, "What is a running board, Grandpa?" My fourteen-year-old grandson said running boards are those things that you see on those funny old cars in that television series known as *The Untouchables*.

That little incident demonstrated to me how things can change or disappear until a chance remark or a question, a child's question, stirs your memory.

■　■　■　■

Earl "Curly" Lambeau
Green Bay Packers, Chicago Cardinals, and Washington Redskins Coach
Class of 1963

A charter enshrinee, Lambeau posted a 229-134-22 coaching record that included six NFL championships. He founded the pre-NFL Packers in 1919.

I am deeply grateful and very happy to be honored here today. Forty-one years ago I came to Canton to get a franchise for Green Bay, Wisconsin. The franchise was issued by Joe Carr at that time and it cost $50, and the last time I looked, the Packers are still in the league. Thank you.

■　■　■　■

Mel Hein
New York Giants Center
Class of 1963

A charter enshrinee, Hein was a sixty-minute regular for fifteen years and an All-NFL selection in eight consecutive years.

Most of us got in last night, and most of us got together for a little while to compare notes and talk over old times. I've knocked heads against most of these fellows, and you should have heard some of the stories that were told last night, and if any of you people doubt that we're not great, you should have been there.

That's the way it is with football, whether you're in high school, college, or the professional ranks. The longer you're away from the sport, the greater you become. And it thrills me to death to think how great I'll be when I'm one hundred years old.

■　■　■　■

Sammy Baugh
Washington Redskins Quarterback
Class of 1963

A charter enshrinee, Baugh was a six-time NFL passing leader, and the NFL passing, punting, and interception champion in 1943.
I feel as the other men on the program who have been up here do. I'm very honored to be inducted into Pro Football's Hall of Fame. But to me, the people who should be honored are the owners who stayed with it back in those days when they weren't making money.

They were losing money with pro teams. They still loved the game and thought enough of it to stay there and lose their money until the game became what it is today. A player didn't have much to lose. When you start putting your own money up and not having anything in return, friend, you've got a little courage then.

■　■　■　■

Bronko Nagurski
Chicago Bears Fullback Linebacker/Tackle
Class of 1963

A charter enshrinee, Nagurski rushed for 2,778 yards in nine seasons and was an All-NFL selection five times.
In the past I've been asked many times if I wouldn't like to return to football. Well, I could tell you right now if I had to face what I've got sitting behind me, nothing could ever get me off the farm.

■　■　■　■

Otto Graham
Cleveland Browns Quarterback
Class of 1965

Graham threw for 23,584 yards and 174 touchdowns. He guided the Browns to ten division or league crowns in ten seasons.

I've had many honors in my day, but I have to admit, this has to be the tops of all of them. I honestly don't think I belong here, but I'll be darned if I'll give this bust back. The greatest honor though for me personally is having Paul Brown come back to give this award to me. In my opinion, he is the greatest football coach ever, and one of my very dearest friends.

■ ■ ■ ■

Bill Dudley
Pittsburgh Steelers, Detroit Lions,
and Washington Redskins Halfback
Class of 1966

Dudley won NFL rushing, interception, and punt return titles in 1946. He was All-NFL in 1942, 1946, and 1947.

There's not much that one, who the game of football has meant so much to as yours truly, can say at this moment. Football has been a part of my life for the past thirty-five or forty—well, the past forty-five years—and I hope it's a part of my life for as long as I live, and particularly this Football Hall of Fame. I feel humble, very humble, to be considered to be a member as well as to be considered a part of pro football because it's great today, it was great years ago when it was first started here in Canton, and it'll be greater tomorrow.

■ ■ ■ ■

Paul Brown
Cleveland Browns Head Coach
Class of 1967

Brown built the Cleveland dynasty with a 167-53-8 record, four AAFC titles, and three NFL crowns. He returned to coaching with the Cincinnati Bengals after induction, from 1968–75.

Presented by Browns Quarterback Otto Graham

It's a very distinct pleasure for me to be back in Canton, just a couple of years after I was honored, being inducted into the Hall of Fame by Paul himself. And, of course, now that I'm coaching, it's pretty hard to get time off to come back and do things like this. In fact, I had to call practice off today in order to get here. This is something Paul Brown would have never done, I guarantee you this. He just doesn't believe in those kinds of things and that's why he was successful, and I probably won't be.

I must admit that I was a normal American red-blooded boy football player that always didn't like my coach and I used to cuss him out like every boy did. I could never understand why he did some things, but I can tell you very honestly now that I'm coaching, I even outdo Paul Brown. And I am very happy that I played under him.

Paul Brown

I want to thank Otto for coming back to do this. I've said many times that he's really not only the greatest player I ever had, but really the basic reason we won so many times. All football players have the same spirit of just the one thing that counted—just whether we win.

I also would like to say this to the people of Canton. I had a rather personal interest in this Hall of Fame and it being in this area. I can remember the meetings that were held real early before this was realized. This was just a piece of ground they were going to pick out, and we'd meet out at Congress Lake and try to figure out whether we could get it to Canton. And I must say, it belongs here.

For any little part that I had in trying to sell the National League people in that, I'm so very glad that I did it. It makes me so very proud that I might have helped a little bit.

■　■　■　■

Bobby Layne
Chicago Bears, New York Bulldogs, Detroit Lions, and Pittsburgh Steelers Quarterback
Class of 1967

Layne passed for 26,768 yards and 196 touchdowns. He also ran for 2,451 yards. His late touchdown pass won the 1953 NFL title game.
This is the greatest moment of my life. I've dreamed of this a long, long time and it's here and, of course, I'm nervous. I feel like I am even now for all the safety blitzes I had to face.

■　■　■　■

Elroy "Crazy Legs" Hirsch
Los Angeles Rams Running Back
Class of 1968

A key part of the Rams' revolutionary "three end" offense, Hirsch caught 387 passes for 7,029 yards and sixty touchdowns.

Presented by Rams Coach Hampton Pool

Football is best appreciated, I think, when we keep our eyes on the field instead of in the statistics books. I think it is best appreciated when you are in the stadium on Sunday afternoon, for you're there with all the excitement. And if you've ever seen Elroy perform on Sunday afternoon, you'll agree with me.

First you saw that peculiar gate of his, that way of running, that got him his nickname. His legs were like the pistons of a car—that is a car with a tank full of Jack Daniels. Then there is his nickname. There have only been two baseball players who had a nickname as good as Elroy's—Jerome Hanna "Dizzy" Dean and George Herman "Babe" Ruth. But no one upon being introduced to Elroy has ever asked "Crazy Legs" who? Anymore than they would ask "Papa Bear" who? You just know who.

Elroy has frequently made a spectacle of himself. Most of you will remember, I'm sure, Elroy's movie, *Crazy Legs*. I know you older folks will, and most of you youngsters have probably seen it frequently on the late show on TV. Like Elroy, it is still running. But *Crazy Legs* was the first movie Hollywood ever made about professional football, and it was a good movie, and I think it had a lot to do with making professional football popular.

In any discussion regarding Elroy Hirsch, you could never forget his will to win and his come-through ability, which only these great ones have. You also must remember his warmth and friendliness. He never was so busy that he could not help one of our rookie players or sign an autograph for a little kid. Elroy now is an executive for the Los Angeles Rams, and he is also husband to his wife, Ruth, and father to his son, Wyn, and daughter, Patty. But to the rest of us, he is Elroy Hirsch, "The End."

Elroy Hirsch

If any of you think this isn't tough, I wish it were a kickoff and I were being clobbered, believe me.

■ ■ ■ ■

Earle "Greasy" Neale
Philadelphia Eagles Coach
Class of 1969

Neale turned the Eagles into winners with three consecutive division crowns, as well as NFL championships in 1948 and 1949. Before that, he played outfield for the Cincinnati Reds, batted .357, and played in the 1919 World Series.

I played in 1917 with the Canton Bulldogs under the name of "Foster," and the Detroit paper came out and picked an all-pro team and they picked Greasy Neale at right end. The reason I covered it up with the fictitious name Foster was because the Cincinnati ball club didn't allow you to play professional football.

Now I'll speak of Jim Thorpe. I saw him in 1919 when I wasn't playing because I was in a World Series that year. I saw him punt three times, Jim Thorpe, in 1919. Each one traveled over eighty yards. He could run the hundred, in uniform, in ten seconds. He weighed 208 pounds, could block, and he played at Akron all by himself, the only man in the backfield.

How I got the T-formation was because I was playing bridge at the University of Virginia with a boy that was studying law, and he invited me over to a restaurant right off Eighth Avenue and Fifty-sixth Street, West Fifty-sixth Street. He had all the officials of Fox Films with him. So I said to him, I said, "I don't understand how you get this play, this special play that you show on TV, on your pictures."

He said, "We tape the whole ball game." I said, "You do?" I said, "What would it cost me for a 16mm reel of the 73–0 game which the Bears had beaten the Redskins down in Washington?" They told me, "Oh, $168." I said, "Get them for me," and then I studied them eight hours a day for the next four months, and I picked out the best that Halas had. I was the first man in the National Football League outside of Halas that ever used the T-formation.

■ ■ ■ ■

Hugh McElhenny
San Francisco 49ers, Minnesota Vikings,
New York Giants, and Detroit Lions Halfback
Class of 1970

McElhenny rushed for 5,281 yards, scored 360 points, and totaled 11,375 total rushing, receiving, and kick return yards.

Presented by 49ers President Lou Spadia

Before telling you of Hugh McElhenny, I would like to make one comment. Like all of us, I have had a great concern in the recent months and years about the future of our country. But I'll tell you, after riding in the parade this morning and seeing the wonderful young people that you have here in Canton, my fears are no longer there. I'm sure this country is good for at least another two hundred years.

While we were leaving San Francisco to come back here, I asked our publicity director to give me a fact sheet on Hugh McElhenny. Well, he handed me four or five pages of records and statistics and looking at them, I was amazed at the accomplishments of this young man. But really, the statistics were hollow because there is no statistic that can describe the beauty and artistry of Hugh McElhenny running. He was simply the greatest runner of all time.

But the magnificent thing about Hugh is that he took this gift of God, nourished it, treasured it, and carried it on to his public. Now his knees don't bend quite as easily, but those great characteristics that made him a fine football player make him today a great father, devoted husband, and real citizen.

Hugh McElhenny

I was asked several months ago what I would say here this afternoon and I felt that I did not need to prepare a speech, for I knew as I stand here before you, the emotional individual that I am, that this would happen to me.

This is the greatest honor that has ever been bestowed upon me, and my credit goes to the athletes that I played with and the second effort that they made to make my runs and my receptions the successes that they were. And I also must thank the teams in which we played, my opponents, for all the mistakes they made to make me look good.

My mother, father, wife, and children accept this honor as I do.

■ ■ ■ ■

Norm Van Brocklin
Los Angeles Rams and
Philadelphia Eagles Quarterback
Class of 1971

Van Brocklin set a single-game NFL record, throwing for 554 yards in the 1951 season opener. He guided the Eagles to an NFL crown as league MVP in 1960.

Presented by Falcons Owner Rankin Smith

His companion through all these years, both good and bad, has been his wife, Gloria, who was his college biology teacher. He was indeed a straight "A" student in biology. No one has had a more stormy or more colorful career than this enormously talented, fiercely competitive, and inspired leader in his chosen profession. Ladies and gentlemen, the inimitable "Dutchman," Norm Van Brocklin.

Norm Van Brocklin

I have in my football career so many things that I have to be thankful for: the people, the times, the events, the ups, the downs, but above all, in football—and some of my fellow inductees have touched on it—is the fact that out of all this we feel as one member of a football organization. And today I feel so insignificant to the great game of football and to all the men that have preceded me in the Hall of Fame.

■　■　■　■

Lamar Hunt
Kansas City Chiefs and Dallas Texans Owner
Class of 1972

Hunt was the driving force behind the organization of the AFL, and he then spearheaded the merger negotiations with the NFL in 1966.

Presented by Patriots President Billy Sullivan

It might be that there is a happier person in the world today than I, but I don't know what his name would be. So today we salute a man who can neither kick, nor pass, nor block, nor punt. The AFL's first enshrine—the incomparable Lamar Hunt.

It was just thirteen years ago today when he launched the AFL on its incredible way. And you know, they laughed when Lamar sat down at that sparsely attended press conference in Harry Wismer's apartment and noted that he was commencing a new league which someday would be an appendage with the established NFL.

The laughter was subdued and has changed to applause only seven years later, when he sat alongside Commissioner Pete Rozelle and Tex Schramm and announced the celebration of a marriage between the fastidious tradition-laden old NFL and the brash upstart new American Football League.

Now that mirth wasn't confined to the press conference room alone. From coast to coast, the new concept was ridiculed, downgraded, derided, and, worst of all, ignored. But since that time, a lot has happened.

Disbelievers became converts. Agnostics became devout American Football League fanatics. And the reasons were numerous for I humbly submit that the man who is being honored here today served more than any one individual in our time to rewrite the pages of sports history to indicate that where there is a will there is still a way. To show that those who are willing to pay the price can achieve success, and the price today as yesterday, and as tomorrow, is hard work.

It took a stern man to shrug his shoulder at the barbs, the scorn, the snobs, and the rebuffs, the scoffing and jeering, the taunting and the batter which were the handmaidens of the American Football in its early days and such a man we are honoring today.

We saw him at league meetings time after time when Plan A would help his team and Plan B would help professional football, and as the night would follow the day, you could always be sure that our honoree would vote for what was in the best interest of the game.

And soon the youngest man among our owners gained the greatest respect of all. The old wise heads in the National Football League—men like Carroll Rosenbloom, who is here today, a man like the commissioner—recognized that when a man with the character of Lamar Hunt was involved, it was insurable and inevitable that the day of the merger would come.

So it seems entirely appropriate, therefore, that he was the first American Football League man to enter the Hall of Fame. He brought the first team that won the final Super Bowl game before the realignment took place. It was he who suggested names on the back of the uniforms. It was he who chose the title "Super Bowl." It was also he who recommended, and wisely so, that the trophy given to the winner of the Super Bowl be named in honor of one of the great figures of the game, the late and revered Vince Lombardi.

Truly the great stars of the game will see the days when more passes will be thrown, more touchdowns scored, more ground gained. History has a habit of repeating itself. But I submit that there will never be a twenty-seven-year-old young man who will more effectively rewrite the story of sports in our times or in the time of anyone to come.

So there is a little word that I would use today. It is *duende*. That is a Spanish word. It means not just charisma, but it is charisma to the nth degree. It is something a little bit above a superstar. It is a man of abounding charm, a man of great character. And I say that Lamar Hunt is all *duende*.

Now it is my distinct privilege to present to this audience the architect and designer, the builder of the sports version of the impossible dream. A truly gentle gentleman, a modest person who has let his actions speak more loudly than his words, an individual who does the common things uncommonly well and who in his soft-styled manner still indicates that when the going gets tough, the tough get going.

I'm sure that the selection of no man in the history of this great shrine—past, present, or future—will be more widely applauded by his peers than that of our great founding father, our guiding light, our pleasant leader, the indomitable Texan, Lamar Hunt.

Lamar Hunt

Everyone's life takes funny bounces and funny turns and it has been my privilege to be associated in football with men such as Bill Sullivan, Wayne Valley, Bud Adams, and Ralph Wilson. They had a dream on which we worked together and it was a very tough fight, this American Football League, and we were able to achieve a degree of success, and I consider them to be among my very closest friends on earth.

It has been remarkable luck for me to be involved with what some people call the game of our times. It's been exciting to see pro football grow and develop. It is really an understatement for me to say that I'm proud to share this stage with this illustrious group that is up here with me today.

No one ever really benefited, I don't suppose, from an association with others as much as I have.

■　■　■

Lou Groza
Cleveland Browns Tackle/Kicker
Class of 1974

Groza scored 1,608 points in twenty-one years. He was selected to nine Pro Bowls, was All-NFL six years, and was the NFL Player of the Year in 1954.

Presented by Browns Coach Paul Brown

Lou Groza embodies more of what I value in the combination of football player, husband, father, son, than any player that I have had. I think it sort of shows you about things when one of the first things he said when he found out he was elected to the Hall of Fame was, "Isn't it wonderful that my mother will get to go to this?"

Lou Groza

As I am here with these wonderful gentlemen that I have become acquainted with, I'm impressed that these fellows are great because they come from wonderful families and they, too, are good family men. I always wanted to be a good son to my own parents, and I wanted to be representative of a good family. I'm pleased that my mother is here and my wife and my children, and really this is my life. This is what it is all about. Any goals that I have set in my life have always been in regard to what is best for them. . . .

I had the ability to go ahead to Ohio State, where Paul Brown invited me to join his team, and how thankful I was that he thought I was good enough to be a part of his football team. However, I couldn't compete scholastically at college. I had to go to the army for three years and there I really grew up. I learned the fundamentals of living because I was in the Ninety-sixth Infantry Division, and I went to Okinawa, and when I got out of the service, I signed a professional football contract and I was part of Paul Brown's team for many years to come.

And there I learned not only that football was important but many other things. And the thing he taught me, I think, was to hold myself out always as a good representative of pro football and to be something that the youngsters would like to be themselves. And I didn't know if I always accomplished that, but I did try to set a good example. And I hope that I have done it.

My future, the kicks I will get out of my future, will be involved with my family. I may have not become familiar with a lot of you fans, but really basically, I think this is what makes a football player work, what makes him want to be good, because he likes to hear you say, "Nice going," to get a pat on the back, but most of all riding up here in the parade today.

I just can't tell you how overwhelming it was to hear the people clapping. Sometimes I wonder when something like this happens to you, "Are you really man enough to say what you want to say so it is all encompassing?" I don't think I have. But I do want you to know one thing. This is what memories are made of. Thanks for the memories.

■　■　■　■

George Connor
Chicago Bears Tackle/Linebacker
Class of 1975

All-NFL at three positions—tackle, defensive tackle, and line-backer—Connor was All-NFL for five years and played in the first four Pro Bowls.

Presented by Bears Coach George Halas

He seems to be physically as massive today as he was in his eight NFL seasons. He towered at six-foot-three and hasn't shrunk over these years. He came in at 240 pounds, and I'll leave it up to him on whether he has added any poundage. The sight of this solid, muscular athlete in action inspired the late sportswriter Grantland Rice to observe, "Connor was the closest thing to the Greek god Apollo. . . . He was Chicago born and bred—he was a premature birth and weighed only three pounds—but he had a lot of growing up to do from the tiny acorn to a mighty oak."

George Connor

I played in the early days and we didn't have reruns. But they have reruns now and I have done some work on television, and I know what one is. The last five months have been a rerun of my life.

I have been so fortunate to hear from former friends and teachers and coaches. Dave Conlin from the *Chicago Tribune* has said that George Connor has had more parties before going to the Hall of Fame in Canton, and that all his relatives are now broke.

My lovely wife comes from a nonathletic family and it has been tough for her to understand all these parties. She thought I should be out working, selling corrugated boxes. But I always try to combine them both.

■ ■ ■ ■

Dante Lavelli
Cleveland Browns End
Class of 1975

Lavelli caught 386 passes for 6,488 yards and sixty-two touch-downs. In six NFL title games, he caught twenty-four passes.

Presented by Browns Coach Paul Brown

I first met Dante Lavelli when I recruited him to go to Ohio State from Hudson, Ohio. His father was a local iron welding working gentleman there. We met the family, and he had great foot speed. At that time, I did not know what a super catcher of the ball he would turn out to be.

He was a running back in our national championship game in 1942 and then went to war like all of us did at that time. As a result, he missed two or three years of his college existence. He was gone long enough that when he came out, five or six years had lapsed, and he was ready to make a living. We took him into professional football with the understanding that he would get his degree, and he did.

He was probably the ultimate all-American boy. The young man didn't drink or smoke. He was the epitome of the kind of person you want to raise to be your son, and he became very special to me.

Dante Lavelli

An honor of this magnitude is never achieved without the help of so many others. I would like to take time out to thank my mom and dad for catching the boat that brought them to this wonderful country of America. I would like to thank my sister, Edith, who played catch with me in my younger years. My wonderful wife, Joy, and my three children, who gave me my inspiration and who sacrificed when I was not home much in my playing days.

Now to let you in on a little secret: I want to thank Paul Brown for sending someone up Highway 91 in Twinsburgh, Ohio, where I was working cutting grass, for changing my mind from going from Notre Dame to attending Ohio State. Paul Brown is the man who made this day possible for me.

■　■　■　■

Alphonse "Tuffy" Leemans
New York Giants Fullback
Class of 1978

Leemans rushed for 3,132 yards, passed for 2,318 yards, and had 422 receiving yards. In 1936, as a rookie, he led the NFL in rushing.

Presented by East High School (Wisconsin) Football Coach Peter Guzy

Tuffy never forgot his high school coach throughout his New York days, occasionally sending me a play or two along with many words of encouragement, and he remained the gentleman that he is in spite of his popularity and success.

So today the dream comes true for Tuffy, which he so rightly has earned and deserved. And for me, the high school coach, whose dream it was to see one of his players so honored, it is a person whom I respect and idolize. It is with great pride I present Alphonse "Tuffy" Leemans to the Pro Football Hall of Fame.

Alphonse Leemans

Ladies and gentlemen, thirty-five years—that's what it took me, and it's worth every bit of it. I have met the finest people in the world. It has been a long haul and a lot of injuries on the way. But I assure you today, after seeing what I have seen, it is worth every bit of those bumps. . . .

My induction today is going to make a little bit of history. Two of us came from a small little place in Alouise, Wisconsin. One was NFL Hall of Famer Ernie Nevers and now Tuffy makes it. . . .

Then I came along and I was drafted with the New York Giants— not the number one pick but the second pick. And I was picked by a young seventeen-year-old boy who is now the president and one of my finest friends, Wellington Mara. I was his first pick and he is my first pick, and I played under another Hall of Famer and a wonderful man, the late Steve Owen. . . .

I am so happy for my family. I mean, I have got to be a success; I have about fifteen or sixteen relatives and my in-laws out there. And I want to say that I am probably the proudest guy in the world and I am so happy that today I never before allowed anyone to call me Alphonse. But you can call me Alphonse today.

■　■　■　■

Lance Alworth
San Diego Chargers and
Dallas Cowboys Wide Receiver
Class of 1978

An All-AFL player in seven seasons, Alworth caught 542 passes for 10,266 yards and eighty-five touchdowns.

Presented by Raiders Owner Al Davis

It is truly an emotional and inspirational experience to be a member of the National Football League, to come here to the Hall and to walk through its exhibits, to stand in the shadows of the great men whom we idolized as young people and in whose glory we all share. It brings a realization of the great debt we owe to them and we leave here every year with a firm resolution that we will never forget that debt.

My life has been years of glory sprinkled with a few days of defeat, but today is a day of glory for me because it is a great honor to serve in this role. I have shared great moments in Lance Alworth's life as well as his sharing great moments in my life.

In 1960, while the great National Football League prospered, a new league called the American Football League was formed, dedicated to uphold the tremendous traditions of professional football that is so brilliantly espoused in this great Hall of Fame. We had a goal. We wanted to make our new young league the finest in all of professional football.

We had money, we had fine brilliant people, fine organization, coaches, scouts, small fan appeal, but above all, we needed great players. In the struggle to sign great players, our league was most fortunate in January of 1962 at the Sugar Bowl, under the goalposts, to sign Lance Alworth for the San Diego Chargers. Lance Alworth said money was not a factor, I want to grow with the young league and the young team.

No one questioned Lance's being destined for greatness, for he was born with physical talent. It was up to him to utilize that talent, and did he ever put it to use. Under the guidance of Sid Gillman, great coach and innovator, Lance with his exploits captured the imagination of football fans throughout the country and gave credibility to the new league with his wide-open exciting football. Pro players in both leagues pointed to Lance as the best at his position, being the first American Football League player whom the NFL people referred to as the point of comparison in judging athletes. In other words, that kid is like Lance Alworth.

The record books show that Lance Alworth was one of the most productive players of all times. He broke the great Don Hutson's record and caught at least one pass in ninety-six straight regular-season games. He was All-Pro seven straight seasons, played in seven all-star games. At the twilight of his career, he joined the Dallas Cowboys and caught their first TD pass in their initial Super Bowl win over the Miami Dolphins. Lance compiled these records against man-to-man coverage, zone, bump-and-run coverages when few had ever seen those, double coverage, triple coverage, and he did it in the years rule makers did not try to restrict the defense.

The records did not tell what really set him apart. He was beloved by his teammates, and I know. He was honored by his foes, and I know. He was admired by the players because he had courage and he had an indomitable spirit, and confidence and a killer instinct that made him the most feared player of our time.

Lance Alworth, the chills go through my body as I hear that roar and I think of all those special people. I can see the faces of many of them as if it were only yesterday. Some of those legendary heroes—Lamar Hunt, George Blanda—are here today. Some have become doctors, dentists, teachers, lawyers. Some are in sports, entertainment, Congress. Others are in less fortunate situations today and sadly some have passed away. But I know wherever they are today, a sense of pride will swell in all of them.

And Lance, because you come here today with credentials that have been passed by few if any, you will enrich this Hall of Fame, you will be their standard there, the first American Football League player enshrined in the Hall.

And so, as the roar of the crowd and my dream stadium become thunderous, I can hear the field announcer saying, "From Brookhaven, Mississippi, where he was a high school All-American, from the University of Arkansas, where he was a collegiate All-American, from the San Diego Chargers and Dallas Cowboys, where he was All-Pro, number 19 in his finest hour, Hall of Famer, Lance Alworth."

Lance Alworth

I guess after hearing that introduction, no one is wondering now why I picked the AFL. Al Davis recruited me and I did go to the AFL. He was a big reason why I did, and Al, I want to thank you for those kind words today, they were really touching. At this point in time, it is hard to get words out. . . .

Al Davis brought me to the AFL and he has been a close confidant of mine in the last four or five years that I have retired. That meant an awful lot to me because when you retire, you are left alone and it is all over, and I want to thank Al for being close to me in that period of time.

Ron Mix
San Diego Chargers Tackle
Class of 1979

An All-AFL selection nine times, Mix was called for holding pen-alties only two times in ten seasons.

Presented by Chargers Assistant Coach Joe Madro

Ron Mix represents all that a professional football offensive line-man should be. Ron was totally committed, with speed, strength, flexibility.

With a great capacity for work and self-critique, Ron would always devote time after practice to further improve his skills. He had no peer as an offensive-line technician. Each snap of the ball was a challenge to this combatant. Ron would select and implement his skills like a surgeon wielding his scalpel.

The combination of his mental and physical attributes prompted my labeling him the intellectual assassin.

Ron Mix

We walk through the Hall of Fame, a great tribute to hard work and the history of professional football, and it just seems to come alive.

I know I looked at those old photographs and I tell you, I saw a great similarity of those players many, many years ago with the old Canton Bulldogs and those that exist today. You see those same thick necks, those same thick shoulders. Their necks and shoulders were made that way from the hard work in the steel mills, digging coal, while they played the game for nothing. And to look at those pictures closely, you can truly see in their eyes the fire and enthusiasm that made men take pleasure in something they risked greatly. . . .

To be a part of remembered history of professional football is truly beyond anything I ever dreamed, beyond anything I sought. My only desire really was to simply be a part of this great game of professional football. I never consciously thought of the honor that is with me today. I tried only to play as hard as I could on every down and to conduct my life off the field and on the field in a way that would make me a better football player. If I were to try to begin to express where I started, I must honestly say, it begins in this great country of America.

You know President Carter says, "Love your country." There is a great much to love about it. It's a country that protects our freedom and allows us to rise as far as our capacity to work and our desires will carry us.

And then I think about my mother, a woman who worked with that quiet dignity and great courage that millions of other divorced women of America do when they are left to raise children on their own and somehow do it by themselves. They see that their children stay in school and see that they are educated and they are imparted with a system of values. . . .

We're judged whether we're a success or not in this world by what we have given to others. Has there been somewhere along the way we have stopped to help others? Have we stopped to help a young boy? . . .

I spent my career in the American Football League and sometimes, in fact just about all the time, when sportswriters asked me if I ever regretted not signing with the Baltimore Colts, my first thought is always, would I have met my wife, Pat, if I would have gone to Baltimore? I promise you that is my first thought.

And through all of this, there is still one thing I must tell you about and that is the players. I can't exclude them, most of whom will not be up here today. They are simply a part of the game, and I have the grandest respect for them.

From the first day you report to training camp, from that first contact drill you play with an injury of some type for the rest of the season, the pressure is tremendous to try to keep playing and you play in front of millions of people, thousands of people in person. You make your mistakes in person and you can't erase them. These players do that.

To them I must recognize their great talent and finally you think about training and you train as hard as you can in the off-season. Yet you know with all that training, once that game starts, and that great explosion of energy takes place, you try to do your best. You are exhausted, and you thank goodness for the time between the plays to rest up again and come back again.

■ ■ ■ ■

Morris "Red" Badgro
New York Yankees, New York Giants,
and Brooklyn Dodgers End
Class of 1981

*A first- or second-team All-NFL selection four times,
Badgro scored the first touchdown in the NFL championship
game series in 1933.*

Presented by Giants Center Mel Hein

In 1930, Red thought he would concentrate on football only, so he signed a contract with the New York Giants. He played from 1930–35, six years. Four of those years he was All-Pro. That's when they only picked eleven men going both ways. The other two great ends at the time were fellows like Bill Hewitt from the Chicago Bears, who was enshrined many years ago, and Ray Flaherty, who was enshrined five years ago. Now we will have Red Badgro, if he doesn't faint before he gets up here.

Morris Badgro

I would like to give you a little rundown on what I have been doing and how football was played way back about fifty long years ago. First of all, the squads at that time were only twenty-two men. Out of those twenty-two men, the eleven fellows who started the game usually had to play sixty minutes; the second eleven seemed to be the substitutes, so you were due for a good sixty minutes. And the passing was very little at that time, and I'll try to explain why.

During that time the football that you see today was nothing like we used. It was a smaller ball and they could pass the ball much easier. We didn't have the dome stadiums and the nice turf they have today, and with that wet old ball playing out in the mud, the game wasn't too interesting.

Now as we know it, it is a game of specialists. Every one of the forty-four men on a team, which is twice as much as we had, everyone is a specialist. They get out and with the remarkable job they can do, they made the game so much more interesting and really the crowd gets a thrill out of this aerial circus.

Now we will get around to what everyone wants to ask me—the salaries. Well, I received $150 a game. Now I thought that was great. I see a lot of people smiling here, but that was a lot of money. I was glad to get it and I'm telling you it was a really great feeling because at that time—I don't know if any of you remember the big Depression, we could buy a hot dog for five cents, a hamburger for ten cents. I paid $3 for a hamburger yesterday and you could buy one for ten cents then and that was the difference. You could also buy a tailored-made suit for $25. Every year from New York we would go back home with a brand-new car costing $400–$500. So in regards to the salary, there was quite a difference. . . .

Now a lot of people say, "Well, you are way out there in a little town in Washington, how did you ever think you would get into the pros? How did they pick you up?" Well, we all know you have to have a lucky break somewhere along in your life, and I think this was one of mine.

Just as I was going back to school my senior year in 1927, I was just entering my fraternity house and out rushed Roy Baker, who had played with Red Grange the year before. He stopped me and said by chance, "Red, do you want to play pro football?" Well, I kind of hesitated and said, "Well, sure, I'll take a shot at it," and two days later I got word from New York to come join the New York Yankees.

Now just think: If I would have been one minute later and had not met Baker coming out of the fraternity house, I would have never played pro football and I'd be missing here today.

■ ■ ■ ■

Sonny Jurgensen
Philadelphia Eagles and
Washington Redskins Quarterback
Class of 1983

Jurgensen threw for 32,224 yards and 255 touchdowns with an 82.63 passer rating.

Presented by Redskins President/
Attorney Edward Bennett Williams

It was 1959, behind a journeyman line, Sonny Jurgensen had been sacked, pounded, weakened, and flattened. And once again he had passed the Redskins to victory.

Coach Lombardi walked to the dressing room and he said this to the press: "Sonny Jurgensen is a great quarterback. He may be the greatest this league has ever seen; he certainly is the best I have ever seen. He hangs in there in the worst of adversity. He's no longer a young man; he's all man."

Sonny Jurgensen

When I look back on my career, I consider myself very fortunate just to have the opportunity to play professional football. You remember I went to Duke University. I think we threw the ball something like fifty-three times my senior year there. I really wasn't schooled for coming into professional football. If it hadn't been for an assistant coach there by the name of Clarence A. Parker, who is enshrined right here in this Hall, telling professional scouts that I had the God-given talent to throw the football, I doubt very seriously that I would ever have had the chance to play.

• • • •

Sid Gillman
Los Angeles Rams, San Diego Chargers, and
Houston Oilers Coach
Class of 1983

The first coach to win division titles in the NFL and AFL, Gill-man compiled a 123-104-7 record.

Presented by Rams and Chargers Assistant Coach Joe Madro

Football is a piece of business, as we all know, and I'm not just talking about athletic talent. You have human insight to select a highly talented staff and many of Gillman's assistants from his original Chargers staff went out to become successful coaches and administrators.

An example, Al Davis—who was an excellent coach—is the managing general partner of the Raiders, who hold the winningest record, not just in all of professional football over the last twenty years but in all of sports. Chuck Noll is a native of Cleveland and a highly successful coach of the Steelers, the only four-time Super Bowl champion.

In June of 1970, Gillman underwent surgery for multiheart artery bypass and by the start of the season, he was back on the firing line, coaching the quarterbacks of the Eagles. Last March he accepted a new challenge, becoming the general manager of the Tulsa, Oklahoma, Outlaws, an expansion team of the USFL. This is extraordinary, considering most of the teams have a much younger coaching staff.

Gillman is keen of mind and young at heart. He continues to explore new football horizons, seeking, searching, finding. He lives in a reality that is always pursuing a dream.

Sid Gillman

I would have been very happy with a college experience, but we came to the pros. And you can imagine starting with the Los Angeles Rams and having a guy like Norm Van Brocklin, golden passer, to Elroy Hirsch, and then to Tom Fears, all three of them are in that building in the Hall of Fame.

And I also had two great general managers, the first of which is Tex Schramm, the tremendous rigger of the Dallas Cowboys, and my second general manager, who is none other than Pete Rozelle, the commissioner of the NFL.

I still think they are probably a little mad at us yet in Los Angeles because at one time, Pete and I combined for a trade that was ten players for one. The one that we traded for was Ollie Matson, who happens to be in the Hall of Fame. The other Joes, I don't know where they are, but God bless them and I hope they are happy.

■ ■ ■ ■

Mike McCormack
New York Yanks and Cleveland Browns Tackle
Class of 1984

A six-time Pro Bowl selection, McCormack excelled as an offensive right tackle for eight seasons.

Presented by Browns Coach Paul Brown

Mike was a very intelligent and intense player. He was our captain. I appoint the captains and I don't appoint them without good reasons. He was our leader and he earned every bit of the honors that are coming to him today. This man exemplifies more of the things that I value in football than anybody I know or I have had.

Mike McCormack

To prepare for this moment, you think about the things in your past, the nostalgic things. You get a lot of strange feelings, a lot of different feelings. My feelings can best be exemplified from a poem that was found in Andersonville prison after the Civil War. It said:

I ask God for strength that I might achieve,
I was made weak so I may learn to humbly obey.
I ask for riches that I might be happy,
I was given poverty that I might be wise.
I asked for all things that I might enjoy life,
I was given life that I might enjoy all things.
I received nothing that I had asked for, but everything I had
      hoped for.
Despite myself, I am a most blessed man.

I would also wish that my parents were here; they are both at peace. I remember when I first started and I was kind of a fat kid who loved the game of football and I would come home at night with cramps. They would rub my legs and get the cramps out of my legs, and they would cover the scrapes and scars, and help me along. I wish they were here to share this moment.

■　■　■　■

Pete Rozelle
NFL Commissioner
Class of 1985

Rozelle negotiated the first league-wide television contract in 1962. He is credited with making the NFL the nation's most popular sport.

Presented by Rams and Cowboys Executive Tex Schramm

Go back to the year 1960. The National Football League was really at a crossroads. It had just lost its commissioner, Bert Bell, who had guided the league since the Second World War. There was a new giant on the scene, television. There was a new league starting. There were a lot of deep problems that faced the league, so deep that the owners at their meeting debated for one, two, three, up to seven days to try to find a man to lead them in the years to come. They couldn't agree.

So they selected what was termed then a "compromise candidate," and that compromise candidate, when they made that decision, they probably didn't know it at the time, they probably made one of the most important and wisest decisions that they could have made. Because that was the decision that they selected a man for the times, a man that was prepared to lead through a new era, and that man was thirty-three-year-old Pete Rozelle.

We are now twenty-six years later honoring that man. But when he was selected, few people realized what they had obtained as their leader. They had obtained a man of tremendous intelligence, foresight, patience, preparation, tenacity, a will to win, and a sense of class. He imparted that through the league and he also had the background to make it work because he was young and had grown with the new giant, television. He was media conscious.

He understood the problems of the media and how to work with them. He had club-level experience. He handled all the threats to the integrity of the game and he handled them with dignity. He went through the pains of growth because no sport experienced the growth that the NFL did in the past twenty-five years to become the number one spectator sport in this country. He brought expansion. We started moving around the league, being truly a National Football League. It was under his direction that the Super Bowl came to be.

From the very beginning he said, "I don't care what it is, what it takes, we are going to do it with class and with style, something we can be proud of." Today it is the single biggest sports event in the country. . . . He is a man who has stood very tall and who you will look upon for many, many years when you think about the NFL. He's probably the greatest commissioner any sport has ever had.

Pete Rozelle

You know it was 1962, right in this area, that I turned the first shovel of dirt for the construction of the first part of this facility. It was with Mr. William Umstattd of the Timken Company. I know that day when I turned the shovel of dirt, I never imagined that I would be standing here today in this capacity. I think that we all get a sense of what it is about. I know in discussing with Lamar Hunt the other evening, he said, "You know, I enjoy so much coming here each year as a member of the Board of Directors of the Hall."

It's like an oasis, an oasis of calm and tranquility. It's like a fix that each year we come here and get a sense of enthusiasm from you people and the sport we represent.

■　■　■　■

Al Davis
Oakland Raiders Owner
Class of 1992

Davis has served in the pros as personnel assistant, scout, assistant coach, head coach, general manager, commissioner, and team owner/CEO.

Presented by Raiders Coach John Madden

I was thirty-two years old when he named me the head coach of the Oakland Raiders. You talk about a day when a fat linebacker at age thirty-two gets named as head coach—and nobody knows who he is—I guarantee you that is a man you can never forget.

I represent everyone he has given a chance to—players, coaches, administrators. Many of them are here because it doesn't make any difference what someone said about you, what someone wrote about you, what someone thought. Al Davis does it one way. Al Davis does it his way. I tell you, "Just win, baby," is one thing. Al Davis is just one, baby. . . .

A maverick? Heck yeah, he is a maverick. Being a maverick is good. He does it his way. But this man has given his whole life to professional football. There is nothing else. He doesn't fish, or hunt, or play golf, or play tennis, or bowl. There is one thing—professional football. And that is commitment—commitment to excellence.

Al Davis

My parents in their own way encouraged me to dominate. I'll tell you this quick story. In Florida, about six years ago, I was seated in a very prominent restaurant with my mother, some of the top people in professional football, some of the top writers, and we were talking about signing players. My mother asked, "How are you doing?" and I said, "I have problems. I haven't signed Todd Christensen, Lester Hayes, and two others. They just want too much money." Her answer was, "Without them, what kind of team are you going to have? Give them the money, you can't take it with you." And I gave them the money.

I learned early on in life that if you are going to lead, if you are going to dominate, the golden rule "Do unto others as you would have them do unto you" is not necessarily right. You must treat people in a paramilitary situation—the way they want to be treated, not the way you want to be treated. To do that, you must first learn about them, learn their cultures, and allow for individual differences.

We never wanted our players, or even our friends, to fit into rigid personality molds. There is a place in this world for mavericks, standing up for principle. Defy custom at times, be right, do not hurt others. That individualism encouraged me to go forward. And my heroes as I was a young boy dared me to dream.

I had come from Brockton, Massachusetts, to Brooklyn, New York, over fifty years ago. I was about six years old. We had no TV, little radio, and eight great newspapers. They were my eyes and ears.

Pro football had little popularity, but I was immediately inspired by two great organizations at the very young age of between six and twelve—the New York Yankees and the Brooklyn Dodgers.

Let me tell you what the Yankees represented—size, power, dynasty, intimidation, the home run, the ability to take players from other teams and put that Yankee uniform on them, and they would play great.

The Dodgers of Branch Rickey were speed, the development of young players, fundamentals, a way of playing the game, and the willingness to pioneer.

I always thought early on you could take the great qualities of these organizations and encompass them into one. As a famous American said, "I had a dream"—a dream to someday build and maintain the finest organization in the history of sports. An organization that would be most imitated, the most respected, and the most feared organization in its field—a standard of excellence by which all others would be judged.

■ ■ ■ ■

Lou Creekmur
Detroit Lions Tackle/Guard
Class of 1996

An All-NFL selection six times, Creekmur was selected to eight Pro Bowls and played on three NFL championship teams.

Presented by Lions Halfback Doak Walker

Without a doubt, Lou wore more pads than anyone I ever saw in pro football. He made the Johnson-Johnson all-tape club, no doubt about that. He taped his hands like a prizefighter. He wore knee pads, thigh pads, shin pads, front- and back-of-his-leg pads, he wore hip pads, shoulder pads, pads on his upper arms. There was no way you could get to him. You could swing at him with a sledgehammer and never touch him.

Lou Creekmur

I've led a pretty lucky life for an old beat-up football player. I never thought that when I went out for football at Woodbridge High School in 1943—yeah, '43—that someday I'd be standing up here at a podium, being inducted into the Pro Football Hall of Fame.

When I was offered a scholarship to William and Mary, there was no question about my acceptance. Imagine Mrs. Creekmur's little boy going to school, going to college. I went down to William and Mary seven days after I graduated from high school. I weighed all of two hundred pounds and was six foot tall.

There's a little thing that some of you guys ought to remember called a World War II going on at the time and I had to go over to Germany for a couple of years. Well, that time that I spent over in Germany was growing time. And I came back from Germany to get back to William and Mary at 270 pounds and six-foot-four. My coaches there at William and Mary sure were happy to see me return. What a difference four inches and seventy pounds make, whoa! They didn't even mind my cigar smoking.

And here's where the "Lucky Lou" label comes into play. I doubt very much that the two-hundred-pound, six-foot Creekmur would ever end up in the pros. But the six-foot-four, 270-pound Creekmur was a different story. . . .

I'd like to say something to the ballplayers. You've got to think about this: there is life after football, and I hope these guys that are playing today try to remember that. There is life after football. And the values you learn in football have to be applied to the real world. Dedication, persistence, and loyalty are still words that have meaning. Yet the block and tackle in the business world as well as on the football field, and opening holes for the boss, will still give you the recognition we all crave.

Don't ever give it up; there is gold at the end of the rainbow, I can attest to that—here I am. Challenges in life I think are there for a purpose, and if you utilize what you learn when you accept these challenges, it's surprising how successful you can become.

■　■　■　■

Wellington Mara
New York Giants Owner
Class of 1997

Mara worked as the Giants ballboy, secretary, vice president, president, and co-CEO.

Wellington also has an extended family. That family is made up of former players and coaches and their wives and their children. I can't tell you, and Well would kill me if I did, how many times some member of that extended family has needed help and Well has been there. I know because he has been there for me.

I became a member of that extended family when Wellington scouted and drafted me as his number one pick in 1952. He also signed me to my first contract, and I won't embarrass both of you by telling you for how much. What I will tell you is, as I grew to know him and he grew to know me, I never worried about a contract. He was always more than fair. Nor did I even bother to sign some of them. Well's word was and is his bond.

I know he won't like this, but I can honestly say Wellington Mara is the most honest and decent man I have ever known. Can that kind of man, one could ask, can that kind of man succeed in the world of pro football? Well, Wellington Mara has been the key ingredient in the Giants' six NFL championships, eighteen division titles, and today Wellington Mara becomes the twenty-fourth member of the Giants organization to be enshrined in the Hall of Fame.

Wellington Mara

Twenty years ago, I presented Frank at the Hall of Fame. What he didn't tell you was that I asked if I could, and that's the only time I ever volunteered for anything. Frank honored me by asking me to present him, and of course, he doubly honors me today by presenting me as he did, and I thank him for that.

Now, despite Frank's very kind introduction, I overwhelmingly feel that I come to you here as a surrogate—someone who takes the place of someone else. If it hadn't been for his untimely death some thirty-odd years ago, Jack Mara would certainly have taken his place alongside our father long ago to form the first father-and-son team in the Hall of Fame.

For it was Jack, together with Dan Reeves of the Rams and George Halas of the Bears, who cast what I think is the most important vote that was ever cast in the National Football League. They, representing the three cornerstone franchises of our league as it existed then, agreed to share television money equally with all teams.

That act of selfless vision made it possible for Pete Rozelle to construct the National Football League as we know it today—the envy and the unobtainable goal of every other sports franchise and sports league. Unhappily, their selfless vision is too little shared by many who today benefit the most from their award.

Seventy-two years ago, my father invested $500 to purchase the New York franchise in the National Football League. He laid down the standards and the principles according to which he wanted the new family business to be operated.

In his time, Jack Mara practiced and embellished those standards and principles far beyond any abilities of mine. I accept this honor today as acknowledgment of my stewardship over that legacy of decency which they handed to me and which I, in turn, hope to hand on to the taxi squad and others.

I'm very grateful for a long life and a lifelong association with the administrators, the coaches and scouts, and especially the players of our great game, for they are the heart and the sinew of our game. If it were not for Frank Gifford, Rosey Brown, Andy Robustelli, Sam Huff, and the many Giants who honor me by their presence today, there would be no Wellington Mara going into the Hall of Fame. They are the people who make it work. They are the people who make it great.

Our beneficent creator has seen fit to give me a long life and large family. And He has used them to show me with crystal clarity the absolute sanctity and the utter inviolability of life, from the womb to the grave, and I am forever thankful to Him for that.

■　■　■　■

Andre Tippett
New England Patriots Linebacker
Class of 2008

*A five-time Pro Bowl selection, Tippett posted one hundred sacks
and thirty multiple-sack games.*

Presented by Patriots Owner Robert Kraft

I'm a lifelong fan of the NFL and became a Patriots fan in 1960, when
the team was created. And in 1971, I became a season ticket holder
and have enjoyed nearly every game since then with my family. Of all
the players I watched and rooted for during that time, I can say, without a doubt, that Andre Tippett was the most dominant defender the
Patriots ever had and one of the greatest ever to play the game.

I will never forget the first time I met Andre. It was on the field
at the old stadium in 1985 and Andre was doing a photo shoot. He
wasn't dressed in his Patriot uniform. He was wearing a white karate
gi with a black belt wrapped around his waist. Now I have met a lot of
football players over the years, but Andre Tippett is the only football
player that I have ever met in his full karate garb and the only one I
know with a fifth-degree black belt. Now, that's an image; I'll never
forget that the rest of my life. What impressed me most that day was
his graciousness. Hearing him talk about the love of the martial arts
and the discipline required to excel at karate, I started to understand
and appreciate how he was able to maintain his individual excellence.

My second meeting with Andre only served to underscore the
depth of his character. It was in 1989, at Mass General Hospital where
Andre was recovering from surgery. I saw Andre in the hospital and I
was flattered that he remembered me. He asked me why I was there,
and I told him I was visiting my son, David, who had just suffered a
very serious knee injury that had ended his wrestling season. Andre
insisted that I take him to David's room so he could offer him words
of encouragement. That visit meant a tremendous amount to my son
and left a lasting impression on me. I didn't own the team at the time.

I was just a fan that he had only met once before. Yet, Andre, who had just suffered a season-ending injury, insisted on visiting my son to cheer him up. To think that this man who was so ferocious and intimidating on the field could be so gracious and thoughtful off of it, to me these are the traits that make Andre so special.

Andre Tippett

As I look out at all these great men sitting here, I can't believe I'm joining this fraternity. I tell our young players to know their history, because you are the living representatives of that history. You have inspired me since I was a young boy, dreaming of one day standing here. In my youth, I watched every game I could. I studied all the great players like Ham, Lanier, Youngblood, Bobby Bell, Lee Roy Selmon, and many more. Some kids play cops and robbers. I emulated you. You are my heroes. Even in my college years, my teammate and I, Brad Webb, would pretend we were the Steelers linebackers in our Iowa black and gold. Brad Webb was Jack Ham and I was Dennis Winston. To my contemporaries, you also inspired me. The linebackers of the '80s. You guys set the standard for how to play the position. You are—we are—the best of the best.

My journey here has been a long one. And it hasn't always been easy along the way. So many people have touched my life. Francis Tippett, my mom—what can I say about my mom? Thank you for teaching me perseverance. Life wasn't easy for us moving from Birmingham, Alabama, to Newark, New Jersey, with not much more than the clothes on our back. Through my mother I learned to be accountable for my actions and understand the consequences of those actions. And with that you better believe my mom—she made me appreciate, understanding what's right and what's wrong. She ruled with love and a whole lot of discipline. Mom, I love you and thank you for that.

I was the player I became because of the great coaches and teammates I was surrounded by. From the day I was cut from my freshman football team at Barringer High School, Coach Frank Verducci instilled in me the proper mind-set to play this great game. My high school model was truth, honor, and light. In truth, Coach Verducci taught us to recognize our strengths as well as our weaknesses and to raise our hand if it was our fault. In honor, he taught us to be proud of our names. He always said, "Rob me of my money and you have nothing, but rob me of my name and you take my most prized possession." In light, coach wanted all of us to get an education. He said, "Only a fool doesn't go to school."

CHAPTER 4

MEMORIES

MARV LEVY

DURING THE 2007 SEASON, THE *FLORIDA TIMES-UNION* published an interview with Jacksonville Pro Bowl cornerback Rashean Mathis in which he was asked the best advice he had received from a teammate. Mathis recalled his second year in the league, 2004, when teammate James Trapp—who went on to become the team chaplain for the Atlanta Falcons—approached him with a question.

"He asked, 'Are your ribs showing?'" Mathis recalled. "I know I'm a skinny dude, so I was like, 'What do you mean? Are you trying to say I'm skinny?' And he was like, 'No, are your ribs still showing?' I didn't know what he was talking about.

"But basically, he just told me, 'Regardless of how good you get, stay hungry. Stay hungry and keep your ribs showing.'"

This was one lesson. There have been plenty of others, along with the mounds of advice that has been dispensed and absorbed.

Hall of Famers heard it, lived it, and, eventually, shared it. These are their memories.

■ ■ ■ ■

Marv Levy
Kansas City Chiefs and Buffalo Bills Coach
Class of 2001

Levy led the Bills to an unprecedented four consecutive Super Bowls. He compiled a 154-120 coaching record.

Presented by Bills, Panthers, and Colts General Manager Bill Polian

It is said that leadership is that unique quality which enables special people to stand up and pull the rest of us over the horizon. By that, or any other definition, Marv Levy is one of the greatest leaders this game has ever known.

His incredible vision for what his teams and players could become— and there are many seated in front of us here today who I think will be up on this podium before long—his magnificent ability to articulate that vision, his boundless kindness and empathy for his players and associates, and his unconquerable will to persevere no matter what the obstacle or odds left an indelible mark on those of us privileged to be led by him.

His famous Marvisms, reflected in a few short sentences from a person, a philosophy, a role model, not only for us, but because of his genius as a teacher, through us for generations to come. Here are just a few:

"Everyone wants to win. The special person has the will to prepare to win."

"What you do should speak so loudly that no one can hear what you say."

"Adversity is an opportunity for heroism."

"Expect rejection but expect more to overcome it."

Words not only for winning, but for living. And words that remind us not only of the lessons learned and battles fought but of the profound respect and affection we have for their teacher.

Cicero wrote that friends multiply joy and divide sorrow. There wasn't very much sorrow in our days together, and Marv, your friends are here today to thank you and multiply your joy as you take your rightful place amongst the game's immortals.

Perhaps the most famous Marvism of all is the most appropriate today: "Where would you rather be than right here, right now."

Marv, there's no place in the world we would rather be than right here, right now.

Marv Levy

When I first walked out onto the practice field as a high school assistant football coach exactly a half-century ago next month, men like Jim Thorpe, Bronko Nagurski, Sid Luckman, and Marion Motley were mythical gods. They still are, and I tread this ground with great reverence for them and for all who reside here. Never did I dream that someday I might be invited to share these same lodgings with them.

How could it happen? Well, it's because of some wondrous people, without whose love, abilities, and counsel I'd not be standing here today.

My father, Sam, by his lifelong example, displayed for me the virtues of an honest day's work and of great personal courage. You as avid football fans undoubtedly have witnessed many exciting runs from scrimmage. But the greatest run I ever knew of was by my father, who during World War I, along with his comrades from the storied Fourth Marine Brigade, raced several hundred yards into withering machine-gun fire, across the wheat fields at Belleau Wood in France. Their valor on that June day, in 1918, succeeded in halting the German army advance just twenty-five miles from Paris.

He was my hero even before I was born. One day, many years later, I telephoned my father to tell him I was leaving Harvard Law School and that I wanted to be a football coach. Thirty seconds of painful silence followed, and then the old marine said simply, "Be a good one!" I hope I haven't disappointed him.

I will never forget that first time I walked into the Buffalo Bills' team meeting room in early November of 1986 upon being appointed in midseason to take over as head coach. Sitting in that room were a young Jim Kelly, Andre Reed, Bruce Smith, Kent Hull, and Darryl Talley, great leaders. So were Jim Ritcher, Pete Metzelaars, Will Wolford, Dwight Drane, Fred Smerlas, Mark Kelso, and Mark Pike. Soon to join them: Steve Tasker, Shane Conlan, Cornelius Bennett, Howard Ballard, Thurman Thomas, John Butler, Kenny Davis, Henry Jones, Phil Hansen, and speedy receivers like Don Beebe and James Lofton.

What an odyssey I lived with those men, with their teammates and coaches, with all the wonderful people in the Bills' organization, and with those incomparable Buffalo Bills fans. For six consecutive years they led the NFL in attendance. Who cared if it was bitter cold or if an angry snowstorm was raging? Their spirits were as tough as linebackers; their hearts were as warm as the thermal underwear I wore during those January playoff games in Orchard Park.

And what about those great players and coaches against whom we competed so fiercely? I'm so proud to have walked the opposite sideline from Hall-of-Fame coaches: Don Shula, Tom Landry, Bill Walsh, Bud Grant, Chuck Noll, Joe Gibbs. And to have walked the same sideline as an assistant to a coach from whom I learned so much and to whom I owe so much, the inimitable George Allen.

My family, all girls, is here. Someone once lamented that given my enthrallment with this game, it's a shame I never had a son. Well, he was wrong. Don't tell me I never had a son. I've had thousands of them, of every size, shape, color, faith, and temperament, and I loved them, every one. And because of them, I still hear the echoes from those sounds which glorify this game. I hear the cheers of the crowd as Thurman or Andre goes hurtling into the end zone or as Bruce . . . Bruce . . . Bruce sacks yet another quarterback.

I hear the grunts and collisions out on the field of play. I hear Jim Kelly calling cadence at the line of scrimmage. I hear Kent Hull's confident Southern drawl as he relays our line blocking schemes to his teammates up front. I hear the thundering footsteps of young men as they streak down the field to cover a kickoff. No one ever did it better than two men here today, Steve Tasker and Mark Pike.

And finally, I hear words spoken to me more than fifty years ago by a man whose memory I cherish. He was my basketball coach and my track coach at Coe College. His name was Harris Lamb. And I will conclude my remarks today by repeating for you what he said to me so many years ago: "To know the game is great. To play the game is greater. But to love the game is the greatest of them all."

Harris, my dear friend, I have truly loved this game, and I love everyone who has shared this passion with me.

■　■　■　■

Steve Owen
New York Giants Coach
Class of 1966

Owen coached the Giants to a 155-108-17 record, with eight divisional titles and two NFL championships.

Accepting on Behalf of Steve Owen, Giants Coach Jim Lee Howell

There's just one little human incident that I want to bring to your attention. We were playing the Browns in one of the crucial games, and his team had been very stingy in giving up touchdowns to the Browns.

And here on this particular day, just before we went in for the half, one of the boys that is now one of the leading coaches in the country let the kickoff roll down to the goal line, where it was recovered by the Browns. They scored and we went in at the half. In came this huge three-hundred-pound man and we thought here that he would tear this young fella apart. He walked up to him, looked him in his eye, and then bent over him and put his arms around him and said, "Jimmy, we'll get that one back for you."

That is a great coach.

■ ■ ■ ■

Gino Marchetti
Dallas Texans and Baltimore Colts Defensive End
Class of 1972

After being voted to eleven consecutive Pro Bowls and All-NFL nine times, Marchetti was named the top defensive end of the NFL's first fifty years.

Presented by Colts and Rams Owner Carroll Rosenbloom

Ernest and Maria Marchetti always had a somewhat normal parental fear that their son, Gino, would be hurt playing football and they advised him to stay out of it and to keep out of other boys' way so they won't hurt you. Every quarterback who played in the National Football League in the 1950s and early '60s wished that Gino had followed his parents' advice.

Gino Marchetti—six-foot-four, 240 pounds of extreme talent—did not listen to his father's advice and Gino wound up instead as the greatest defensive end in the history of pro football.

When I retired Gino's number, I said to him and to the people in Memorial Stadium that he was a legend in his own time. To say to you that Gino Marchetti was a great football player doesn't begin to describe this man. It is like saying that the Taj Mahal is a nice place to visit or that Abraham Lincoln was an outstanding president of the United States.

Through most of my adult life, and particularly during my ownership of the Baltimore Colts, I have witnessed closely the swings in our society, the changes in our young people—some moving up, some sliding down. Inevitably, the question arose, "What sets one person apart from another? Why does one prosper and another fail?" I think that I have found that answer in Gino.

In the National Football League, he was an all-time defensive end at six-four, 240. This was not really big compared to the current rosters. And yet, more than any single man, Gino is credited with creating the crashing style of the modern defensive end play.

Marchetti played in every pro football game but for one from 1955 through 1965. The one he missed was because of a broken leg in the 1958 championship game, the first break of sudden death ever in pro football. Right on the sideline he refused to leave until he saw his team tie it up in the final seconds of regulation time. Of course, he had saved that game with the never-to-be-forgotten tackle on Frank Gifford in a critical third-down play. Not because God had given him a body better than others, but because he took what God gave him and got more from himself than he ever thought he would be able to give.

The greatness that is within him will be with him for the rest of his life. He had an outstanding and unending commitment to excellence, a willingness to submerge himself individually within a group effort, courage, an acceptance of pain, and a love for what he is doing and a notation of achievement, respect for worthy adversaries, and, perhaps most important, the realization that not all in life can be success and victorious.

Gino Marchetti

I was fortunate enough to be associated with an organization like Baltimore and Carroll Rosenbloom, fortunate enough that they didn't believe in the old theory that a lot of people have today that an athlete should be lean and hungry to play the game of football.

Lucky enough for me that Carroll grabbed me one time in San Francisco—that is exactly the way he approached me. We were voting championship shares that day and I had gotten the call that the big man wanted to see me. So being nervous, when the owner wants to see you, you say to yourself, "Now what did I do wrong?"

So I went to his room and he came out dressed very casually and sat down and he said, "Hey, you dumb hillbilly! What are you going to do with the rest of your life?"

At that time, I was playing and I was going home, tending bar, working in a factory, very happy, very content. And he showed me the way to better myself and make a better life for my family. And through him and the organization, I have grown, and I think that any man or any player that was fortunate enough to be within that organization should be very thankful.

I was at a banquet a few years ago in Baltimore when a guy gave a definition of a successful person. And he said that a successful person is somebody that loves to do something and is smart enough to get somebody to pay him to do it.

So I sat there and thought, "Man, that takes care of everything." You know if you want to be a bartender or a janitor or a mechanic, and you're smart enough to get somebody to pay you, you are successful. And I thought, "Here I am, just a kid smart enough to get Carroll Rosenbloom to pay me to do what I love."

■　■　■

Jim Parker
Baltimore Colts Offensive Lineman
Class of 1973

Parker was the first full-time offensive lineman elected to the Hall of Fame. He was All-NFL eight consecutive years and voted to the Pro Bowl eight times.

I would like to tell you fans here in Canton, Ohio, and all over the country, just how I got started in football.

If you were at the Mayor's Breakfast yesterday morning, you saw a picture of me when I weighed 106 pounds, and I wanted to be just like my oldest brother. He was a football star and I looked at him every time he came home and I idolized him.

So I went to my mother one day and I said, "Ma, I want to play football." She said, "That's good, you can be the waterboy." I said, "I don't want to be the waterboy, I want to be a star like my brother on the football team." So she said, "Well, why don't you give it a try?"

So I went out for the high school team at fourteen and 106 pounds, and I came home one day so beat up, black and blue all over, and she said we have to fatten you up. She started preparing all of the starchy foods for us because meat was at a ration at the time, and I started working out every day, and she tolerated this all the way through high school. I just worked out and I started gaining weight.

When I was having trouble at Ohio State University, I called home and I got inspiration from my mother. And when I was having trouble at Baltimore with the Colts making the team, I remember one day I called her. I called home and I was worried about the pass protection and they said, "Don't worry about it and have a little faith in God and everything will be all right."

Raymond [Berry] said I had the team made because I was the first draft choice. But I kept a suitcase packed for the eleven years I was there.

■　■　■　■

Larry Wilson
St. Louis Cardinals Safety
Class of 1978

Wilson intercepted fifty-two passes, including a streak of at least one in seven straight games in 1966. Wilson also made the "safety blitz" famous.

Larry Wilson had all the grace and the poise and the speed and the agility and whatever it took to be a great defensive football player—in spite of my coaching.

Because as we would have practice sometimes, one boy would break down the field on a forward pass, which we were using in those days, and he would break behind Larry and I would turn around and say, "Wilson, what in the devil is the matter with you, letting that fellow break behind you?" And Larry would say, "Sorry, coach, but I'll not let the ball get back there."

Well you know, it took almost nearly a year to be smart enough to realize that Larry didn't need my help. Many a receiver broke behind Larry Wilson, but I have yet to see a quarterback throw one behind him.

I do want to finish with one thing I think you will always remember. After Larry's last game with the Big Red, the people of St. Louis as you know them, a fellow named Stan Musial had some little standing in that community. In fact, he had so much standing they built a big bronze statue of him at one end of the stadium. After Larry's last game, the people of St. Louis met one night and they raised $80,000 to build a bronze statue at the other end of the stadium of Larry Wilson, the greatest in professional football.

But ladies and gentlemen, Larry Wilson would not let them take the money for a bronze statue, though there had been a precedent set. Larry said, "Add two rooms to the children's hospital."

Larry Wilson

Being inducted into the Hall of Fame is very meaningful to all of us and it is a point of time where we can share our joys with different people. All of us look back to our families first of all and say, "Hey, thank you for standing behind us, for fighting, for loving, and for sharing the time that you did with us." I really think in my lifetime of playing football I gained from them their determination and desires, which is what made me what I was out on the football field. All you had to do was turn around and look at them and they said, "Go get them."

Like Ray Nitschke, I liked to hit people. I enjoyed it. I feel that one thing about football today that every youngster who's competing should know is go out and enjoy yourself. It can be drudgery, but I would just hope and pray that each one of your sons will have the same opportunity that I have had, to compete in football and to have fun.

And I would say to you that this is a great game, this is the epitome of what every one of us played for—to be standing in front of the shrine and to be honored with a statue and with a picture saying you are the best.

I'll say to you, this is a great game. We all can find fault in it. We argue about the salaries that we are paid, we argue about the rules changing. I'll say to you, be positive. This is number one.

■ ■ ■ ■

Doug Atkins
Cleveland Browns, Chicago Bears,
and New Orleans Saints Defensive End
Class of 1982

An eight-time Pro Bowl selection and an All-NFL selection four times, Atkins played seventeen years and 205 games.

Presented by Bears Executive Ed McCaskey

I remember one time standing next to Coach Clark Shaughnessy at a practice session at St. Joseph's College in Rensselaer, Indiana, and he said to me, "Now I will show you who the great athletes are."

He blew his whistle, tossed the football to the defensive squad, and told them to play volleyball utilizing the goalposts. As we watched these giants batting a football back and forth, Clark turned to me and said, "The greatest athlete on the field is Doug Atkins."

Weeb Ewbank, who signed him to his first pro contract, said of Doug, "Doug Atkins is the most magnificent physical specimen I have ever seen." In a recent TV interview, George Halas was asked what he thought of Doug Atkins and we have it on tape, so I know it is true. Coach Halas said, "Doug Atkins was the greatest defensive end I ever saw."

Doug Atkins

Football has been good to me. I have enjoyed lots of it and some I haven't enjoyed so much. Of course, Coach Halas has kept my spirits up and aggravated me every once in a while. One time the coach and I were talking about contracts and we were talking about a matter of $500, and we got into a pretty heated argument. Coach Halas said, "If I give you that money, you would only spend it." I said, "Coach, that's what I want it for!"

■ ■ ■ ■

Bobby Bell
Kansas City Chiefs Linebacker
Class of 1983

An All-AFL/AFC selection nine times, Bell scored nine touchdowns, including one on an onside kick return.

Presented by Texans, Chiefs, and Saints Coach Hank Stram

Number one, Bobby always had the capacity to see clearly and believe strongly. He thought he could do anything and do it better than anybody else.

Number two, he had a great attitude. He wasn't a stock market player; he wasn't up or down. He was always the same. He was great. He loved to practice, he loved to play. He had a lot of faults, but he knew when to play and when to work.

Number three, he didn't permit himself to be susceptible to the negative influence of other people. He knew what he wanted and if there was any kind of a problem on the squad, he would try to help it. He believed in what he did and what we did. That is why we went on to enjoy the great success and enjoy being one of the winningest teams in the history of professional football during that short span of time.

He also had a great capacity to follow through with a resolution once that resolution had passed. Now a lot of people say, "I'm going to do this," and "I'm going to do that," and when the time comes, they get out of the mood and they don't do it. Bobby was not that way. Once he made up his mind, he was going to do it.

Bobby Bell

Leaving the security of Shelby, North Carolina, for the University of Minnesota was a traumatic experience. There was no family, no friends, and the pace we had to set was demanding. But Coach Murray Warmath knew my concerns and helped weather my problems. With Coach Warmath, it was a never-ending battle, it was academic.

There was that determination that he instilled into us athletes, student first, athlete second. And we played with so much determination and we studied with that much determination. We went to class with that determination, we competed with that determination, we graduated with that determination. So you cannot be surprised that while on the football field, we played with determination.

There was always one thing he told me. He would say, "Bobby, I can read about you in the newspaper, but be prepared for life after football."

■ ■ ■ ■

Bobby Mitchell
Cleveland Browns and Washington Redskins
Running Back/Wide Receiver
Class of 1983

Mitchell scored ninety-one touchdowns, eight that came on kick-off and punt returns. He compiled 14,078 combined yards.

Many of the immortals enshrined here in these hallowed halls have gained their fame as great runners, some as great receivers, and still others as great returners. But only Bobby Mitchell can combine all these skills in a way no one ever has before.

Bobby Mitchell

From the University of Illinois, Paul Brown sent a scout to talk to me about football. At the time, I had only seen two professional football games in my life. I saw the Bears play a couple of times on TV, but I really didn't have much interest in professional football. I loved track. My ticket was to wait for the Olympics in 1960. My wife said, "No way," particularly not when Paul was going to give me $7,000.

He induced it by saying, "You will be the next great flanker back, Ray Renfro will be retiring next year." Of course, Ray played another ten years.

But once I signed the contract and received my bonus, Dick Gallagher—who was head of this Hall before Pete Elliott—came to me and said, "Mr. Brown said you will be running the ball." My wife already had spent the bonus. So I had to show up to the Cleveland Browns, scared to death at 173 pounds.

But Paul Brown taught me all about taking care of family, and he talked to me about security, all of those things I've used in my life to bring me to this point.

I was fortunate to be in the backfield with the great Jim Brown. My first four years were, therefore, very easy. It was Jim Brown up the middle, Jim Brown to the left, Jim Brown to the right. And occasionally a pitch out to Bobby Mitchell.

I then was traded to the Washington Redskins, which started a very beautiful association with them. As [the Redskins owner] Mr.

Marshall said to me, "We are taking you out of the shadows of Jim Brown." We didn't win a lot of games, but we cared about each other.

My wife went through all of this. She has worked hour upon hour for many a year. On that day when I wanted to call it off because I didn't want to go to training camp, she talked to me about what we wanted out of this. I think of the number of times that she would walk behind me so I could shine. I had the glory, she had all the stress, and I just hope that sometime during this lifetime I can find the way to say to her that I think she has been a great partner.

I miss my mother. I wish she could be here today. God, how she would laugh. She would be extremely happy that her son has made it to this point. She never understood the game, crashing into one another, beating up one another, and she never understood why they wanted to hit her son. And she always wanted me to run faster and beat them back. Mother, I love you, and I'm still around, and I beat them.

■ ■ ■ ■

Willie Brown
Denver Broncos and Oakland Raiders Cornerback
Class of 1984

Brown intercepted fifty-four passes for 472 yards, including a seventy-five-yard interception that he returned for a touchdown in Super Bowl XI.

Presented by Raiders Owner Al Davis

Presenting Willie Brown, the magnificent horseman who delivered fear and interceptions upon all the great wide receivers of his time; who for more than three decades, and in the years to come, will be the standard of excellence by which cornerbacks are judged.

Only time, the great robber, beat Willie Brown at the corner. But time could not defeat him, as the legend Willie Brown will live on in this Camelot which is the National Football League's Hall of Fame.

Willie Brown

A long time ago, I told Al Davis that if I ever made the Hall of Fame, he owed me $1 million, so Al, I guess this is the day and we'll deal with it when we get back home.

But I have always believed that if you can dream it, you can do it.

■ ■ ■ ■

Willie Lanier
Kansas City Chiefs Linebacker
Class of 1986

Nicknamed "Contact" for his ferocious tackling, Lanier inter- cepted twenty-seven passes and also keyed the Chiefs' upset vic- tory in Super Bowl IV.

Presented by Chiefs Owner Lamar Hunt

In August of 1945, Harry Truman was president of the United States and the NFL as an entity was struggling to keep the sport alive with a roster of makeshift teams. Doak Walker and Bobby Layne were in the Merchant Marines together and V-day was just a few weeks ago. But in that scenario in Clover, Virginia, a baby was born to the Robert Lanier family. I want to say Clover in this case must have meant the four-leaf kind because it was indeed a lucky day for the football fans of America.

Later a teenaged Willie Lanier furthered his education at a school called Maggie Walker High School in Richmond, Virginia, and judg- ing by Willie's later financial acumen, which is substantial, that school was indeed prophetically named after the first black female bank pres- ident in America.

Willie Lanier

It is difficult to explain how you really feel when you stand here and realize that a stadium such as Fawcett Stadium is just like any basic stadium in the country. You play on a field the same size all over the country and you wonder at what point you really decide to try to maybe be a little bit better.

But I think if there is one thread that runs between all of us who happen to be here, it's that there was a tremendous amount of dedication and a belief that we had the skill to perform. Not at a level above others, but we set some sights that were only amongst ourselves and doing that allowed us to stand before you today.

This is something that should be strived for, and I think it is important for all young people that try to make decisions that would affect their lives in the future that they recognize that these kinds of events are possible for all of you out there, regardless of background and circumstances.

■　■　■　■

Jim Langer
Miami Dolphins and Minnesota Vikings Center
Class of 1987

A six-time Pro Bowl selection, Langer played every down during the Dolphins' perfect season in 1972.

I've had a lot of people ask me how the Dolphins accomplished what they did and how did they tick. I would like to read you one sentence. This is Don Shula talking in the early 1970s, and I quote:

"I feel you set a goal to be the best, and then you work every waking hour of every day trying to achieve that goal. The ultimate goal is victory, and if you refuse to work as hard as you possibly can towards that aim, then you are just cheating yourself. What we want to do is dedicate ourselves to establishing a standard of excellence in the future just as the Packers did in the past. That is the challenge."

And ladies and gentlemen, we believed that to a man for all the time that I spent in Miami.

■　■　■　■

John Henry Johnson
San Francisco 49ers, Detroit Lions,
and Pittsburgh Steelers Fullback
Class of 1987

A member of San Francisco's "Million-Dollar" backfield, Johnson
rushed for 6,803 yards and fifty-five total touchdowns.

It's a funny thing. My football career started and ended in Pittsburgh. Back in Pittsburgh, California, my high school coach Tom Cureton was a confidence builder. He gave me a lot of chances to play ball. He gave me the idea that I could accomplish a lot of things in sports if I wanted to and if I worked. That was the secret—if I worked. . . .

I would like to say something about the principal I had in high school, Mr. Sphere, and some of the teachers I had back in Pittsburgh High School. They were dedicated teachers. They helped me develop my confidence. I think what we need today is for those people to think more about those people around them in high school. Listen to what they are telling you, not only to keep your grades up, but about staying away from drugs and the importance of hard work.

I think [Lions Hall-of-Fame quarterback] Bobby Layne liked me because I had the same attitude he had. We played hard all the time. We didn't want to lose, we didn't ask any questions, and we didn't give any answers.

I played in the famous green backfield when I started out with the San Francisco 49ers—Joe Perry, Hugh McElhenny, and Y. A. Tittle. I learned teamwork with those fellows. We were good because we worked together as a team. To them a good block was just as important as a good run. I know because I did a lot of blocking for those guys and it made me feel good.

My greatest moment in pro football was winning the championship in Detroit. The season taught me never to quit and never to say die. We were behind on many occasions, but we came back to win. Bobby Layne said throughout all those games that we were winners, and believe it or not, we did win.

Old-timers were driven by pride, not dollar signs. They looked at it as performance, not press clippings. After I left pro football, all these values really started to mean a lot to me. Working hard, never giving up, having confidence, this is what kept me going.

■ ■ ■ ■

Jack Ham
Pittsburgh Steelers Linebacker
Class of 1988

Selected to eight consecutive Pro Bowls, Ham also helped the Steelers win four Super Bowls while recovering twenty-one fumbles and intercepting thirty-two passes.

Presented by Penn State Coach Joe Paterno

Jack was a professional, even when he was in college. I don't use the word professional as far as being paid for something. To me, the professional is the one who knows what he is doing all the time and, therefore, he is consistently at a higher level than anybody else.

I have been asked a hundred times in the last couple of weeks, "Do you remember the greatest game Jack Ham ever played?" And I can't. Jack never played a bad game for us. He had ten or eleven tackles, he'd block a punt, he'd intercept a pass, he'd recover a fumble because he was hustling. He was always consistent. He always tried to do the best with what God gave him.

His strong, poised character, his commitment to professionalism—he really gave a lot of unsure and unknowing kids a standard, a standard to practice, how to handle themselves, how to work under tremendous pressure. He was always in that huddle calm, cool, no matter what the situation was. And he really was a leader in his own quiet way, a leader that is hard for me to describe to you.

But you can't have a good football team unless you get a team committed to get a little bit better every day in practice. You've got to prepare yourself to practice well, and Jack Ham did. He didn't waste time out there on the practice field. He came on that field to get better, and he came off that field better, and I think every day until he hit his peak physically, Jack Ham was a better football player because of what he did.

As far as the Hall of Fame, let me share with you a thought that came to me when we were riding in the parade. I said to Jack, "You guys and we in football don't realize what a terrible burden and responsibility we have. To see over two hundred thousand people come out there for the parade with the enthusiasm and loyalty that you have to this game, and what it means to you, and what it does to the quality of your life, is an awful responsibility to us."

We have no more heroes anymore. We don't have Lindberghs because when we put someone up in space, it's the technology that's the hero. We can't have military heroes anymore. Our social heroes, the Martin Luther Kings and the Kennedys and the Sadats, the burden of trying to make the world better was so awesome they were assassinated. So we really don't have the kind of people who have been their heroes.

Our heroes come from our sports world, and that is what you have today. You have legitimate heroes, and Jack Ham is a legitimate hero. There are people that get enshrined in the Hall that give the Hall more honor than they receive.

Jack Ham is one of those people.

Jack Ham

Joe Paterno taught me a lot more than just to be confident in myself and that playing better football should not be the most important thing in your life. I have grown to know Joe better now since I left Penn State. The better I know him, the more I respect Joe Paterno, the man.

It was only a year ago when I was out in the audience and watching Joe Greene, the cornerstone of our football team. I saw him accept the greatest individual honor a football player can receive—to be inducted into the Pro Football Hall of Fame. I watched Joe mention almost all the players on our Super Bowl years, name for name, and I sat in that audience and was proud to be among the names he mentioned.

I don't get nostalgic too often, but seeing this crowd and a lot of old friends reminds me that you people are a great part of why we were a championship team for many years. People, fans, visiting teams hated to come into Pittsburgh and play. They knew that not only did we have great players but probably the greatest fans as well. And it was almost impossible for them to win.

I hope all of you remember this road to Canton because all of us will be traveling this road in future years, and I guarantee you it will be an annual event to help honor some of my teammates who were part of the greatest football team in the history of the NFL.

■　■　■

Stan Jones
Chicago Bears and Washington Redskins
Guard/Defensive Tackle
Class of 1991

Voted to seven consecutive Pro Bowls, Jones was the first to rely on weight lifting for football preparation.

Unfortunately the person that probably should be here and get a high respect from me would be my father, who died before I graduated from college and never saw me become an All-American. And his greatest hero was Red Grange. Red Grange represented the highest pinnacle that man could ever expect to reach.

He often said to me that the main thing about sports—he never played football, he was never healthy enough to play—but the thing about it was that you challenge your opponent.

I remember he came down to the University of Maryland, and he only saw me play one game, and he saw the game and I said after it, I said, "Dad, I didn't play very well." And he said, "No, you didn't, but you challenged the guy you played against. You made him a better football player." And I will never forget that.

■ ■ ■ ■

John Riggins
Washington Redskins and New York Jets
Running Back
Class of 1992

Riggins ran for 11,352 yards and scored 116 touchdowns. He was the MVP of Super Bowl XVII with 166 rushing yards, including a game-winning forty-three-yard touchdown.

Presented by NFL Commissioner Paul Tagliabue

Whenever John Riggins was handed the ball and smashed his way through the line of scrimmage, the voices of teammates, fans, and broadcasters seemed to rise as one. He could go all the way. Riggins could go all the way. Today Riggins has gone all the way—all the way to the Pro Football Hall of Fame. . . .

He once said, and I can quote him: "Everything I have done has been in fun. I see myself as an entertainer and the football field is my stage. If there wasn't anyone in the stadium, I wouldn't be there. What makes it fun is the cheering of the crowd, the fans."

John, from one of those in the crowd who cheered, I take the opportunity to say thank you from all of us. We appreciated what you did and you made it fun.

■ ■ ■ ■

John Mackey
Baltimore Colts and San Diego Chargers Tight End
Class of 1992

The second tight end to be inducted into the Hall of Fame, Mackey caught 331 passes for 5,236 yards and thirty-eight touchdowns.

Presented by AFL Players Association President Jack Kemp

I want to thank you for being introduced as the father of one of the quarterbacks of the Philadelphia Eagles. I was in Philadelphia recently, giving a speech, and the emcee got carried away and introduced me as the father of the quarterback of the Philadelphia Eagles.

A very distinguished gentleman in the back of the room stood up and said, "He doesn't look like Randall Cunningham to me." I am not Randall's daddy. I am Jeff [Kemp]'s daddy. But we would like to have his arm, and his money.

When John was picked by Ben Schwartzwalder to go to Syracuse, Coach Schwartzwalder sent him three airline tickets. He sent them to his mom and dad, and the Reverend Mackey said, "We can't accept an airline ticket; we will drive. I don't want you beholden to anybody, John Mackey."

When I first started off speaking to all the players of the AFL and NFL, John Mackey didn't say a word. He didn't talk for the longest time. Finally, after the meeting was over, I said, "John, why didn't you speak longer?" He said, "Jack, my papa taught me to listen. He said if you listen, you will be the smartest man in the room. You will know what you know, and besides that, you will know what other people know."

Mackey was the smartest man in the room.

John Mackey

When we found out that I had been inducted into the Hall of Fame, Jack said to me, "John, I just want to tell you something. You know John Unitas never threw you a pass because you were a minority. John threw you a pass because, first, he knew you would get open and second, he knew you would catch it and third, he knew you would know what to do with it." That makes me feel good because it is very important that we evaluate people on the basis of their performance alone.

My father, Reverend Walter Mackey, used to say to me when I was in high school, "Son, I know you scored a touchdown, but where are your feet?" I had no idea what he was talking about. I want him to know he is eighty-seven years old and I know he is watching, and I want to tell him first I love him and second, I know where my feet are. I keep them placed on the ground so I keep my head out of the clouds.

I didn't know what that meant as a little boy, but I know what it means today; I understand now.

■　■　■　■

Jim Finks
Minnesota Vikings, Chicago Bears, and
New Orleans Saints Administrator
Class of 1995

Finks developed the Vikings, Bears, and Saints—all teams with losing records—into winners.

Presented by Bears Executive Ed McCaskey

He was admired at all levels throughout the league for his integrity, his ability, and his creed of, "Do the right thing." He was tough and fair and believed that building a football organization was the secret to success on the field. Each year the Chicago Bears invite the alumni home for dinner and a game. Those who can't come might write a letter as their most memorable experience as a Bear. Our fearless safety of yesteryear, Doug Plank, wrote a letter that, with your permission, I would like to read now.

"I had just completed my third year as a starting free safety. Since I was drafted in the twelfth round, my salary qualified me for low-income housing. I was attempting to double my salary. After I submitted my initial offer to Jim Finks he immediately countered with a 50 percent reduction in my increase. Intimidated by his position and negotiating ability, I explained I would have to discuss the offer with my wife before I made a decision. After my response, the room became very quiet. He stared into my eyes for what seemed an eternity. Then he said, 'Doug, you go home and talk to your wife. I'll go home and talk to my wife. I hope she doesn't think I offered you too much.'"

Accepting on Behalf of Jim Finks,
His Son, Jim Finks Jr.

He had a great sense of humor. Anybody who survives in the National Football League for over forty years better have a sense of humor.

A reporter asked him after a game about some questionable calls by the officials. His immediate reply was, "I'm not allowed to comment on lousy officiating." And we both enjoyed reading that quote in the paper the next day. To sum up what Jim Finks was all about, he kept these words written on a piece of paper in his wallet at all times.

"If we are ever unlucky enough to have it made, then we will be spectators instead of participants in life. It's the journey, not the arrival, that counts. Does the road wind uphill all the way? Yes, until the very end." Jim Finks was known as a former Steeler, Viking, Bear, but it is no coincidence he left this world a Saint.

■　■　■　■

Mel Renfro
Dallas Cowboys Defensive Back
Class of 1996

Selected to the Pro Bowl in each of his first ten NFL seasons, Renfro intercepted fifty-two passes and also added 842 yards on punt returns and 2,246 yards on kick returns.

Presented by Cowboys Coach Tom Landry

The Cowboys had their eye on Mel from the start. We knew he was going to be an outstanding pro and first-round pick. But an off-the-field incident in 1963 almost ended Renfro's football career.

President John F. Kennedy was assassinated two weeks before the draft. When Renfro heard the disastrous news, he banged his fist on a mirror and severed a nerve in his hand. Like other NFL teams, we weren't too sure if the nerve was going to be okay. So we took a calculated risk and picked a defensive tackle in the first round hoping that Mel would last until the second.

And boy, were we lucky that he did.

Mel Renfro

As a child, I was fortunate. My parents grounded me in the church. They taught me right from wrong and they taught me to believe in the Ten Commandments.

There were many other people who were inspirational to me along the way. I remember my fifth grade teacher, Mrs. Honeywell. She pulled me aside when I was ten years old and she said, "I see something special in you, Melvin. One day you are going to be someone." I didn't know what she meant. Oh, I knew I could run a little faster than some of the other kids, but she saw in me a vision—a vision of a professional athlete. She encouraged me to stay in the right path. I never heard from her or saw her again after grade school. But I took her words to heart and I stuck with athletics.

What can you say about Coach Landry that hasn't already been said? He's a fine Christian man. Tom Landry is a great teacher. We soon came to realize that if we had faith in him, played where he wanted us to play, did what he wanted us to do, that we would be successful. In retrospect, many years later as I was reading the scripture, I saw Coach Landry's methods.

All the time he was training and teaching, he was doing it from principles in the Bible. He was never threatening. And he never mentioned Christian principles or beliefs, but that is what it was. I know it now.

■　■　■　■

Mike Haynes
New England Patriots and
Los Angeles Raiders Cornerback
Class of 1997

The Defensive Rookie of the Year, selected to nine Pro Bowls,
Haynes intercepted forty-six passes during his career, including
one in Super Bowl XVIII.

When I went to Arizona State, I wanted to be a wide receiver. Like a lot of kids playing football, you want to see your name in lights and people reading about you in the papers. Well, at wide receiver, quarterback, running back, you can get that. Not at lineman, not at defensive back, usually. It's usually defensive backs that are getting beat in those news highlights and some wide receiver is looking pretty good.

But at Arizona State, they had injuries in the secondary and I was a freshman. It was the first year that freshmen could play varsity and they moved me up to the varsity squad. I was third-string free safety. Before you knew it, I was actually starting. I got a couple of interceptions in the games, had some nice runbacks with those, showed a little bit of what I could do.

It was then that I started this trek to be a defensive back. If I was going to be one, I wanted to be one of the all-time best. And it was hard work there, with a lot of work from a lot of coaches and a lot of players that were at Arizona State.

For those of you young people out there who want to play the game of football, I want you to know some of the things that it really took from me and maybe you will learn from my experience. I loved the game of football. I loved it. I revered it and I really appreciated it. And I knew to be a good player at that game, I had to work hard. I had to understand what 100 percent was all about and I had to understand that that goal kept moving higher because the better I got, the higher the standard became. And that's why you hear people talk about giving more than 100 percent—because it's possible, because it keeps moving.

So, young people, set your goals high, it can happen for you. Get the most out of your abilities—that's what Frank Kush taught us in college and that's what I think young people who take anything seriously should try to do. Remember, there are no limits.

■　■　■　■

Anthony Muñoz
Cincinnati Bengals Offensive Tackle
Class of 1998

An All-Pro choice in eleven consecutive years, Muñoz went to eleven straight Pro Bowls as well.

Presented by His Son, Michael Muñoz

I'm going to use this time to say thanks to my dad for what he has meant in my life.

Dad, thank you for always being there. By coming home when you could have gone out with the guys. Or by not taking jobs so you could watch me and Michelle play basketball and football. Thank you for taking us with you whenever and wherever you could. I never remember watching you play but I always remember being there.

I remember going to Spinney Field, I remember going to Pro Bowls, trying to catch Reggie Roby's mile-high punts, getting Bruce Smith's autographed shoe, and getting Howie Long's practice jersey. I thank you for keeping us in your heart when you're away on the road. By bringing us gifts or calling us on the phone to let us know that you love us. Thanks for always being there.

And thank you for always being consistent in your work ethic. I remember Michelle and I would go to Sycamore High School and you'd be running and you would run and run and run. And me and Michelle would say, "Are you done yet?" And he would start his sprints.

And thank you for being consistent in your walk with the Lord. You've always been consistent in leading our daily prayers, no matter what happens, good or bad, easy or hard. I've seen you trust God and be consistent in what you say and what you do. Thank you for always being there, always being consistent, but most of all thank you for always being a real person. You've been my model. I learned to say "I'm sorry, I was wrong" from you being big enough to admit your mistakes. You have modeled humility. I have learned to respect women because of how you respected and loved Mom.

You've also been my mentor. You've taught me technique, strategy, moves, and drills. You've taught me how to let my actions speak louder than my words. And to make people more important than things.

And finally, you've shown me how to be a man. Recently, in Ontario, California, where you grew up, his former classmates and friends all had the same basic thing to say about him. Everybody knew who the big man on campus was—except for one person, and that was him.

Humility always has been a hallmark for your life. You've showed me strength under control and how to be tough while still being tender. You are a real man.

Anthony Muñoz

A lot of times when we strive to get to the pinnacle of our profession, it's like a triangle. You reach the pinnacle and you have a broad base of people that make that possible. I had those people, lots of people.

It was people like my brother Joe, who's right here in front—Joe, stand up—and his wife, Barbara. It was individuals like my brother Joe and my brother Tom, who is not here today, that taught me, "You just go out and play and let your playing do the talking. You don't have to say anything. Be competitive, be intense, but let people see your humility."

I think about all the opportunities I was offered, the encouragement, the instruction I was offered. And it allowed me to do only one thing and that is offer my life, make my life an offering.

See, because in my second year in the NFL, I knew I wasn't motivated by money, I knew I wasn't motivated by the notoriety. And I sat in my hotel room the night before the season opener and there had to be more to playing in the NFL. And I realized as I looked through the scripture that there is more than playing in the NFL. That I was to present my body as a living sacrifice and that was my way to worship God.

■ ■ ■ ■

Ozzie Newsome
Cleveland Browns Tight End
Class of 1999

Newsome finished his career as the all-time leader among tight ends with 662 receptions for 7,980 yards.

Presented by Browns Running Back Calvin Hill

I stand before you to talk about my friend, Ozzie Newsome, and the qualities that make him special for me. And these are qualities that transcend statistics or receptions, and yet were essential for his success on and off the field. Ozzie is grace. And not just the grace of an acrobatic reception, but the grace of congratulating an opponent after a bitter loss. The grace of consoling a teammate after a critical mistake. And I know, because I made one of those mistakes against Denver in 1981, and the first arm around my shoulders was Ozzie Newsome.

Ozzie is dependability. One of the greatest coaches whose bust is in this building, Vince Lombardi, once said that "ability is important, but dependability is critical." And for Ozzie, whether it was practice or games, or even more important, a verbal commitment to a young kid to be there, he was there. You could etch his word in stone.

Ozzie is humility. We call him "The Wizard of Oz." When he was introduced in Cleveland, they would put up "The Wizard of Oz." I heard people in the parade today yell "Wizard" and he would chuckle, almost embarrassed. Because with his greatness comes a deep humility.

Ozzie is class. Twenty-one years ago, when I first came up to Cleveland, he showed me a telegram he got from Bear Bryant. He was embarking on a professional career and Bear Bryant was just telling him some things, and he ended that telegram by saying, "Ozzie, keep your class." And for twenty-one years, he has kept his class. . . .

See I know what it means to be the father of a son. As a father, you hope to impart all the right values by example. But you know, it takes a village. And there are others in that village that help. And when my son was five years old and he first met Ozzie, he was someone I used as an example outside my house—an example of grace, an example of humility, of dependability, of class, of family. And so it excites me because I've talked about Ozzie to my son for a lot of years. And he's watching, and he's going to see this man that I have used as a role model for him go into the Pro Football Hall of Fame.

Ozzie Newsome

At some point during my career, I was at a dinner and I heard Hall of Famer Paul Warfield talk about Hall of Famer Jim Brown and the passion he had for the game. Paul related the story of how Jim drove all night so he could be at the very first practice for the College All-Star Game. That's passion.

I've come to understand and appreciate passion, playing for thirteen years in front of what I consider the greatest football fans in America. We've got great fans here from Buffalo, great fans here from New York. But I want to give you your official welcome to Cleveland's "Dawg Pound."

Along the way, in order for any of us to achieve, there had to be some mentors. I had one of the greatest college football coaches to ever walk a Saturday afternoon, a man by the name of Paul "Bear" Bryant. Just ask some other fellow Alabamians that have come before me; they've talked about Coach Bryant. I think we all can agree that the lessons that he taught us while we were there are the lessons that we are living right now in our lives. That's how special a man he was.

■ ■ ■ ■

Eric Dickerson
Los Angeles Rams, Indianapolis Colts,
Los Angeles Raiders, and Atlanta Falcons Running Back
Class of 1999

Dickerson rushed for 13,259 yards,
including an NFL record 2,105 in 1984.

Presented by Rams Tackle Jackie Slater

I have known Eric Dickerson since 1983, and by his own admission, he'll tell you that I've changed and grown, as we all do. But there are a few things about Eric Dickerson that I have found to be as consistent today as they were in 1983. And those qualities consist of the following: an unshaken loyalty to his family and his friends; a willingness to take responsibility for his shortcomings and to try to improve; and, last but not least, Eric's supreme confidence in his abilities that he felt came directly from God, almighty.

Eric Dickerson

When I go back and think about people who have really changed my life in certain ways, who comes to mind most definitely is John Shaw of the Rams.

Now if you know John Shaw, he was the general manager of the Rams at the time. John Shaw and I could not see eye to eye on anything. Me and him had an argument one day in his office about who led the league in rushing.

I'm saying, "John, I led the league in rushing." "No, you didn't," he tells me. "Yes, I did." "No, you didn't." "Yes, I did," I said. "John, get the book." And he did and he said, "Oh! You did lead the league in rushing." It was just amazing.

But one thing I can say after all the years, and you step away from the game of football and you sit back and you get to know a person on a one-on-one basis, it makes it a bit different.

John and I, we had lunch about three years ago—and I don't even know if John remembers this—but we were sitting in a restaurant and we're talking about the old times, the old teams, the old players, and he said to me, "Eric, I don't want you to think I'm saying this because you're in front of me, but I just want to tell you, you were the greatest running back I've ever seen in my life."

To me, that meant more than all the contract disputes I'd ever had. To me, it just laid everything to rest for someone to take notice of my talent and say that. And John, I just want to thank you for that moment. I don't know if you remember it, but I remember it very well.

Last of all, my dad never saw me play in the National Football League. He only saw me play in high school because he passed away. He would go sit in the stands and he would sit there and read his Bible while I played and while I practiced. And I'd go sit beside him after practice and he'd say, "Son, let me tell you something. This is great. But I want you to understand one thing. You can gain the world, but don't lose your soul."

And at one point, I never understood what that meant—gain the world but don't lose your soul. And as an older man, I understand. I really do understand now.

These are things we will soon pass up and leave behind but my dad loved me so much, and I loved him so much, and he would always say these words to me: "Son, all you do, do what you might, things done by halves are never done right."

And as I played in the National Football League, I think I did it right.

■ ■ ■ ■

Dan Hampton
Chicago Bears Defensive Lineman
Class of 2002

Despite enduring ten knee surgeries during his career—five on each knee—Hampton still finished twelve seasons in Chicago with eighty-two sacks and four Pro Bowls.

Playing the game of football will teach you so many things. How lucky was I that as I learned to compete in this game, that the good Lord had me go to Chicago, where I got to play with one of the greatest competitors of all time, number 34, Walter Payton. I've got to tell you something: I got to play nine years with Walter Payton. Man, it wasn't because Walter was the biggest or strongest or fastest that he was the NFL's all-time leader in yardage. It's because he had the biggest heart. . . .

In every player's life, you get a certain coach that really touches your soul. Buddy Ryan was from Oklahoma, I was from Oklahoma, and right off, we hit it off.

As a first-round pick, I really felt like the Chicago Bears expected an awful lot of me. I started playing pretty good at the end of my rookie year, and I got a little bigheaded. I thought I was doing a pretty good job and we go into Pittsburgh my second year, when they had this juggernaut. And we go in there, and I swear, not only do I not make a play but I'm not even on the film. It's like I walk into a spaceship or something. You don't even find me on tape.

The next morning we come into the meeting after getting beat about 40–0. Buddy is standing up in front of the meeting and he's got tears in his eyes. And he says, "You know, Big Rook, I thought we could count on you. With you playing the way you're capable of, you give us a chance to be special. Now if I can get some other guys to show up and they have a great game, man, we've got a chance to really have a great defense. But if I can't count on you to be the player that we expect, man, we're dead. We'll get gutted week in and week out."

I went home and I didn't sleep for three days. And I realized then that what he used to say is true. Football is not a game where you make a living; it's not about making money. To us, the guys that really care about it, it's about winning. It's a game of finding the difference in people, looking in their hearts and seeing who's willing to compete and to make a difference. And who wants to be a man.

I remember my very first awards banquet. I was the first one in high school to make All-American and I went to the awards banquet and I sat down right in front, thinking I'm going to get some awards. And boy, I couldn't wait when the head coach, Bill Reed, said, "Our offensive lineman of the year is . . ." and I thought to stand up, and he says, ". . . Lee Monroe."

I said, "That's okay, I play both ways, I'll wait." The next thing he said is, "Our defensive lineman of the year goes to . . ." and I was about to stand up again and he says, ". . . Rodney Jansen." I'm saying, "Wait a minute, what's up with this?" Then I remembered we had the big award, the Red Devil Award, and I thought, "Oh yeah, that's me." And he said, "Our 1975 Red Devil Award winner of the year is . . ." and I stood up, and he said, ". . . Fernando Weathers," and I immediately led a standing ovation for Fernando Weathers.

But I realized right then that maybe you're not as great as you think you are. Man, I'll tell you what, this is a humbling game. The thing that coach told me in high school is, "The reason I didn't give you those awards, Dan, is because the guys that you played with, they played just as hard, and they cared just as much, and they practiced just as long, and they bled just as much, they sweat just as hard, and they're not going to get a chance to go to college. And you are because the good Lord has given you a great gift. So instead of these awards, you think about honoring the good Lord and His gift to you by going and making the most of your talent."

■ ■ ■ ■

George Allen
Los Angeles Rams and Washington Redskins Coach
Class of 2002

Allen never suffered a losing season and ranked tenth in coaching victories at the time of retirement.

Presented by Rams, Chargers, and Redskins
Defensive End Deacon Jones

My experience with George Allen began in 1966, when he was hired to lead the Los Angeles Rams out of the depths of despair. I remember walking into the locker room that first morning and seeing little signs plastered all over the place—little sayings that you might find posted on a grammar school wall, one-liners that seemed ridiculous. The Rams had not had a winning season since 1958, and we needed a miracle worker, not a schoolteacher. We all looked at each other and shrugged. But then we met Coach Allen. And that was exactly what we got—a miracle worker of the utmost degree.

He drove us to make the most of ourselves, and he made us winners. And we learned to love those little sayings of George Allen. Teamwork, hard work, pride, determination, and competitive spirit. Every stop he made, every level of football he coached, he had a winning season using these five points that I believe make a champion. Through George Allen's leadership, forty men made a total commitment to our coach and to winning.

George Allen is the only coach in the history of the NFL to have coached twelve years or better and never had a losing season. He taught us that the harder we worked, the luckier we got. And boy, did we get lucky, and stayed that way, through his tenure.

I recently read a quote from George, and I remember it like it was heard yesterday. "I have told my team," said coach, "that God, family, and football are the three most important things in their lives. During the season, football comes first. And we all should have some leisure time. Leisure time is the five or six hours you sleep each night."

Yes, that exemplified George Allen and the ethics he required when you worked for him. Often times, it's best to describe someone in their own words. And I can find none better that exemplified Coach George Allen than these words: "In sports, the only measure of success is victory. We must sacrifice everything to this end. The man who can accept defeat and take his salary without feeling guilty is a thief! I cannot think of a thing that this money can buy that a loser can enjoy. Fancy cars, clothes, parties, and pretty women are only window dressing. Winning is the true goal. Only the winner's alive; the loser's dead, whether he knows it or not."

Accepting on Behalf of George Allen,
His Son, Former U.S. Senator George Allen

I know if my father were here today, he would tell you all, "Gosh, this sure is a great day to be alive!" But I feel that George Allen is with us all, in the living spirit of all those who have gathered to celebrate this pinnacle of football honors, joining with this great class of inductees and their presenters.

My father would have celebrated with a typical glass of milk—maybe even allowed one blackberry brandy. But he would also say this honor is a team victory. He would give thanks to God and say, "This is a victory for all of the players, coaches, and staff who were on our teams."

In 1990, my father remarkably turned Long Beach State into a winner, and in what turned out to be the last weeks of his life, he penned an article for *Sports Illustrated* about, what turned out to be, enduring values.

"At a time when concepts like working together and being positive seem old-fashioned to some people," he wrote, "it's reassuring that those ideas still have value. I learned that players need the same things they needed in 1948—discipline, organization, conditioning, motivation, togetherness, love. No matter what a player did, I usually gave him another chance. It wouldn't have helped to kick players off the team, because then I wouldn't have had a chance to work with them."

George Allen loved his players, he loved his coaches, he loved the game. To my father, I hope you are enjoying this reunion because many of the gang's all here to celebrate the contributions you made during your inspiring life. Thank you for the blood and spirit that you gave to your family, and to the joy of life that you gave to all your winning teams and their fans.

Coach Allen, you are with us all in our hearts and in our memories.

■ ■ ■ ■

James Lofton
Green Bay Packers, Los Angeles Raiders,
Buffalo Bills, Los Angeles Rams, and
Philadelphia Eagles Wide Receiver
Class of 2003

Over sixteen seasons, Lofton caught 764 passes for seventy-five touchdowns and a then-record 14,004 yards. He was voted to eight Pro Bowls.

Presented by His Son, David Lofton

Growing up in a home centered around football, I've always had dreams of playing in the NFL. I share these dreams with many of my peers not knowing that it would take more than a dream to make my aspirations become a reality. And even though I had a dad with first-hand experience, I often overlooked his advice. He would try to help me realize what I had to do to achieve these dreams but I often didn't want to make the sacrifices that he often preached about.

I think back to the summer before my freshman year. At the time that I was probably the most frustrated with my dad than I've ever been. As a normal fourten-year-old, I saw the summers as a time to stay up all night watching TV, playing around, and sleep in the next day.

My dad had slightly different views than me. He would wake me up before seven in the morning and would take me out to the track with him and then to the health club to lift weights and I hated it. And every morning I would let him know it. I thought he was crazy. Even if I had a friend spend the night, he would make them come out to the track with us. It's probably why none of my friends wanted to ever come to my house after the first time.

Every morning I would complain and ask him why he had to wake me up early. My friends were on vacation, and I had to get up and work out. He would always tell me that in football there's no substitute for strength and no excuse for the lack of it. He explained to me that if I wanted to make it to the next level that it was going to take extra work. Looking back at those times, I'm ashamed for not trusting his expertise. He was just pushing me to be the best I could be and taught me that being a great athlete takes sacrifice. That season, I realized how much I had benefited from all the work outside that at one time I despised.

I now look at that summer as a turning point in my athletic career. My dad taught me how not to settle for mediocrity, to expect the best from myself, and how to achieve it. Without his advice, support, quotations, and early-morning wake-up calls, I'm sure that I wouldn't be where I am today.

James Lofton

During my first three years at Stanford, Jack Christiansen—another Hall of Famer—was one of my coaches. And at Stanford those first three years, I was a role player. Okay, I'll be honest; I was a nonstarter, a benchwarmer. But that was in the fall.

In the winter and spring, I was tutored and influenced by Payton Jordan, my track-and-field coach. He had been the coach of the 1968 Olympic team. Coach Jordan, by word and deed, taught me to think like a champion, to practice like a champion, to perform as a champion. But, above all, despite where you are, believe that you would always become a champion. Thank you, Coach Jordan.

In the fall of 1977, a sweeping change came to the Stanford University campus and my path to the Hall of Fame really got a jump-start. A young man with slightly graying hair was hired as the new football coach. Bill Walsh had not reached genius status then, he was just a smart guy. But he did have some pretty good pass plays, although the first installment of the "West Coast" offense got off to a slow start.

My first game as a starter my senior year, zero catches, zero yards. Bill, as he preferred to be called, came over to me and sat down next to me in the locker room. And he told me that I'd be okay, that I would catch a dozen passes in a game. And I'm thinking, "Yeah, the coach is just blowing a little smoke up me. Here's a guy who's been riding the pine for three years and he's telling me I'm going to catch a dozen passes in a game."

But a dozen it was by the middle of the season against the Washington Huskies. Thank you, Bill Walsh, for having confidence in me when my own was pretty low. Thank you.

■ ■ ■ ■

Barry Sanders
Detroit Lions Running Back
Class of 2004

A ten-time Pro Bowl selection, Sanders rushed for 15,269 yards, including at least one thousand in ten seasons. He scored ninety-nine touchdowns. He was the NFL's co-MVP in 1997.

My first year as a nine-year-old was a memorable year for me because I think that a couple years before that, I had been bugging my dad about letting me play, and he thought I was too small, believe it or not. So he wanted me to wait until I got a little older. I went and joined the team because I went to football practice with an older kid and I had to join up, regardless of what my dad said. I was scared of my dad growing up, but let consequences be what they may, I was going to join the football team.

I played on good teams and bad teams, and some teams I played a lot and other teams I never got in the game. But I was always glad to be part of a team and going to practice and just being part of a special unit going out every weekend or whatever with the same purpose and goal in mind. And in that way, I felt special.

I can think of the day where I learned a precious lesson from my father. My sophomore year in high school, I was fortunate enough to be on the junior varsity and I played a little bit of cornerback, and I returned punts and kickoffs. We were just a little bit outside of our town, Wichita, playing against a team. And it was a very close game and the fourth quarter came, and it was close and I was in there catching the kicks, and I wouldn't run up and catch the ball. I wouldn't run up and catch the punts.

But after the game on the ride home, my dad asked me . . . because it was sort of unusual, he never really said anything about what I should do on the field, he saved his advice for off the field, and trust me, he had plenty of advice for that.

He asked me, "Barry, why weren't you catching the punts?" And I was like, "Well, Daddy, it was a close game, and I didn't want to run up and drop the punt and cause us to lose the game." He said, "Son, you can play the game the way it's supposed to be played. Don't be scared to make mistakes. In life you're going to make some mistakes. Even if you wanted to stay in bed all day and avoid the whole world, that's not the answer, especially in the game of football. You're going to make some mistakes. Go out and play the way you're capable of. The coach has you in there for a reason, he has confidence in you."

That was some of the best advice I think I've ever gotten, because as a young player you want to do everything right and it doesn't always happen that way. As Mr. [Chris] Berman pointed out, sometimes I did lose yards on a run, but it wasn't for a lack of trying. And I can credit William Sanders for that great lesson that allowed me to be a great player, to be here today.

■　■　■　■

Art Monk
Washington Redskins and
New York Jets Wide Receiver
Class of 2008

A three-time Super Bowl winner, Monk caught 940 passes for 12,721 yards and sixty-eight touchdowns. He was the first receiver to catch more than one hundred passes in a season.

My class and I had a luncheon with all the Hall of Famers yesterday. And as we were eating and some of them started standing up and talking, I took a moment to just look around the room, and I focused on the face of each and every Hall of Famer that was in there. And I suddenly realized that I was sitting in the middle of a room of the greatest athletes that have ever played this game.

Some played just because the love of the game. Some broke through the color barrier and persevered through the struggles of racism, and others sacrificed for the benefit of those who follow in their footsteps.

And for me, it was a privilege for me to be sitting in that room with them, some of which I never knew, some of which I've watched in awe growing up, wanting to be like them, emulating them, and others that I've had the opportunity to play with, compete against. And even though they were my competitors, I greatly appreciated and respected their abilities. And I loved playing against them because they were the best, and they helped bring the best out in me.

And now to be standing here next to them as one of them is truly an honor and an awesome, awesome moment in my life.

There's a scripture that I think about almost every day and I've come to personalize it to my life. It says: "Lord, who am I that you are mindful of me?" And the Apostle Paul says, "Think of what you were when you were called. Not many were wise by human standards. Not many were influential. Not many were born of noble birth." And when I look at my life and how I grew up, I certainly had none of those qualities or benefits.

But I understand, and I know that I'm here not by in and of my own strength but it's by the grace and the power of God upon my life, who I know gave me favor along the way and who provided opportunity and room for me to use my gifts.

From the time I first picked up a football I fell in love with this game. It's all I ever wanted to do. From playing tackle in the streets of White Plains to playing in the stadiums in the NFL, I never, ever imagined it would take me this far. It's taken a lot of hard work and sacrifice and the belief from people and times when I didn't believe in myself. I've experienced some exciting moments. I've met some extraordinary people and I have a lot of great memories that I will never forget.

This is the icing on the cake for me, and I take it very seriously. And I'm extremely honored to now be included with this group of elite athletes and to do so with my Class of 2008. I will wear the banner with pride. And I will represent it well.

■ ■ ■ ■

Gary Zimmerman
Minnesota Vikings and
Denver Broncos Offensive Tackle
Class of 2008

A member of the NFL's All-Decade Team in the '80s and '90s, Zimmerman blocked for Steve Young in the USFL and John Elway in the NFL.

Presented by Broncos Owner Pat Bowlen

When Gary asked me to be his presenter, my first concern, I guess, was that I was going to have a difficult time explaining how good he really was. An offensive lineman doesn't usually get very much attention. Gary wanted very little of it. But there's no doubt in my mind that for five years he was the mainstay of our offensive line and the major reason that we were able to go and win our first Super Bowl in 1997.

One of the things that Gary was very good at was inspiring his teammates. And when he arrived in Colorado, in Denver, he sat his other four offensive linemen down and he said: "This is what we're going to do. We're going to work our tails off. We're never going to talk to the press, and we're going to have our own corner of the locker room." And from that moment on our offensive line, in my humble opinion, became one of the better offensive lines in football. And they were really under the tutelage of Zimmerman, better known as "Zim."

One of the problems that Gary suffered with was he had a very bad left shoulder, which is something you don't want if you're playing left tackle. And I'd watch him every game, and I would watch him go through the motions of a lot of pain, but I don't think he ever gave up a sack. And it was unbelievable that he could play at that level with an arm that he could only lift this high.

When it came time for him to retire, in his mind, it was right after the Super Bowl in San Diego, Super Bowl XXXII, and I remember vividly we were all partying and having a great time, and I looked in the back of the room and there were the five offensive linemen standing in the back with a beer in their hands and just watching this party go on.

So I said, "I've got to approach these guys. I've got to get them involved in the fun." And I went back and I said: "Gary, why don't you guys come on out and sit down at a table and drink your beer there and maybe get into some dancing and stuff. And, oh, by the way, Gary, I can't wait until next year." And that's when he dropped it on me at the Super Bowl party. "Mr. B, I'm done." That was the end of my evening.

The last thing I'd like to say is something that really comes from my heart, and I will try not to cry. Zim, the Broncos love you. We love you for the way you conducted yourself, for the kind of guy you were, and for the great player that you were for us and for the entire game. I mean that from my heart. I can't talk up here anymore. I'm about ready to start crying.

Gary Zimmerman

In 1980, I signed my letter of intent with the University of Oregon. I chose Oregon over other schools because it was the only college that would sign me as a middle linebacker. While dressing down for the first practice, I thought how strange it was that I was number 75. After practice the coaches pulled me aside and explained that my future might be on the offensive line. The Dalai Lama once said that not getting what you want is sometimes a wonderful stroke of luck. The point I'm trying to make here is that nobody starts out wanting to play the offensive line position; it's just where we end up.

Being an offensive lineman requires its own special qualities. And this is why there's such a unique bond among us. We are an inconspicuous group who defend our quarterbacks as if they were our mothers. We open holes for our running backs. Our job is to make the team's stars shine. The O-line position is a cohesive unit, a collection of individuals. If one member of the unit fails, we all fail. We need to be thick-skinned because if things are not going well, the blame is often directed at us. And when things are going well, it's just another day at the office. There's often ten ways to block a play. So a lineman needs to be intelligent and able to make split-second decisions to changing defenses. We must be physically tough because we play the entire game making contact on every offensive play.

And, finally, offensive linemen conform to the herd principle. It's not good to be singled out for good or bad, and that's why it's difficult for me to stand up here alone getting this incredible honor. There should be a stage full of guys up here standing here, receiving this honor with me.

When I began playing in Denver, I came to know the curse. The curse happens to tackles that have an amazingly talented quarterback, like John Elway, and you are responsible for protecting his blind side. What happens is the night before the game you get little or no sleep knowing that if you screw up you will forever be known as the guy who lost the franchise. Like clockwork I would wake up between 4:00 and 4:30, flop around for a while, and finally get up. Many times I would just go to the stadium with our trainer, Steve Antonopulos, who, by the way, I would like to extend a huge thanks for all your friendship and the hundreds of hours you spent getting me ready to play on Sundays. I would also like to thank John. It was worth every sleepless night.

CHAPTER 5

PASSION

JOHN MADDEN WITH
AL DAVIS

EACH FEBRUARY, EVERY NFL TEAM SENDS ITS COACHES, executives, and trainers to Indianapolis to test the top college football prospects physically, athletically, medically, intellectually, every way possible.

Yet for all the manpower, money, and time each team invests, the process could be streamlined and simplified with one basic question posed to each potential pro player:

How important is football to you?

Whenever football is as important as anything else in a person's life, the player's chances of succeeding in the sport rise dramatically. It is the same with any person in any field. The more important their livelihood is to them, the more they care about it, the greater the chance is they will succeed.

Some men make it to Canton more on their passion than their talent. The passion that was obvious in their play is evident in their words.

■ ■ ■ ■

John Madden
Oakland Raiders Coach
Class of 2006

Hired at the age of thirty-two, Madden compiled a 112-39-7 record. He owns the best regular-season winning percentage among coaches with one hundred wins.

Presented by Raiders Owner Al Davis

Let's go back to Oakland for a moment. Let's go back to the 1970s. Let's fill that stadium one more time with the staff and the administrative people who poured their heart and soul into the Raiders. Let's go back to the great Raider warriors who are here today, and to those who are no longer with us, but whose memories we cherish, and those great warriors who are watching up there today who will lead us in the future.

I say let's line you up under the goalposts one more time, one more time, and have you introduced all individually once again to the roar of that Oakland crowd. We can never forget those great moments. The roar would be deafening to see you trot out in those black jerseys, silver helmets.

John Madden, the chill goes through my body as I hear that roar and think of all those special people, but seeing you, John, down on the sidelines prowling those sidelines, yelling at officials, that flaming red hair, those arms moving left and right, screaming at Raider players, and, most of all, winning football games.

But that is fantasy. Fantasy isn't the answer here today. But what is not fantasy is you coming up to this podium to be enshrined into the Pro Football Hall of Fame. Ladies and gentlemen, the great John Madden.

John Madden

The Hall of Famers behind me, that's what it's all about. I was reading the NFL stats and history book. That's what you do when you ride a bus. When you don't fly, you read big old thick books like that. But they had a chapter on history. The first page in the chapter of history was a list of the Hall of Famers. I said, "That's right, they got it. That is our history."

The players that played before us, the players that played when they didn't have face masks, when they had leather helmets, when we got this thing started, the players that played in smaller stadiums, didn't have the medical thing, didn't have anything. They laid the foundation for this great game, and we should never forget it. I say the NFL teams, you ought to honor your history more. Sometimes we tend to get caught up in the players, the games now. Honor your history. Bring back the Hall of Famers. Bring back their teammates. Let the fans show their appreciation to the history.

I know going in with these guys is so special. We always talk about immortality. Some of us think maybe we will be immortal, that we'll live forever. When you really think about it, we're not going to be. But I say this, and this is overwhelming, mind-blowing, that through this bust, with these guys, in that Hall, we will be forever. You know, when you think of that, it just blows your mind. It's forever and ever and ever.

You have to stay with me a moment on this one. This is a little goofy here. You're going to say, "There is old Madden being goofy again." But I started thinking about this after I got voted into the Hall of Fame. The more I think about it, the more I think it's true. Now I know it's true and I believe it.

Here is the deal: I think over in the Hall of Fame, that during the day the people go through, they look at everything. At night, there's a time when they all leave. All the fans and all the visitors leave the Hall of Fame. Then there's just the workers. Then the workers start to leave. It gets down to there's just one person. That person turns out the light, locks the door. I believe that the busts talk to each other.

I can't wait for that conversation, I really can't. Vince Lombardi, Knute Rockne, Reggie White, Walter Payton, all my ex-players, we'll be there forever and ever and ever talking about whatever. That's what I believe. That's what I think is going to happen, and no one's ever going to talk me out of that. And these guys in there are going, "Oh, no, hope I don't have to put up with his BS for an eternity."

This is a celebration. It has to be fun. To have Al Davis here is something special. I mean, if it weren't for Al, I wouldn't be here. He was a guy that gave me an opportunity. He was a guy that hired me forty years ago, brought me into pro football. He was a guy that made me a head coach when I was thirty-two years old. I had two years of pro coaching experience. Who the heck names a guy thirty-two years old as a head coach? Al Davis did. But he not only named me head coach, he stood behind me and he helped me and he provided me with players, with great players. As he was saying, nine of the players are in the Hall of Fame. I mean, those are the types of players that he provided me with.

He stood behind me not only the ten years I was the head coach, but he stood behind me for the last forty years. Al Davis is a friend, always has been a friend. I remember I had the opportunity to induct him into the Hall of Fame. At the time I said, you know, talking about loyalty, what a guy Al Davis was. I said that he's the guy, you know, if you had anything happen, you had one phone call, who would you make that phone call to? I said it would be Al Davis. All these years later, I got an opportunity, I got voted into the Hall of Fame, I had a phone call to make for a presenter. And I called Al Davis.

I just talked to my mom. She's watching. Hi, Mom, I love you. I was talking about how excited I am, how I haven't slept in three days, my mind is mush. She just said, me, too. She has the same feelings. She's not right here, but she's here in spirit. She's a special person that's been with me for the seventy years of my life. I know that my dad, who died in 1960, is up there looking down and laughing.

My mom's probably laughing right now, too, because when I was like a sophomore in high school, I was playing in summer baseball. I was playing on three or four different teams. I told my dad, "I'm going to drop a couple of these because I want to get a job to make some money." My dad said, "I'll give you a couple bucks, go caddie, make a few loops, you'll be okay." He said, "Don't work. Once you start work, you're going to have to work the rest of your life."

My dad worked hard. He was a mechanic. The reason I say that he's up there laughing right now is because I listened to him and I continued to play, and I have never worked a day in my life. I went from player to coach to a broadcaster, and I am the luckiest guy in the world.

If there was a Hall of Fame for families, my family would be in the Hall of Fame—my wife, Virginia; my two sons, Joe and Mike. They talk about how hard coaches work. They work eighteen, twenty hours a day. They sleep on a couch. They don't come home. You know, that's not the hard job. The hard job is a coach's wife, believe me. The job of the coach's wife, she has to be mother, father, driver, doctor, nurse, coach, everything, because the coach is out there working. When anyone is appreciated, they have to appreciate their wife. I have the greatest in Virginia. Thank you. Stand up, you deserve it. After all those years putting up with me, you deserve to stand up and take a bow on this day.

And my two sons, Mike and Joe, I'm so proud of them. They're not only my two sons, but they're my two best friends. When they were kids, I used to take them to practice on Saturdays. I'd take them to the Pro Bowl. I coached the Pro Bowl way too many damn times. I used to take them to the Pro Bowl, Super Bowl, every time I could. Those were special times.

As I look back now on my coaching career, I think of my family, I think of the days that we spent together. I say this to coaches everywhere: If you ever have a chance to take your kids with you, take them. Don't miss that opportunity. Because when it's all over and done with, when you look back, those are going to be your fondest memories.

I just want to say in closing that it's been a great ride. I want to thank everyone who has been along for any part of it. Speaking of great rides, I was lucky enough to be carried off the field after we won Super Bowl XI. I was told it took like five or six guys to lift me up, then they dropped me. But that's okay, because that was me and that was them. They aren't going to carry me off. You carry him off for a while—boom!—you dump him on the ground. But it was the happiest moment of my life.

Today feels like the second time in my life that I'm being carried off on the shoulders of others. Yet instead of off the field, it's into the Hall of Fame. Instead of five or six guys today, I ride on the shoulders of hundreds of friends, coaches, players, colleagues, family. I just say this: I thank you all very much. This has been the sweetest ride of 'em all.

■　■　■　■

Weeb Ewbank
Baltimore Colts and New York Jets Coach
Class of 1978

Ewbank is the only coach to win championships in both the NFL and the AFL. He led the Colts to championships in 1958 and 1959, and the Jets in 1968.

My selection into the Pro Football Hall of Fame was the most thrilling honor I have ever received. Having played and coached football since high school, which is practically all my life, and now to be enshrined, has to be the epitome of all football. The only thing that could be better than this enshrinement would be for me to attain what all of you and all of our goals would be, and that would be reaching heaven and eternal life.

Football is a great game. It is more than a way of living. It has been a labor of love to me. Lucy, my number one assistant who has been with me for more than fifty years, once said after several attempts to get my attention at the breakfast table on a Monday morning after a ball game, she said, "You know I just realized, your eyeballs are not round; they're oval." All coaches' wives know well what kind of fanatic it takes to be a football coach. I hope they all will be rewarded in heaven. . . .

Little do you people realize that it is much more fun socializing with this group than it is trying to make out game plans to negate their extraordinary abilities as football players. I have been walking by Lance Alworth all day, and it's the same thing—I haven't caught him yet.

■　■　■　■

Dick Butkus
Chicago Bears Linebacker
Class of 1979

Butkus was All-NFL six times and a Pro Bowl selection eight times, and he recovered twenty-seven fumbles.

Presented by Illinois Coach Pete Elliott

Anyone who ever saw Dick Butkus play knows he was a superior player immediately. His tackling was devastating, his instincts were absolutely unbelievable. But the thing that sets him apart from every other athlete I have known is his great, great intensity.

Dick played the game like it ought to be played, all out, all the time, every game, every practice. Dick Butkus is a yardstick, a yardstick for linebackers of all types. He is also a yardstick by which any athlete can measure the intensity of his own personal effort to try to reach the goals that Dick has established.

Dick Butkus

To be truthful, I dreamed of being a great football player as far back as I can remember. I decided to take one step at a time and wouldn't settle for less. I knew God had given me the physical aspects needed, now it was up to me.

I felt my goal and my dream was in sight when I entered professional football. Finally, after eight years of preparation, my opportunity was before me. Yes, I was secretly afraid I would stumble and did many times. There were times I needed more energy and more strength and more vitality to do all that I felt I must do. Anxiety and apprehension would fill my mind. I knew my family, coaches, fans, and also, first of all, my God was counting on me. I also felt that there was something so great in me that nothing in this world could defeat me or hold me back if I kept myself humbly in contact with these people. . . .

I consider being inducted into the Pro Football Hall of Fame as the top of my dream. For only on the top can I see the whole view. And I can now see what I have done and what I can do from now on. I have a new vision and a new goal now, and that is simply to be a better husband and a better father and a better person.

■ ■ ■ ■

Mike Ditka
Chicago Bears, Philadelphia Eagles,
and Dallas Cowboys Tight End
Class of 1988

The first tight end selected to the Hall of Fame, Ditka caught 427 passes for 5,812 yards and forty-three touchdowns. He played in five consecutive Pro Bowls.

Presented by Bears Defensive End Ed O'Bradovich

This great building that stands behind me was built on character, dedication, responsibility, and ability. No one exemplifies those characteristics better than Mike.

When Mike first came to the Chicago Bears, he showed a level of intensity, a burning desire, and a sense of dedication that all his fellow teammates admired. Mike's practice habits were something to behold.

The games were played on Sunday, but as far as Mike was concerned, they could have been played on Tuesday, Wednesday, or Thursday, because Mike always gave that extra 10 percent that it takes to be a true champion and leader.

To gain respect and to be a leader takes time and effort. Mike accomplished it in one year. We're all proud to see Mike be the first tight end enshrined in the Pro Football Hall of Fame.

Mike Ditka

I want to thank the NFL for what it stands for, for the men who played the game for what it really is. It is a tremendous thing, gang. I don't know any other way to put it, but you've got to love the game. It is just the greatest thing, the greatest feeling being up here. Being able to play every day, to practice every day, to be a part of it, to say that you played against Ray Nitschke, or you played against Doug Atkins, or you knew Marion Motley—any of this is what it's all about.

In life, many men have talent, but talent in and of itself is no accomplishment. Excellence in football and excellence in life is bred when men recognize their opportunities and then pursue them with a passion. I think that sums up what the players of the National Football and the Pro Football Hall of Fame stand for. They recognized an opportunity and they went after it.

I have a lot of heroes in life and one of my heroes is a man named Abraham Lincoln. And Lincoln had a little statement that he made about himself that I kind of think applies to me. I try to live by it—don't always make it, but I try.

And he made a simple statement that says this. He said, "If I were to try to read, much less answer, all the attacks made on me, this shop might as well be closed for any other business. I do the very best I know how—the very best I can; and I mean to keep doing so until the end. If the end brings me out all right, what's said against me won't amount to anything. If the end brings me out wrong, ten angels swearing I was right would make no difference."

Fred Biletnikoff
Oakland Raiders Wide Receiver
Class of 1988

In a career in which he compiled 589 receptions for 8,974 yards, Biletnikoff had at least forty catches in ten straight years. He was named MVP of Super Bowl XI.

Presented by Raiders Owner Al Davis

The will to win has been a dominant theme of the Raiders organization. No player in the history of the organization has epitomized that will more than Fred Biletnikoff. I will remember him most because he hated to lose. Like the owner speaking to you, he was a sore loser. . . .

Raiders football has always been an emotional game and Raiders fans everywhere must get emotional when they remember Fred Biletnikoff. The loose sleeves flying on your silver-and-black jersey with the famed silver number 25, your socks hanging down below your bony knees, the long blond hair flowing below the back of your helmet, the stick'em on your stockings, the black eyes, and those hands, those magnificent hands extended at the last second to pluck the football out of the sky. You know, Fred gave credibility to the credo that plain old-fashioned was not passé.

Thousands of young Americans were reminded that hard work, dedication, and devotion still reap the rewards of victory. Genius comes in many configurations. It comes in great size, in great strength, great speed, and, maybe once in every decade, in great artistry. A man will walk softly into the valley of giants and he will make you wonder, "Where is the body? Where is the strength? Where is the speed? How is he going to play a giant's game? How is he going to compensate?"

And then you hope and you watch and then you wait and a miracle will happen and you will discover that this man can play the game. He can beat you not with great skill physically, not with great athletic skill, but with artistry, timing, and execution. That was Fred Biletnikoff. When he had to catch a football he went for it as if it were in heaven, and nobody was going to stop him from catching it. Nobody could.

Fred Biletnikoff, you are a great artist who for fourteen glorious seasons used the football field as your canvas and your magnificent hands as palette and brush to paint unforgettable moments for football fans everywhere. You go to the Louvre, del Prado, the Hermitage, and you will find the miracles of what men have wrought with his hands. Now it's Freddie's turn. From this day onward, the National Football League Hall of Fame will commemorate the miracles Freddie wrought with his hands.

While we cannot preserve Fred's works on a wall, we can treasure the memories of his artistry in this one hall, the great Hall of Fame. Fred Biletnikoff, a great student of the Raiders' famed passing game, who always knew where the sideline was, who always knew where the first-down line was, and, more important, always knew where the goal line was. He loves his team, he loved his organization, he loved the great game of football.

■ ■ ■ ■

Terry Bradshaw
Pittsburgh Steelers Quarterback
Class of 1989

The MVP of Super Bowls XIII and XIV, Bradshaw threw for 27,989 yards and 212 touchdowns.

Presented by CBS Broadcaster Verne Lundquist

Just last Monday night in my home in Colorado, I was chatting with a close friend about the events that were coming up this weekend. He is a retired air force pilot, a historian, and a member of the collegiate Hall of Fame because of his All-American days at West Point, so I value his insight.

We talked a little bit about the specific events of this morning, of how this honor will be the single highest honor that can be paid of these four men. But we talked in more general terms about the role of sport in our society, throughout the ages. Of how from the time of recorded civilizations those civilizations have venerated their athletes, the Greeks, the Romans, a multitude of nations since then, including us. We do so, my friend said—and his name is Robin Olds—we do so because those who have accomplished in sport have the potential to give us a higher plane. They can provide a mirror so we can see what we can become. They do that especially when through a quest of their athletic accomplishment, we glimpse their humanity. We see them prevail and we also see them stumble and fall. We relish their joy because we recognize their pain. Ultimately the best overcome. And the best of the best we put into the Hall of Fame.

For two decades, Terry Bradshaw has lived his life in public. We have known his triumphs and we have known his tragedies. For twenty years we have glimpsed his humanities, we have seen him prevail. There is, I believe, engrained in each of us, a small hope that we will be remembered after we are gone, that somehow those who come years from now will know that we were here, that we lived, that we loved, that we laughed, that somehow we mattered.

For most of us, that desire is very fervent, but the dreams are highly improbable. But for Terry Bradshaw, today that dream becomes a reality. Generations unborn today will come to Canton years from now, they will hear his voice, they will see his face, they will watch his exploits. And no doubt they will say then, as we do today, we whose memories are more fresh and fervent, "Boy, wasn't he something?"

Terry Bradshaw

When I got the phone call, those of you that know me know that I'm not a man that hides his emotions well. I went nuts. I went crazy, which I already am anyway. I jumped around, I ran around the house outside, I just lost it for three days. I said, "I can't believe this," and then I stopped and I said, "What does this mean? What does this all mean?"

It means that, yeah, you're one of the best that ever played, and I said, "No, wait just a second, wait just a second. What it means is that in football, you never get anything that you don't share with people. You don't get elected to the Hall of Fame by yourself."

So, thank you number 88, Lynn Swann. Thank you number 82, John Stallworth. Thank you, Franco Harris. Thank you, Rocky Bleier. What I wouldn't give right now to put my hands under Mike Webster's butt just one more time—thank you, Mike. Sam Davis, left guard, I love ya—thank you, Sam. Moon, who never knew he played in the National Football League—thank you, Moon. Jon "Cowboy" Kolb, my left tackle. Larry "Big Boss" Brown, my right tackle, and two of the finest tight ends that I never had more fun playing with, one Big Baby Huey, Benny Cunningham, I love you, thank you. And Randy Grossman, the greatest set of hands a tight end ever had, thank you. Folks, Jim Smith, Calvin Sweeney, Theo Bell, and I can go on and on, every one of them. It takes people to get anything done. We didn't get in here by ourselves.

Hey folks, I went to my dad in 1955 and I said, "Pop, I'm going to play in the National Football League." I was seven years old, we lived in Camanche, Iowa. He said, "That's right, son, move on." So I did and I got a ball. He gave me a Sears and Roebuck ball and I learned how to throw that sucker. He said it has got to last a year, and it had gotten real ripped. I took this clothes hanger and threaded my shoe strings through it to hold it together. That's commitment, isn't it? That's what it takes. I wanted it so bad. Not to get in the Hall, but just get in the NFL.

I was drafted by the Pittsburgh Steelers in 1970. Now folks, we didn't have a love affair when it started. Y'all called me "Ozark Ike" because I was big and white and dumb acting. Said I was Li'l Abner. Said I couldn't spell "cat." And I never understood what you wanted from me because all I thought was, "Hell, we're supposed to win. Isn't that what we're supposed to do up here—just win?"

We the Steelers, all my boys, all of them, we loved to win. God, we loved to win. I want every one of you loving me. I want you clapping for me. I don't want you booing me and when we won you clapped. But it takes people.

All our careers, we were blessed with great people around us. I'm a fortunate quarterback to have so much beautiful talent, so many wonderful athletes to go out and get the job done. It allowed me to be the kind of person I was, to go out and be aggressive and to attack and have fun and tell jokes and cut up with reporters who still haven't figured me out yet. That was fun. I enjoyed that, I got a kick out of that.

But folks, when it's all said and done, the crowd finally goes home, and we're left with our thoughts, we sit back and we say, "It's the people you share it with."

■ ■ ■ ■

Ted Hendricks
Baltimore Colts, Green Bay Packers, and
Oakland/Los Angeles Raiders Linebacker
Class of 1990

Hendricks intercepted twenty-six passes and blocked twenty-five field goals, extra points, and punts.

Presented by Raiders Owner Al Davis

Thank you, Ted, for having the charismatic presence in every game you played. You were the epitome of just win, baby, just win.

Thank you, Ted, for having such an awesome tolerance for pain and not at all for defeat. It took indestructibility to do what this guy did, but he played in 215 consecutive league games, the most ever played by a linebacker, the most in the history of the National Football League.

Thank you, Ted, for your commitment to excellence and the will to win you provided as a defensive team captain.

Thanks for being such a winning force in every one of the four Super Bowls that you played, three with the Raiders, and his teams won all four.

And lastly, Ted, from all of us, thanks for exemplifying the great Raider spirit and individuality of carrying that silver-and-black insignia so proudly and distinctly on your uniform and in your heart.

As you go into the Hall of Fame, we advise you that you bring your silver and black. There are six legends named Shell, Upshaw, Otto, Brown, Biletnikoff, and Blanda that have been waiting patiently for a linebacker and we could no less than send in the very best there is.

I want you to think of all the great stadiums—Pittsburgh, Miami, Kansas City, Dallas—and as the crowd roars in my dreams and the stadium becomes thunderous, I can hear the PA announcer saying, "From Hialeah, Florida, where he was the high school All-American, from the University of Miami where he was a college All-American, from the Baltimore Colts, the Green Bay Packers, the Oakland, and now Los Angeles, Raiders where he was All-Pro with every team, number 83 in his finest hour, the indestructible Hall of Famer, Ted Hendricks."

■　■　■　■

Lem Barney
Detroit Lions Cornerback
Class of 1992

A seven-time Pro Bowl selection, Barney intercepted fifty-six passes that he returned for 1,077 yards. He also scored seven defensive touchdowns and four on special teams.

Presented by Lions Defensive Back Jim David

Lem Barney was simply a natural and a true champion. But the stats do not give you the whole picture of Lem Barney.

You see some players today think of football as an individual sport. Lem never forgot football as a team sport. On the sidelines and in the locker room, he was just as valuable to our team as he was on the field. He never failed to lend a helping hand, give advice, or take advantage of a situation to help raise the morale of our team and our level of play.

All of this is so important today because Hall of Famers, as positive role models, must exhibit championship qualities on and off the field.

Lem Barney

For once in a lifetime a man knows a wonderful moment, when fate takes his hand. This is my moment. I've said all along, for many years, success, accomplishments, and achievements are no good unless you have someone whom you love to share this with. Today you share this moment with me.

Life does not always deal us a fair hand, but the hands that life deals us, we must play them. We must play the game of life in order to win, and win at all costs. No one ever dreams of getting to this spot once he comes into the NFL. If anyone ever dreams of getting into the Hall of Fame, he is having a nightmare. When dreams of being able to utilize his God-given skills and talents and attributes to make them manifest and make them fruits. I believe my skills and talents were manifested.

Football for me for twenty years was a way of life. I enjoyed it. I whistled while I worked and every opportunity I had, I tried to promote victories and wins. Life has been good to me and if I die tonight, I wouldn't die blue because I have experienced great things in life.

Love, I believe, is our most motivating factor we could have in life. Love, love for self. Love for God. Love for your family. Love for your friends. Love for your coworkers. Love for your community. And love for this country. Love is our most powerful weapon. Someone once said that love was the only game in town that is not called off because of darkness, and love is powerful.

I would like to culminate my acceptance by rendering what I believe is the world's greatest love song ever written, penned by one of the world's greatest lexicographers, a great disciple, Brother Paul. It comes from Corinthians 1:13, and simply states:

Though I speak with the tongues of men and of angels and I have not loved, I have become a sounding blast or a tinkling symbol. Though I have the gift of prophecy to understand all mysteries and understand all knowledge and have all faith so that I could move mountains and have not love, I am nothing. Though I bestow all my goods to feed the poor, though I give my body to be burned and have not loved if prophets be nothing. For love is long suffering, but love is kind. Love envied it not, love wanted not, and love is not all puffed up. Love does not behave itself unseemingly, does not seek her own, love thinketh no evil. For love rejoices not in inequities, but love never failing but whether it is prophecies they shall fail, where there is tongues they shall cease. Whether there is knowledge it shall vanish away. The last of those scriptures it says and now abideth hope, faith and love, but the greatest of these three is love.

I thank you very much, God bless you and I love you.

■ ■ ■ ■

Jimmy Johnson
San Francisco 49ers Cornerback
Class of 1994

A five-time Pro Bowl selection, Johnson had opposing quarterbacks avoid throwing to his area. He intercepted forty-seven passes that he returned for 615 yards.

The very first year of my junior varsity competition under Coach Les Ratzlaff I learned all the x's and o's and fundamentals of football. Coach Ratzlaff taught me how to be proud when I was a winner and how to be humble when we came up on the short end.

I worked real hard for Coach Ratzlaff but unfortunately, early in that very first season, I got bumped around quite a bit—whirlybird left and right—and at the end of one of those early games, I came up with a tremendous stomach cramp, and it hurt.

That was a Friday night, and I had pains throughout Saturday, throughout Sunday, went to school on Monday, and Monday evening I went to the hospital for a checkup and found that I had to have an operation. I had to have an appendectomy. I had the operation, convalesced for a very short time, and came back to the team. This is where I think I learned the biggest lesson in the game of football and sports.

Coach Ratzlaff asked me to be his manager, and at first I turned him down because I wanted to be a football hero, a high school standout, and I didn't accept. But after talking to Coach Ratzlaff a couple of days, I saw the picture he wanted to give me. He was giving me the opportunity to get another view of the game of football and once I saw this, I accepted his offer to be comanager of the 1954 Kingsburg High School junior varsity football team.

Coach Ratzlaff explained to me that I could be just as important to this team by being there and showing my leadership and doing all things that managers do. Within the scope of that year, through this small window of opportunity presented by coach, I really learned how to love the game of football.

Being away from the game of football for one year, I came back with a passion as a sophomore. I came back to make up for all the time I lost by missing that one year, and I decided at that particular time that I would not be denied no matter what the odds.

For sure, throughout my career, I've been confronted with many situations that it didn't look like I could fight my way through. But that first year gave me an opportunity to look at football and decide why I really wanted to play it, and I decided I was going to play because I loved it. I loved it with a passion. And that's the way I approached the rest of my career.

My presenter, Rafer Johnson [a gold medalist in the 1960 Olympics in Rome], is in fact my hero, and that is an amazing thing in itself. Most young men growing up usually have a hero in another town, another city, another country, and they will write to this individual, receive an autographed photo, and then tack that photo up on the wall and worship that photo. No such problem for me.

I had a brother living with me on a day-to-day basis that I was able to talk to, ask the pertinent questions, get the pertinent feedback, and get corrected in my direction if needed. I must say I must give my brother Rafer credit for everything that I have accomplished in the field of athletics. And I just wish we could split this trophy right down the middle because he surely deserves half of it.

■　■　■　■

Tommy McDonald
Philadelphia Eagles, Dallas Cowboys, Los Angeles Rams, Atlanta Falcons, and Cleveland Browns Wide Receiver
Class of 1998

McDonald caught 495 passes for 8,410 yards and eighty-four touchdowns.

Presented by NFL Films Writer/Producer Ray Didinger

Tommy McDonald is here today for one reason. He followed his heart. He had a passion for the game of football and a desire to be the best and he wouldn't let anything stand in his way. That's why he is here today. Not because it was easy. Because for Tommy, it never was. Not because it was destiny, because then it wouldn't have taken this long. Tommy is here because he refused to listen to all the people who told him it was impossible. The high school and college coaches who told him he was too small, the pro teams that ignored him in the 1957 draft. They didn't realize that inside that jackrabbit body beat the heart of a lion.

Tommy McDonald was a great football player. But he's much more than that. He's an inspiration to every young person who's ever been told he wasn't big enough or fast enough or good enough. He's proof that the greatest strength is still the strength of the human will. He's proof that you don't have to stand tall to stand for everything that's good in life as well as in athletics. Tommy was five-foot-nine and 172 pounds when he played in the National Football League. Today, he becomes the smallest player enshrined in the Pro Football Hall of Fame. And that makes his accomplishments all the more remarkable.

You had to see him play to know how special he was. If I had one wish for the NFL today, in this era of billion-dollar TV deals and million-dollar contracts, it would be that more players played the game the way Tommy McDonald played it. If they gave as much, cared as much, and loved it as much as he did, we'd all have a lot more fun. Tommy just didn't play the game, he embraced it. He played the game the way we played it as kids at recess, like he was afraid that any second the bell would ring and he'd have to go back to class.

He was the last player in the league not to wear a face mask. He had his jaw broken in the 1959 league opener but he played the next week with his jaw wired shut and he still scored four touchdowns to beat the New York Giants. That was Tommy McDonald.

He was the smallest man on the field yet, in the fourth quarter, with the game on the line, there wasn't a better receiver in all of football. That's not just my opinion. Norm Van Brocklin himself said it. And if the "Dutchman" were here today to see Tommy join him in the Hall of Fame, I'm sure he'd say, "It's about time."

Tommy McDonald

Oh boy! God almighty, I feel so good—so good. Can you hear an amen back there? Yeah, you got that, baby. Move over Ronald McDonald. There's another McDonald in Canton, and we're both going to sell hamburgers—Big Macs and Little Macs.

Do I look excited or do I seem a little like I've won the lottery or the jackpot? Yes! I'm in! I'm going into the Hall of Fame! Yes!

My mom isn't here, she's eighty-eight years old. She's in a wheelchair and Mom, I want you and Dad to know that I wish every kid in the United States would have had you as a pop and mom. You gave the love, the support, and everything that I needed in life. You made my brother and myself your whole life. My dad, he died in '94, but he's standing right here. In fact, Ray Nitschke's standing here also. Can you see him? Number 66! Yeah, right there!

Thank you, Canton. I love it!

■　■　■　■

Jack Youngblood
Los Angeles Rams Defensive End
Class of 2001

A seven-time Pro Bowl selection, Youngblood played in a club-record 201 consecutive games. He played in five NFC championship games and one Super Bowl.

Presented by Rams Defensive Tackle Merlin Olsen

1971 was not an easy year for Jack Youngblood. The transition to professional football was not as quick as Jack wanted it to be. He was struggling, quite frankly. He was learning lessons, some of them quite painful—like the day he was playing against a 320-pound tackle, Bob Brown, who played with the Oakland Raiders. Bob would put two huge pads on his forearm, and he'd beat on Jack's chest. After the game, Jack looked like he had been run over by a truck.

But maybe the low point that year came after a loss when in front of the entire team, our head coach, Tommy Prothro, looked down at Jack and said, "Youngblood, you may be the worst player I've ever seen."

Jack Youngblood's story could have ended right there. One of the reasons it didn't was because Jack believed in himself. While most of us were worried about Jack staying on the roster, Jack was telling his roommate, who happened to be my brother, Phil, "How am I going to make the All-Pro team if I don't get more playing time?"

And interestingly, at each step along the way, there were those telling Jack Youngblood, "You're not big enough," or "You're not strong enough," or "You're not good enough."

Well, Jack, you're here today to have your name inscribed with the elite of pro football, the best of the best. And Youngblood, you may be the best damn football player I ever saw.

Jack Youngblood

I played this game with a passion. It was more like a love affair, a lucid love affair. It alternately intrigued me, it frustrated me, and it rewarded me. But it always kept me returning, giving me a momentary taste of satisfaction but never enough.

We didn't accomplish all that we set out to do. I didn't sack the quarterback every time I rushed the passer. I didn't make every tackle for a loss. I guess no one could. But it wasn't because I didn't have the passion to, the desire to. I hope that showed when I played the game.

CHAPTER 6

TEAMWORK

STEVE YOUNG

ON ANY SINGLE PLAY, THERE IS A QUARTERBACK WHO takes a snap, an offensive line that makes its blocks, and someone who tries to score. Nobody makes it to the end zone on his own. Similarly, no one earns a scholarship, a trip to the Pro Bowl, or induction into Canton on his own. No one.

What sometimes is overlooked is that there are more teams than just in sports. Family is a team. Neighborhoods are teams. Congregations are teams. Businesses are teams. Any unit that fails to work as a team is asking to fail. As Hall-of-Fame coach Vince Lombardi once said, "Individual commitment to a group effort—that's what makes a team work, a company work, a society work, a civilization work."

And it also helps send players to the Pro Football Hall of Fame.

■　■　■　■

Steve Young
Tampa Bay Buccaneers and
San Francisco 49ers Quarterback
Class of 2005

Young led the NFL in passing a record-tying six times. He passed for more than thirty-three thousand yards and 232 touchdowns. He was the MVP of Super Bowl XXIX and elected to seven Pro Bowls.

Presented by His Father, Grit Young

By junior high he gravitated to quarterback and he started to learn the art of passing. An ironic thing happened about that time. He was thirteen years old and I had a week off and I said, "What are we gonna do, kids, for vacation?"

And Steve says, "I wanna go to Canton, Ohio, to the Hall of Fame." And all of the other children said, "What? We're not gonna do that."

And he prevailed, he wanted to come here. And so we drove to Chicago, stayed with my sister, and then we came down and went to the Hall. We actually got a picture of Steve at thirteen years old in front of the Hall of Fame. And of course we had to go on to the chocolate factory at Hershey to satisfy the rest of the children.

Steve Young

Ironically it was my mom who kicked off my football career with a bang as she charged the field when I was eight years old. She was upset that another kid had neck tackled me and knocked the wind out of me. She knew that neck tackling was illegal and since no penalty was called she felt it imperative to rush the field and help her little boy. I was scared to death as I saw her sprinting across the field—with good speed I might add—assuming she was coming to give me a kiss or something.

Imagine the visual: late 1960s—twenties-aged woman, lady in a dress, on a football field, purse on her shoulder, big sunglasses, high-heeled shoes aerating the field. In horror, she passed by me and grabbed the kid from the other team. Adrenaline pumping, she picked up the boy by the shoulder pads and told him that the hit was illegal and that he better not do it again!

Mom, now you know why we never gave you any field-level tickets over the last seventeen years.

Sid Gillman would tie my feet with a rope and taught me that playing quarterback was an art form. He'd always gravely say, "This is not a game, it is a canvas and you are Michelangelo."

I loved Sid. He convinced me not to listen to the many people who believed at that time, in the mid-'80s, that you could not be a great quarterback if you could scramble. Go figure. Times change, it never made much sense to me anyway.

Football is a unique sport. There is no statistic, no touchdown or passing yard, that is accomplished by a single person. The rarest of sports in that you cannot do it alone.

Just think about the times you have achieved something on your own. How great was the celebration compared with when you achieved something when you were on a team? Whether in sports or in a business or with your family, the celebration is so much richer and enjoyable when it is with other people.

My favorite moment still was the five minutes after the Super Bowl when we were alone in the locker room. Just the fifty players and coaches kneeling in the Lord's Prayer, then looking up at each other and realizing that, yes, we're world's champions. No media, no one, just us. That feeling when you do something great together is like no other. No MVP or passing title can compare to the feeling.

That is why football players talk about the camaraderie with a deep sense of passion and commitment. It is the sport that when one of your guys says, "I've got your back," it is not figurative. You depend on them physically and emotionally.

A Hall-of-Fame career is loaded with hundreds of best friends—guys that have your back. I am overwhelmed today to think about the great men that I knew in my seventeen years as a pro, that taught me about what it means to play as a team with all your heart, might, mind, and strength. Men who shared my passion for working together to get it pushed across the line, despite injury and fatigue. Many were my heroes while I played with them and only more so now that I don't. This honor for me today is also an honor for all those that I played with.

The season of an NFL player is fierce, unlike baseball and basketball where you play lots of games, in football it's only sixteen. You can't afford to lose. The routine of training camp, the tricks we played on each other, the hang time with the boys, the gallons of sweat left on the practice field. The drama of who would be the starting players, the daily routine of tightening the cleats, smelling the newly cut grass, laboring through the films, getting constant feedback are all things I will never forget. The anticipation of playing the Cowboys on Monday night, the rhythm of the three-step drop, the thrill of the two-minute drill, the memorization of all the plays and the multiple options Bill Walsh forced me to learn are lasting memories.

Cinching up the shoulder pads and pulling up the socks, walking out into the tunnel and seeing a stadium full of red, Blue Angels buzzing over the stadium like today, the "Star Spangled Banner," all leave an indelible impression on my mind. I think we all love the game because it in some way is a microcosm of our lives in four short quarters over a three-hour period. Filled with twists and turns, unexpected and thrilling, and can leave you breathless and heartless at a flip of a coin. How exciting—makes me want to strap it on again.

When I first came to San Francisco, I soon realized that I was watching the Michelangelo that Sid Gillman had years ago prior spoken about. It was art in action and I was privileged to be holding the palette. Joe Montana was the greatest QB that I had ever seen. I was in awe.

I was tempted many times by the opportunity to play for other teams, but I was drawn to the inevitable challenge to live up to the standard that I was witnessing. I knew that I was a decent player, and for some reason God blessed me with the big picture knowledge that if I was ever going to find out just how good I could get, I needed to stay in San Francisco and learn even if it was brutally hard to do. I had the faith that the opportunity would create itself at the appropriate time. I was tough to live with during some of those years, but as I look back I am thankful for the struggles and trials that I had and for the opportunities that were given to me.

When the opportunity for me opened up, being a regular quarterback was no longer an option, I would have gotten booed out of Candlestick so fast that I had to rise to the new standard of performance that Joe set. I many times thought about quitting as I heard boos during my sleepless nights, but I feared calling my dad. I knew what he would say, "Endure to the end, Steve."

Football is the only major sport that plays with a ball that is not round and given that, there is destined to be some unique bounces. No career, no matter how great, is smooth all the way through. But one thing is sure; if you are lucky enough to make it a career, you cannot play very long without a love of the game. The game demands too much of you physically, emotionally, and even spiritually to stay in it if you don't love it. I don't care how much you get paid, you show me a six-, eight-, or ten-year veteran of the NFL and I'll show you a man that loves the game by definition.

Money isn't the key at the moment of impact. I have seen a lot of guys play for money in practice and warm-ups, but I have never seen one play for money at the point of contact. You cannot buy a football player on game day. He plays for the love of the game. That is why it is impossible for money to ruin it.

I love the game of football. It is an amazing sport that teaches kids and adults powerful lessons that can contribute to making us successful human beings. I love that so many people are drawn to the game—you can see here today—it is no surprise to me, and I encourage others to get involved in the game and to allow your children to play, as long as properly coached. Teamwork, accountability, dedication, trust, faith are a few of the lessons that my teammates and I have learned over seventeen professional seasons.

I have thrown 107 interceptions in my career. Every time without fail, there is a moment when all of your teammates look back at you and say, "Why did you throw it to THAT guy?" either by the words out their mouth or by the look on their face, the latter even hurt more. All of the mitigating circumstances and excuses came rushing into your mind: the receiver turned the wrong way, the lineman missed the block, the ball was wet, it was tipped by a defensive player.

And on and on, you can think of all the excuses. It was years before I learned the tough lesson that my teammates didn't respond to the mitigating circumstances. Despite the fact that the excuses were true, they did not care. I thought that I lost them with the ducking of the original question, "But why did YOU throw it to THAT guy?"

The bottom line was that the throw I made messed it up. I learned to turn to my teammates and say, "I messed up, it's on me, but WE are going to go down and score next time down the field, what do you say?"

I know my teammates and friends can attest that I like my options and have a hard time deciding, but when you grow up having big linemen ask you tough questions about your decision-making skills, it has a lasting impact on you.

Learning to be ultimately accountable for my throws has taught me an enduring lesson in life. You must own up to your mistakes and then, more importantly, repent or fix the problem.

I used to hold on to the ball despite the fact that my receiver was open because I couldn't see him. I'm a lot shorter than Dan. Many times the big linemen blocked my view. It was Mike Holmgren who yelled at me one game and said, "Jerry's open. Why didn't you throw it to him?"

I said, "I couldn't see him."

"Well, you better start seeing him."

Thanks for the tip. I'll be sure to start seeing what I can't see as soon as I see it. But it made me pause; maybe it would be good for my career if I just threw it where I thought my receiver was. I had just seen him a second ago, I knew where he was headed. Throw it—simple. Go on faith and knowledge. You can believe that I have learned that lesson many times. Trust your instinct and let it fly.

Think about it, there are fifty guys on a team with fifty different personalities, different races, religions, socioeconomic backgrounds, geographies, family histories, education, interests, trials, on and on. Most of the guys have very little in common but for their passion for football. Championship football cannot be played without a sense of love and respect for your teammates.

When the game starts, all our differences become unimportant, there becomes a sole focus on a common goal, and you embrace and appreciate the unique gifts people bring. It is amazing to see players rise to the level of expectation and work together for a common goal.

Football is the great metaphor for life. For me, it will never again be third-and-ten late in the fourth quarter down by four at Candlestick Park. Nothing in life can be like those great moments.

■　■　■　■

Y. A. Tittle
Baltimore Colts, San Francisco 49ers, and New York Giants Quarterback
Class of 1971

Tittle threw for 33,070 yards and 242 touchdowns, including the thirty-three in 1962 and the thirty-six in 1963 that helped him become a two-time league MVP.

Y. A. Tittle came to the Giants in 1961 in what was to have been the twilight of an already illustrious career. Without a warning, the twilight became brighter than noontime.

Y. A. Tittle

I feel that the game of football is a game played by people. I really and truly do not completely buy the oversophisticated ideas of computers and the game being played without feeling. Thank goodness it hasn't come to that. I think that all people that play football are motivated by other people. I can't believe that a football player can really play when out there alone because so many people must influence his potential greatness—if you call it greatness—and I know that has happened in my life.

I also promised my wife that I wouldn't do this, either, that I would introduce her and mention her especially as someone that has inspired me because she truly has shared my love for her with that of football. And also she also inspired me in some other ways where she reminded me so many times after so many interceptions in some of the games and asked me so many times, "Was I really color-blind?"

I know all the years that I played we never won a world championship that I so much wanted. We came close three times, but I will really settle for this because this is about the height of all my dreams.

■   ■   ■   ■

Bob Lilly
Dallas Cowboys Defensive Tackle
Class of 1980

The foundation of great Dallas defensive units, Lilly played 196 consecutive games and in eleven Pro Bowls.

Presented by Cowboys Coach Tom Landry

I realize that you don't recognize me without my hat, but I'm glad to be here today.

Back in 1972, I was commenting on Bob Lilly at an all-sports banquet and I made this quote: "There won't be another Bob Lilly in my time. You are observing a man who will become a legend."

I am still of the same opinion today because I have watched too many game films of Bob Lilly in action. He spent a whole career wading through two or three blockers to achieve his great record.

Bob Lilly

As we were riding in the great parade through Canton today prior to the ceremonies, it looked like we were going to have a downpour of rain. I looked over at Coach Landry and I said, "Coach, so many times in the history of our practices, you have called the rain off because you have a direct line upstairs." And he called the rain off.

I just want to tell Coach Landry how much I appreciate the fact that he stayed up all night to fly in an airplane out here to introduce me today before you people. The fact that he introduced me today has a lot more meaning than you would think because there were basically three men in my life: my father, my coach in college, and Tom Landry.

This is the tough part. My father died ten years ago, my coach in college died a year ago. These were the three men who influenced me most.

I guess to sum it up, I deserve just a small part of the award today because it took teamwork as it does with everything in the world, our country, our cities, our states. They all work because of teamwork and because we have a country which allows us freedoms to choose our occupations and our professions and as the people who had the foresight to do things that were tough when they had to be done.

■ ■ ■ ■

Bob Griese
Miami Dolphins Quarterback
Class of 1990

Griese led Miami to three AFC titles and wins in Super Bowls VII and VIII. He threw for 25,092 yards and 192 touchdowns.

Presented by Colts and Dolphins Coach Don Shula

If I ever had to define what a winner is, I could do it in two words—Bob Griese. It is no coincidence that Miami enjoyed unprecedented success during Bob's fourteen years with the Dolphins.

He had great ability, but what set him apart was intelligence and leadership, intangibles that can't be measured statistically except in the final score. Bob simply didn't know what it meant to lose. He was a thinking man's quarterback, a chess master, moving all his pieces brilliantly.

He was a genius at calling the right play at the right time. The double overtime game against Kansas City, he pulled out a play we hadn't used the whole time, a run to Larry Csonka, our fullback, that gained thirty yards that set up the field goal that helped us get into the playoffs and eventually into the Super Bowl. But that is typical of Bob, being one of the smartest players I ever coached. But he also was one of the most unselfish.

I remember when we played the St. Louis Cardinals on Thanksgiving Day in 1977. He threw six touchdown passes in a little over three quarters of play. The record was seven. I said, "Bob, do you want to go for the record? We have a big lead."

He said, "No, coach, let the backup quarterback play. He needs the experience in case something happens to me later on."

Bob Griese

I was never a great talent. I mean, I couldn't carry anybody by myself. I wasn't a guy like Roger Staubach or Terry Bradshaw. I needed help. I needed help and I got a lot of help in Miami. I am the first to admit, give me some good players, some good players around me, and I can do some stuff that may give you some problems defensively.

If there is any lesson to be learned from me going into the NFL Hall of Fame, it is to the young people. You don't have to be the biggest or the strongest or the fastest or the quickest or the prettiest to be successful as long as you have desire and determination and you have heart and you have some intelligence and you have some persistence and you are consistent.

And yes, maybe if you are stubborn, you can be successful and be successful in life.

■　■　■　■

Franco Harris
Pittsburgh Steelers and Seattle Seahawks
Running Back
Class of 1990

Harris rushed for 12,120 yards and scored one hundred touchdowns. In nineteen postseason games, he ran for 1,556 yards and was MVP of Super Bowl IX.

Presented by Steelers Wide Receiver Lynn Swann

Franco was my roommate for eight years in hotels the nights before football games. We were friends. I lived with this man and I watched the intensity.

I would talk to him at night while he would tell me how badly he wanted this championship game. When he put that helmet on and he was pacing in that locker room, walking back and forth, gathering all of his forces together to take on the opponent, everybody got charged for that. Everybody saw the intensity in Franco Harris and everybody knew if we had the chance to score, we had to do it because Franco was there leading the way.

We won four Super Bowls on the shoulders and the legs of Franco Harris. I am a wide receiver, and I'm almost embarrassed to admit that the Steelers could win just on Franco's legs and not on catching the football.

Franco Harris

I always thought, "How can I help my team? Can they count on me when it was needed?" Then you think what makes your talent come through, what makes it work, what makes you work, and the answer is to be with the right teammates.

God knows I was with the right teammates; they were great. You see, I was able to achieve goals beyond my wildest dreams because of the people who surrounded me. They brought out the best in me, they made me rise to new heights, they made me a better ball player. And at this time, I can't find a better way than to just say thank you to my offensive linemen.

During that era, each player brought their own little piece with him to make that wonderful decade happen. Each player had his strengths and weaknesses, each his own thinking, each his own method. Each had his own. But then it was amazing. It all came together and it stayed together to forge the greatest team of all times.

My teammates were men of character with a lot of heart and soul. This was the team I belonged to, a team that will live forever. Remember living those moments? Do you realize how great those moments were? Did you savor them? God, did you see Lynn Swann in Super Bowl X, unbelievable juggling, acrobatic catch? Rocky Bleier in Super Bowl XIII leaping to catch that ball in the end zone for a touchdown. Do you remember? Do you remember John Stallworth catching that pass in Super Bowl XIV over his shoulder for that touchdown? It was great. We remember.

But while we were playing we never knew what the future would bring. We never knew at that time we were building a Steeler wing to the Hall of Fame. We never knew. But now you always will know that you saw the best. You will know it because it says so right here in Canton for all to see.

The Pittsburgh Steelers are here to stay. Remember.

Bill Walsh
San Francisco 49ers Coach
Class of 1993

*With a 102-63-1 record, Walsh guided the 49ers to three Super
Bowl titles—XVI, XIX, XXIII—in ten seasons.*

Presented by 49ers Owner Eddie DeBartolo Jr.

What Bill achieved is not only well-known but has become the standard by which coaching careers are now judged.

His style of leadership included the amazing ability to introduce innovative techniques without destroying traditional concepts. His role as a visionary never caused him to ignore the present. Bigger was not necessarily better to Bill, nor were the strongest always the best.

He emphasized the fact that personal motivation was as important as physical gifts and that the mind and soul deserved as much attention as the body.

Bill Walsh

At one point, San Francisco was in the absolute doldrums morale wise. There had been an assassination of the mayor, and the city was in the doldrums, and the city was ridiculed by many people. Well, after three years, we had a victory parade through Market Street. We turned the corner and there were three hundred thousand people. There were older people and there were younger people. There were black people and there were white people. There were Asian people, there were rich people and rather poor people. There were people of every gender, every interest.

All of a sudden the city came together, the city became San Francisco again, the city became a world champion for the first time. The 49ers turned around an entire state and a great city. We had more impact than you would ever think on our young, our old, and the way people feel about themselves, each other, and their city. We became world champions and we continued to be world champions for four Super Bowls in the '80s. Well, I have heard about great teams today, but we will play anybody, I will guarantee you.

People have asked, "How did you become a successful coach?" People talked about scripting the first twenty-five plays, they talked about our innovations on offense, they talked about individual players, but maybe I can relate this on behalf of our whole group today. The game is for the players. Its leaders are the players, its participants are the players, its coaches are there to help facilitate it.

Now what is leadership? Well, leadership is what developed with the San Francisco 49ers, that each man was an extension of the other. When Joe Montana threw the ball, Randy Cross was an extension of him. When Freddie Solomon caught it, he was an extension of Randy Cross, and when Randy Cross blocked he was an extension of Fred Dean who was the extension of Ronnie Lott who was the extension of Milt McColl.

So it was a chain link that was linked together by a group of men who learned to demand a lot of each other, to love each other, to care for each other, to make sacrifices for each other. They look over at each other, one group is sacrificing at that moment, the next group will go out there at the next moment.

So you will find the players who play for their families, their loved ones, that they are playing for each other, they will sacrifice, they will do anything for each other. And I take great pride in that part of it because I think the 49ers demonstrated we played for each other and we cared for each other, and that is championship football.

■ ■ ■ ■

Chuck Noll
Pittsburgh Steelers Coach
Class of 1993

When he retired, he was the only coach to win four Super Bowl titles—IX, X, XIII, XIV.

Presented by Steelers Owner Dan Rooney

There are times, though seldom, when something happens, when everything comes together, and a group of young men become a special team; where their accomplishments give them a time in history for the way they reach success, not only being the best, but doing so with unselfish determination, making the goal together, and that happened in Pittsburgh. It was a glorious time.

A team begins with leadership. In 1969, a thirty-five-year-young coach arrived with the commitment and the ideals to be the best. He assembled players with similar ideas but had to convince them and the entire community to believe the goal was possible—not an easy achievement. The start was rocky, but he never deviated and he stuck to the basics. Small victories came, and they began to believe possibly they could be the best.

We are not here today to celebrate statistics; the accomplishments speak for themselves. We are here to consider achievement—not just the greatness of winning seasons, two hundred victories, or even four Super Bowls, or even the greatest teams ever, but the accomplishments of men reaching a level collectively to be the best they could be; men of character doing the job together.

All the people of that team belong here. They all deserve to be enshrined in Canton because he led them to greatness and they were the best.

Chuck Noll

The single most important thing we had in the Steelers in the '70s was an ability to work together. It was called teamwork, and you know, it is tough to describe that.

You use that word and the thing that stuck out in my mind is that we had a lot of people who didn't worry about what someone else did. If someone else was having a tough time on a particular day, they reached down and did a little more. They got the thing done. Whatever they had to do, they did to win. There was never a reason to let down.

Right now you hear about teamwork, and it is defined as fifty-fifty.

That is a falsehood. There is no such thing as fifty-fifty. You do whatever you have to do as part of the team. You may have to carry somebody.

We had an offensive line when we were playing Houston that was decimated with the flu. Our offense couldn't move the ball; we had an injury to the quarterback. It was a time when maybe our defense and our special teams could have said, "Hey, let's fold our tent and go home." It didn't happen that way.

We had a bunch of guys—Joe Greene, Jack Lambert, Jack Ham, Mel Blount—they would get together and reach down and what they did was eliminate the running attack. When they tried to run the ball, there was Joe Greene in the running lane; there was Jack Lambert hammering on. When they went back to pass, Joe Greene and L. C. Greenwood were all over Dan Pastorini. They just took the ball away from them and we had the ball in scoring territory and were able to kick field goals. That, to me, is teamwork. Another week the offense carried it while the defense struggled.

Right now we have a society of confrontation. We have male against female. We've got blacks against white. We've got labor against management. Well, you know the shame of it is, some people have made progress through confrontation.

But I can't tell you how much you can gain, how much progress you can make by working as a team, by helping one another. You get much more done that way. And if there is anything the Steelers in the '70s epitomized, I think it was teamwork.

■ ■ ■ ■

Charlie Joiner
Houston Oilers, Cincinnati Bengals, and
San Diego Chargers Wide Receiver
Class of 1996

Joiner caught 750 passes for 12,146 yards and sixty-five touch-downs. At the time of his retirement he played 239 games in eighteen seasons, the most ever for a wide receiver.

This is a wonderful game that we are involved with. It is a team game. It is where forty-five to fifty men come together to perhaps form a great team.

I was fortunate enough to play on many great teams. And on those great teams, we would work together, play together, strive together, run together, do everything together to achieve one goal and that was to win on Sunday afternoons or Monday nights or whenever we played.

There was one characteristic that was very good about all these teams that I played on, especially the very good ones. We had the attitude that we would never, never quit. There is one thing that I would like to teach the youth of America. That would be to never, never quit.

Don't let someone tell you that it can't happen. Pursue your dreams with all the energy and experience that you have.

■　■　■　■

Tom Mack
Los Angeles Rams Guard
Class of 1999

Mack never missed a game in his 184-game career and he was elected to eleven Pro Bowls.

I walked away from football twenty years ago, went and did something totally different. But I guess I always believed that someday I would get the opportunity to come here. And what I kind of wanted to talk about today was believing how important it is. Because when it's all said and done, belief is really the theme that made me come here and made most of the fellows that came here in the past.

First, a belief in God. Second, a belief in yourself. And third, because it is a team game, you really do believe in each other as teammates. You work hard together, you live together, and you die together. But being together is really what it's all about.

Football, to me, is a team game, and I'd like to believe, and I think it is America's game. The secret is that you have got to believe. You know the nice part is, we believed in each other.

I'd just like to give you a little quote about vision. Vision without action is a dream. Action without vision is work. Vision with action moves mountains. So if I can leave you with anything, it's this—you should continue to believe in God, continue to believe in yourselves, and, maybe most important, in almost everything you do, continue to believe in each other.

■　■　■　■

Howie Long
Oakland/Los Angeles Raiders Defensive End
Class of 2000

An eight-time Pro Bowl selection, Long was named to the NFL's
All-Decade Team of the '80s.

Presented by Raiders Assistant Coach Earl Leggett

In 1981, as we were preparing for the upcoming draft, trying to put players in our draft order, I was sent out to scout a college senior at Villanova by Mr. [Al] Davis. I had seen some tapes of his regular-season and postseason games. So I scheduled a workout and made the trip to Villanova and his workout was very impressive. I returned to the Raiders and in our draft meeting, I recommended him as our number one draft choice. Mr. Davis had seen some of the same qualities that I had and drafted him in the second round. Howie came into minicamp and we went to work.

I would hope that you coaches who want to be coaches, no matter what sport, could have someone who is as focused and determined as Howie. He knew exactly what he wanted. Not only did he have the qualities that you put in the measurable categories such as strength, quickness, and size, but his greatest assets were the intangibles.

Posted around our defensive line meeting room were certain slogans. And one that I really tried to drive home, it goes like this—I want to surround myself with players who will pay the price to become great, then become their leader. Howie was the best leader that I have ever been associated with, not only in his professional life but in his personal life. He has a knack of raising everyone a notch higher. He had total focus, he was a student of the game, but, more important, were the intangibles.

Number one: his ability to tell when he had leverage on opposing players. Two: his outstanding work ethic. And three: the total fear of not being successful.

Now listen one more time. Thirteen years, eight Pro Bowls, three-time Lineman of the Year, onetime Defensive Player of the Year, one-time Comeback Player of the Year, First Team All-Decade for the '80s. In those thirteen years, I thought Howie became the most disruptive force in football.

Howie complained that I never said he did a good job. I always told him, "That's what you get paid for." But now is the time to say: "Howie, good job—a job well done."

Howie Long

In the eighty years of the National Football League, over eighteen thousand men have played this game, many great players. Of those eighteen-thousand-plus players, 171 have ended up in this final glorious destination. Of those 171, only seven have been defensive ends. I, for one, believe that being inducted into the Pro Football Hall of Fame is the most prestigious individual honor in all of sports.

Baseball has been called America's pastime, and since my retirement, through my three sons, I have come to appreciate the ability of baseball to bring families closer together and, in particular, father and sons. In my opinion, baseball is America's pastime. But football is truly America's passion.

I think back to something Earl Leggett said to me way back in 1981 when I first arrived at the Raiders and, keep in mind, I was not a very good football player when I did arrive there. He said, "Kid, if you work hard and you do what I tell you to do, I'll make you wealthy beyond your wildest dreams, and I'll make you a household name in every home in America."

Well, Earl, we missed free agency by a few years, but I have to admit I'm a hell of a lot more famous than I could have ever dreamed.

▪ ▪ ▪ ▪

Ron Yary
Minnesota Vikings and Los Angeles Rams Tackle
Class of 2001

A seven-time Pro Bowl selection, Yary started in four Super Bowls and five NFL/NFC championship games.

Presented by Vikings Assistant Coach John Michels

Ron's stance was not a thing of beauty. In fact, I had another coach ask me why I didn't try to change it. My reply was: "Why? He does all we ask and more with the stance that he has."

Ron was responsible for teaching me that you can't force some people into molds. This has helped me tremendously with other "not-by-the-book" players.

My favorite Yary story is one that occurred during a Rams game when Ron was having some difficulty against Jack Youngblood. He came off the field after a bad series and I was waiting there. We sat down on the bench and I began my tirade. I think in the middle of this one-sided talk, I made reference to my playing ability and how I would have handled this situation with no trouble. I made a few more references to my skills when Ron, who was sitting down at the time, looked me right in the eye and stated very quietly, "John, you must have been a hell of a football player."

The bench erupted on either side of him as people burst out laughing. Needless to say, my credibility at that time was shot to hell.

Ron Yary

A few weeks after it had been announced that my career had been honored with this great tribute, I received an unexpected congratulatory postcard from a high school teammate of mine that reads: "If one advances confidently in the direction of his dreams and endeavors to live the life which he has imagined, he will meet with a success unexpected [in] common hours."

Today I'm here to tell my family, my coaches, my teammates, and my friends that I lived the life that I had imagined. I advanced confidently in the direction of my dreams of today, with many of you present. We've come here to Canton, Ohio, to celebrate and to share this great honor on what I consider to be football's most hallowed ground.

I would like to leave everyone with my personal insight about the game of football that we honor today and what makes football the great all-American sport. Every play and every block that I ever made was to help our running back gain more yards or a quarterback and a receiver complete the pass; it wasn't for individual glory, but for the benefit of the greater good—the success of the team.

This is the creed of the offensive lineman that defines the spirit, the American spirit, which is built into the fabric of football. All men who have played this game at any level identify with this creed, whether it is a kid on a high school football team or the great NFL player.

For no other sport in the world can offer up to its participants this internal yearning that exists within all men, this creed, this all-American spirit. This yearning inside of all men in which I speak of is called sacrifice. And it is in the soul, in the very essence of American football.

Therefore, if I can leave anyone with one thought, I hope you will remember this: To those who unselfishly taught me everything you knew, I owe it all. And beyond anything else, you taught me that no one makes it into the Hall of Fame on his own.

■ ■ ■ ■

Troy Aikman
Dallas Cowboys Quarterback
Class of 2006

A six-time Pro Bowl selection, Aikman led the Cowboys to three Super Bowl wins, passing for 32,942 yards and 165 touchdowns.

Presented by Former Cowboys Offensive
Coordinator Norv Turner

A couple years ago during an interview, I was asked if I got to coach one game, who would I choose as my starting quarterback. As you saw today, there's a lot of great ones to choose from. But it was really a very easy question for me to answer. I told them I'd choose Troy. The interviewer politely asked me why. I said, "Because I want to win."

I further explained my answer. Troy was consistently the most accurate passer I've ever seen. What fans saw on Sundays, his teammates saw every day of the week.

Another one of Troy's real strengths was his ability to bring out the best in everyone around him. Troy was driven to be the best, and he expected the same from everyone around him. I really felt that was Troy's drive, along with Coach Jimmy Johnson's leadership, that had accounted for the Cowboys going from worst to first.

Troy's greater strength as a player was his ability to focus and stay focused in the most unusual circumstances. Troy had the ability to make the play when it mattered the most. You know, after a game, a lot of times you have those "ifs." You know what I'm talking about. "If we completed that ball on third-and-four, we would have won the game." You also have those "whys." "Why did they throw the ball in that situation? We could have given it to Emmitt?"

With Troy, you didn't have those "ifs" and "whys." The best example to me was in the '92 championship game, with four minutes left in the game. There were no "ifs." Alvin Harper ran a slant. Troy hit him right between the numbers. Alvin ran down the field inside the ten, and took Troy, himself, and the rest of the Cowboys right to the Super Bowl.

If you look at Troy's greatest plays, they came in the most critical situations. If you look at his greatest games, they came against the best teams and they came in the playoffs. Troy is one of the most unselfish players to have played. He knew the things he had to do to give his team the best chance to win. In an era of superegos, he never let his get in the way of winning. Super Bowls were more important than statistics.

Troy Aikman

Jimmy Johnson and I arrived in Dallas the same year, 1989, both fresh from college, both eager to prove ourselves. Didn't take long to see that Jimmy was unique, and it wasn't just because of his hair. What struck me most about Jimmy was his fearlessness.

Some coaches play not to lose. Jimmy always played to win. Some guard against overconfidence. Jimmy insisted on it. Jimmy's boldness set the tone for a young group of players who didn't know much about winning but were eager to learn. Jimmy was the right coach at the right time for the Dallas Cowboys, and I'm grateful to have been given the opportunity to play for him. . . .

A high school coach once told me, "In life, you have a lot of acquaintances, but very few friends." For most, that's probably true, but not for me. The many friendships in my life are what made me feel every single day like I'm the luckiest guy in the world, and I thank all of you for being here today.

In closing, I'd like to share something that a close friend used to tell me back when I was playing. He'd say this when times were tough, maybe we'd lost a close game, I'd thrown the deciding interception, or the grind and the rigors of the season were beginning to take their toll on me. What Norv Turner would say was this: "Sometimes we have to remind ourselves that these are the jobs we've always dreamed of having."

Norv was right. For as long as I can remember, all I ever wanted was to play pro sports. A lot of kids want that, but very few actually get the chance. I was able to live a dream. I played professional football. That I was able to do so with so many great players and coaches and win three world championships and wind up here today with all these great men in gold jackets, well, it's almost too much to believe.

CHAPTER 7

CAUSES

ALAN PAGE AND
WILLARENE BEASLEY

OVER TIME, FOOTBALL HAS SEEN ITS FIRST AFRICAN
American player, its first African American quarterback, its first African American quarterback as a Super Bowl winner, its first African

American head coach as a Super Bowl winner—all before the first African American president.

They have gone on and on, the firsts. There have been so many that there aren't many left, which might be the surest sign of the progress that society and football have made.

For this, a debt is owed to the men who made it possible. They endured what today's players do not have to. They fought for that cause, as well as for other causes.

Some spoke out for underprivileged children, others for players' pensions, and still others for the NFL Players Association. But the most popular and significant cause was race, the subject of multiple induction speeches.

Men spoke eloquently, thoughtfully, and passionately. They helped pave the way for the players of today, and for society to be what it is.

■ ■ ■ ■

Alan Page
Minnesota Vikings and
Chicago Bears Defensive Tackle
Class of 1988

Page played in 236 consecutive games and four Super Bowls. He won the league MVP in 1971.

Presented by North Community High School (Minnesota)
Principal Willarene Beasley

All of us who know Alan Page know that he has strong philosophical views regarding the education of sports. Alan believes the involvement in sports makes for a healthy body and mind, and he warns that sports is just a short-lived career, that one must be prepared for a second career.

Alan states that education and sports go together and we, as parents and community leaders, make sure it works. Education and sports benefit all of us.

Alan says that we must put these in proper perspective. Sports must be used as an incentive for young people to get an education and not as a substitute. Alan warns, "Do not major in football. Play the sport, it is good to play the sport, but learn to read and to write, and develop marketable skills." If a student can be a winner in sports, a student can be a winner in education.

Alan has said on numerous occasions that people like Martin Luther King and Jesse Jackson have made many sacrifices so we can all share in the American dream. I would submit to you today that Alan Page, too, is helping to fulfill that American dream.

Just as Alan has played defensive tackle for the Vikings and the Bears, now through the Alan Educational Foundation, his defense is tackling problems.

Alan sums it up best in a poem by Alfred Lord Tennyson and I will just do an excerpt: "I am a part of all that I have met."

And so as we pause for the enshrinement on the front steps of the Hall of Fame, Alan Page stands tall not only in his six-foot-four stature, but as he writes his own page into history as a profound, prideful symbol of success.

Alan Page

Football was very good to me, and my good fortune has continued in my chosen career as a lawyer. But in that world where I now work, professional accomplishment is measured on a far different scale over a much longer period of time. So I find it a bit strange to again be the object of this much attention for what I accomplished many years ago, in a very narrow field of endeavor called football.

As my football career ended, many of my contemporaries were already beginning to make their impact felt in society. And they continue to—healing the sick, creating jobs, defending people in trouble, and seeking peace among nations. Very few of them will ever receive the lavish tribute that someone like me has received here today for playing a game called football.

It's hard to say what today's inductees will mean to future generations, but for now we are still looked upon as role models. And role models have an obligation, I think, to relate to the needs of the future, and not just relate to the deeds of the past. It's certainly okay to enjoy the glory and the truths of bygone days. But I think all the men you see here today reached the Hall of Fame because they couldn't be satisfied with their past performances. So as I try to give meaning to this occasion for myself, I want to focus on what I can do for the future.

On this occasion, I ask myself, "What contribution can I still make that would be truly worthy of the outpouring of warmth and good feelings I have received today?" And the answer, for me, is clear: to help give other children the chance to achieve their dreams.

I don't know when children stop dreaming. But I do know when hope starts leaking away, because I've seen it happen. Over the past ten years, I've spent a lot of time speaking with school kids of all ages. And I've seen the cloud of resignation move across their eyes as they travel through school, without making progress. They know they are slipping through the net into the huge underclass that our society seems willing to tolerate. At first, the kids try to conceal their fear with defiance. Then, for far too many, the defiance turns to disregard for our society rules. It's then that we have lost them and maybe forever. But this loss is not always as apparent as the kid who has dropped out of school for life on the street. I've seen lost men in the National Football League.

When I played for the Vikings, there was an occasion where we had a new defensive line coach and he wanted us to read the playbook to learn it and probably wasn't a bad idea if you could read. There were nine players in the group, three of us read pretty well, two so-so, the other four had a difficult time and struggled. It was painful for them, but it was painful to watch for all of us. And we shared their pain.

These same young men were once the heroes of their schools, showered with recognition and praise for their athletic performance and allowed to slide in the classroom. And for their time in the NFL, at least, they were the lucky ones because they had beaten the long, eighteen thousand-to-one odds to make it that far. But without reading skills, what were their chances of finding employment once their playing days were over?

We are doing no favors to the young men from Miami and Chicago and Philadelphia and L.A., if we let them believe that a game shall set them free. At the very best, athletic achievement might open a door that discrimination once held shut. But the doors slam quickly on the unprepared and the undereducated.

We are at a point in our history where black teenagers constitute the most unemployed and undervalued people in our society. And instead of making a real investment in education that could pay itself back many times, our society has chosen to pay the price three times: once, we let the kids slip through the educational system; twice, when they drop out to a street life of poverty, dependence, and maybe even crime; and a third time when we warehouse those who have crossed over the line and have gotten caught.

The cost of neglect is immense—in dollars and in abuse of the human spirit. We must educate our children. We don't have a choice. Once we've let it reach this point, the problem is virtually too big and too expensive to solve. But we can make a difference, if we go back into the schools and find the shy ones and the stragglers, the square pegs and the hard cases, before they've given up on the system . . . and before the system has given up on them.

Then we say to those children: "You're important to our world and to our future. We want you to be successful and have the things you want in life. But being successful and reaching your dreams takes work. It means being responsible for yourself. It means being willing to go to class and doing your homework and participating in the opportunity to learn, then you have no right to complain about the unfairness if you are not willing to do that. You're not alone in all of this. But only you, the student, can do the work that will make you free.

"If you wait until college—or even until high school—to get serious about an education, you may be too late. It's hard to go back as an adult to learn what you missed in the third grade. It's important to dream, but it's through learning and work that dreams become reality." We must, as I said, educate our children.

But we can't preach responsibility to our children if we don't accept it ourselves. We as parents—especially in the black community—must accept that we bear responsibility for our children. We must work with them. Not just by developing their hook shots or their throwing arms, but by developing their reading and their thinking abilities, and if we don't have the skills ourselves to pass on, we can still encourage them, reward them, and praise their academic accomplishments. We can educate our children.

We shouldn't put down athletics, because that teaches children the value of teamwork and disciplined effort. But we must insist that our children take school seriously. And if they can't handle the demands of both, then maybe athletics should go. Finally, you and I, all of you out there, all of you who hear and see this speech, can make a difference as members of our communities. We can't just leave it to the schools, or the social workers, or the police and the legal system. We ultimately pay the cost of our educational system's failures. But we also have the solutions without our power. If we educate our children.

We can support the schools and the teaching profession instead of complaining about them. We can honor students and teachers who excel with the same rewards and recognition that we honor our coaches and our athletes. As it stands, how can we expect kids with poor self-esteem and shaky reading skills to pursue academics when often the only reinforcement they get is athletics.

Now these words may seem simple to the people on the front lines who have seen too many of the lost and too few of the victorious. The jobless single mother may have too little hope for herself to share some with her children. To the kid surrounded by drugs and violence and acres of rotting city, a job in a law firm may seem as unrealistic as me being here on the steps of the Hall of Fame today. And so we, who have been insulated by our successes for a loss of hope, must not turn our backs on these children. We must not concede their lives to the forces that have worn down so many children.

Yes, the things I'm suggesting are simple. But I've learned from school, from football, and from the law that even the biggest, scariest problems can be broken down to their fundamentals. And if all of us cannot be superstars, we can remember to repeat the simple fundamentals of taking responsibility for ourselves and for the children of this country. We must educate our children. And if we do, I believe that will be enough.

■　■　■　■

Dick "Night Train" Lane
Los Angeles Rams, Chicago Cardinals,
and Detroit Lions Cornerback
Class of 1974

A seven-time Pro Bowl selection, Lane intercepted sixty-eight passes for 1,207 yards and five touchdowns. As a rookie, Lane intercepted an NFL record fourteen passes.

A total of eighty-one enshrines are in just by coincidence—that was my playing number. I would like to pay a personal and heartfelt tribute to my teammates—the other players who were not so fortunate to last as long as I did in the National Football League. They didn't reach the glory, but they were men who made the business what it is today. They are the cornerstones of this foundation of the NFL. Those were really the days.

We didn't fly first class. We didn't stay at Holiday Inns. We didn't even have Gatorade. We just played some of the best football ever. We were paid at least $3,500 and I didn't make that much more, yet I still maintained the perspective of the definite sense of professionalism. I find it disturbing today that when professional football is the most popular sport of America, the future of the NFL is in limbo.

I can only hope that the offers of the owners, the coaches, and the players past and present will direct toward betterment of the league and not for personal gain. I can only hope that the owners can understand that football was, and still is, and always will be, the game for the players and the fans who fill the stadium and shout their names, inspiring them on through the thrill of victory and the agony of defeat.

I can only hope that while the players are striking for improvement, that the black players will take this opportunity to band together and deal with the problems of no black coaches, no general managers, and no quarterbacks in the NFL—or, should I say, a few. It is not fair or pardonable for blacks to be treated like stepchildren in pro football. It was wrong in my day and it is wrong today.

In the league that we have established, management must realize that times have changed and must adopt a new philosophy and different approach with the players and the game. I know that some people voice opinions that retired players shouldn't have an opinion about the present situation between the players and management. I disagree because these players are fighting for some of the very things that I wanted in my career.

■ ■ ■ ■

Bill Willis
Cleveland Browns Guard
Class of 1977

A four-time All-NFL player, Willis was one of the first African American men to play pro football. He signed with the Cleveland Browns one year before Jackie Robinson broke the color barrier in baseball with the Brooklyn Dodgers. Willis's success opened the doors of sports to other African Americans.

Presented by Browns Coach Paul Brown

First of all, I want to thank Bill for asking me to have the honor of presenting him. When you are a football coach, you never know for sure just what some of your players might think of you and, as you know, I have never been known for my humor or being much of a comedian.

If there is one thing that stands out about Bill, it would be his quickness and speed. I think he was the quickest down lineman in the history of football. I always likened his defensive charge to that of a snake going at them.

I first got to know him at Ohio State, where I was coaching. He came there with his high school coach, Ralph Webster, who was always telling me about this guy. They played on our national championship football team of 1942 at Ohio State. I went into the navy and when I got out, we started the Cleveland Browns.

We were at camp at Bowling Green and I had an idea. So I called the sports editor of the *Columbus Dispatch*, and I said, "Would you please try to find [Bill Willis] and bring him to Bowling Green, and all you have to do is just have him ask for a tryout." I had him get a hold of [fullback] Marion Motley, and just come up and ask for a tryout. Well, they did, and the rest is history.

I say this to you so we understand each other. This was no social idea. I am looking for guys to play football, for people who are men among a bunch of men, and this guy really measured up.

Bill Willis

I have often said that Paul Brown saved my life, and if it had not been for Paul Brown, I am certain I would not be here receiving this honor today. Because it was he who afforded me the opportunity to play pro football when it was not the popular thing to do.

I was the first black to play in the All-American conference and Paul Brown arranged for me to play. Without fanfare, he simply gave me the opportunity to make that ball club of his, and in his own quiet way, he did have to defend his actions in those days.

It also was a week later that he brought [Hall-of-Fame running back] Marion Motley to camp. Motley and I became fast friends because we had to be fast friends. We had to go through a lot together and we had to depend on each other. However, we not only depended on each other, we had our teammates to depend upon.

When I first started playing with the Browns many years ago, I had no idea whatsoever—the thought never entered my head—that one day I would be standing here selected to go into this Hall. I had but one purpose and one goal in mind in those days and that was to make the ball club and do the very best I could to make my club the winning team.

Playing the game of football, I did learn the secret to success. I tell every young person that there is a formula for success. That formula is to always do the very best you can with what you have, wherever you are. And you will find if you do the very best that you can, under any and all circumstances, that the best will come back to you. The best has come back to me. It has been a long time coming.

I say to you Paul Brown, you are a remarkable fellow and one day someone really ought to write a book about all of the innovations that this man brought to modern-day football. Many of the things that we see today, many of the formations, many of the plays, many of the techniques, were brought about by Paul Brown.

One of the innovations that anyone would have to write about in this book is the process of you introducing a player to the game of football who was selected for his ability to perform and not for any other reason. It was because you gave me that opportunity, Paul.

■　■　■　■

David "Deacon" Jones
Los Angeles Rams, San Diego Chargers, and
Washington Redskins Defensive End
Class of 1980

A unanimous all-league selection in six consecutive years, Jones specialized in quarterback "sacks," a term he invented.

Presented by Rams and Redskins Coach George Allen

In this year of elections, when so many groups are debating the merits of hundreds of candidates, it is with great honor to participate in the election of a man that dedicated fans across the nation will agree was one of the finest defensive players in the history of modern football. David "Deacon" Jones, number 75, a premier defensive end for the Rams, Chargers, and Redskins, is the candidate.

I had the great pleasure of coaching David on both the Rams and the Redskins, and I can truly say that regardless of who wins the presidency this fall, the first cabinet appointee should be Deacon Jones as secretary of defense.

David Jones

Violence in its many forms is an involuntary quest for identity. When our identity is endangered, we feel certain we have a mandate for war.

In 1957, David Jones—a tough, unwavering, outspoken student from the black South Carolina State College—declared his own private war against the racial injustices that were prevalent at the time, the inadequacies facing him in education and in business. He lodged his own campaign of aggressions against a group of society that would spark his persistence and determination and reinforce his identity for many years to come.

This quest for identity had its roots in Eatonville, Florida, when, at the age of fifteen, there were no neighborhood boys clubs, there were no local YMCAs, there were no Pop Warner little leagues. Thus the tribe and trial began with David forced by the circumstances of his surroundings to formulate his own game plan, devise his own strategy, never losing sight of that vision of success.

The self-determination would lead him to develop the nickname "Deacon," to institute the head slap for which he would eventually become known, and to create the term "sacking" the quarterback.

It is with great pride that I reminisce with you today about that young tenacious student that remained true to his vision, and it is with great pleasure that I stand before you to receive the supreme recognition of the professional football world that honors the joy and admiration of one's own ability. Early in life I learned that all life is a purpose for struggle, and our only choice being a choice of a goal.

I'd like to share five points that make a champion. They are teamwork, hard work, pride, determination, and competitive spirit. In all champions is the feeling of excitement in solving problems, the delight of taking on a new challenge, and the eagerness to meet another hard challenge.

The "secretary of defense" would like to leave you with one last thought. Every man is free to rise as far as he is able or willing. But it is only the degree to which he thinks or believes that determines the degree to which he will rise.

■ ■ ■ ■

Gene Upshaw
Oakland Raiders Guard
Class of 1987

The premier guard of his era, Upshaw played in ten AFL/AFC championship games, three Super Bowls, and seven Pro Bowls.

Presented by Raiders Owner Al Davis

Gene Upshaw came to the Oakland Raiders in 1967 out of Little Texas A&I as a first-round draft choice in the first AFL-NFL draft. He captained the west team in the college All-Star game. Gene, when drafted, was approximately six-foot-five, 260 pounds, and he had never played guard in his life, and he did not want to play for the Raiders. He thought they were renegades. Today the word is "mavericks."

On the stand today is twenty-one Super Bowls, eleven victorious Super Bowls in the group, and the reason I bring it up is that there is one person on this stand who was there for all of it. He was there as a player. Gene Upshaw, you were there. And I take you back to the Oakland Coliseum, and I can hear the roar of the crowd and the chills go through my body and I can see those famed silver-and-black uniforms.

Gene Upshaw, I can see you walking to the center of the field to greet the opposing captain with the famed number 63 on your jersey, the while collar, the white-taped forearms, that Raider battle-scarred helmet in your hand.

You know, the Raiders have always believed that what wins is great players and great organization. Gene Upshaw was the consummate organizational player. He wore that Raider uniform with pride, he wore it with poise, he wore it with class. He was a star amongst stars. But he was a man for all seasons. He was the thunder and lightning of the awesome battles, but also the serenity and wisdom of the council room.

It is a great honor and a privilege, and I offer my respect and remembrance to the Upshaw family. They have been a great part of my life, and certainly it has been an emotional and inspirational experience for me to be here today.

In short, as if it were ordained from the beginning, Gene Upshaw was born to achieve excellence and to achieve eternal enshrinement in our own Valhalla, our own Mt. Olympus of legendary heroes, the National Football League Hall of Fame.

Gene Upshaw

I am involved in a pretty controversial position as a representative executive director of the Players Association in the National Football League. The advancement, the strides that we make as a union, will be rooted in my upbringing in Texas, my college career, and the years I spent with the Raiders. We will do the right thing, we will do what is best for the players. We will remember what it takes to play the game of football.

It takes players, it takes owners, and it takes fans. I love the game of football. I love what it has given me. This is the greatest honor you could ever receive as an individual and I must say, I will cherish it. But I don't walk in the Hall alone. I walk in there with everyone I met, everyone that has had a part of my life, everyone that has pushed me when I didn't feel like going.

I had what it took because I was afraid to fail.

■　■　■　■

Carl Eller
Minnesota Vikings and
Seattle Seahawks Defensive End
Class of 2004

A fixture on the Vikings' "Purple People Eaters" defensive line, Eller was an All-Pro five times and selected to six Pro Bowls.

Presented by His Son, Regis Eller

I cannot count the times growing up when I'd been introduced to someone, and the first thing they would say is, "Oh, you're Carl Eller's son." I'd always respond, "Yes, but my name is Regis." Like many other sons of renowned people, I've tried most of my life to distance myself from simply being my father's son, to be recognized for myself.

However, when my dad honored me by asking me to be his presenter and give this speech, I started to think about who my father is and what I'm distancing myself from. I began to recall my childhood memories and what I believe are indicative of the Carl Eller I have been fortunate enough to call my father.

My dad taught me that it's okay to take risks as evident by his acting career. He took risks whether it was on the field or on screen, but no one can say he lived his life by sitting on his hands. His filmography includes such films as *Busting*, *Taggart*, and *The Black Six*. You haven't seen them? Me neither. They weren't exactly general release films.

One of the funniest things is the parts that he tried out for but did not get. In such films as *Throw Yo Momma from the Train*. You know *Meet Joe Black*, it was originally *Meet Black Joe* starring Carl Eller. Of course, *The Black English Patient*. All great films of course, but the credits and roles always listed him as big black man. Obviously, they were roles that really tested him as an actor.

My dad didn't always take himself seriously, thank God, but he definitely took his roles in life seriously. My dad operated a drug treatment center for many years. And I remember how important his clients and their sobriety were to him. As a kid I did not understand when my father would come home from work emotionally distraught and unable to interact with me. My mom would explain it. A client of my dad's rehab center who had been making good strides toward sobriety had inexplicably left the program prematurely. My dad would be visibly shaking in fear for the patient. Dad took this as a personal failure and it resonated through him. However, he wore his disappointment on his sleeve because it was impossible for him not to. However, he would never give up, and he relentlessly attempted to get that client back into the program as if fighting for his own sobriety.

These instances prove to me that my dad does not live his life for himself but, rather, an entire community revels in his accomplishments, just as a whole community shares in his defeats. His work and care for people within his community is undoubtedly one of his life's works. As you will hear in a minute, I can proudly say my dad always tried to use his fame to effect meaningful change.

In my dad's early years with the Vikings, he purchased a home in north Minneapolis when most of his teammates were leaving the inner city for the suburbs. He elected to live in an underprivileged black neighborhood and still lives there today.

My dad always told me, "Son, you have to give back." And if you talk to people in north Minneapolis today, you will unquestionably hear a story about how Carl Eller has helped them or someone they know and what it means to have Carl Eller as a part of their community. As caring as he was with the people he tried to help, he was even more so with his children.

I remember Dad surprised me with tickets to the Twins game. On our way back from the game, a woman ran a red light and hit us directly on my side. The first memory I have of that accident is my dad holding my hand telling me everything was going to be all right. But I could see in his eyes how scared he was for me and how badly he wanted to take my pain away. He didn't leave my side the night I was in the hospital or for the next two weeks. I'll never forget that day. It is the day I truly learned of his love for me and he shows the same affection with all his children. He has given me a vision of the caring a father should give his son and a vision of the father I want to be and everyone should have.

So when I think of who my dad is, I realize he is all these things—the struggling actor, the passionate drug rehab counselor, the good citizen, the consummate father, and, yes, the football player. So, today, if someone asked me, "Aren't you Carl Eller's son?" instead of saying, "Yes, but . . . ," I say, "Yes, yes I am. And my name is Regis."

Carl Eller

I asked a question: "To what do I owe this great honor?" And it's a good one. What can I do with this great honor of being inducted to the Football Hall of Fame Class of 2004? My answer is that I want to use this platform to help young African American males to participate fully in this society.

I know that we must give young African American men a message that will lead them in the direction differently where from many of them are headed today. I want that direction to be headed towards the great universities and colleges of our nation, not to the prisons and jail cells.

African American young men as well as young women must know that they are part of the establishment and not separate from it, that they are part of this great America. They must know that their parents and grandparents and their grandparents' parents before them helped build this great country. And parents, yes, we do have a great challenge before us—maybe the greatest in history, and that is that we must teach our kids the value and importance of education, teach them to be members of this society, to participate fully, and have a respect for country, laws, and customs. Show them that if they want this country to do the right thing that we must do the right thing and to teach our children to be actively involved in everything that's going on in this country.

Barack Obama is a fine young man and a great example. But he is not unique. Contrary to what we see in our media-controlled establishment—we're in a media-dominated society which has focused on the negative in the African American communities and other communities of color—there are hundreds—if not thousands—Barack Obamas out there.

We must educate our children, that's the paramount challenge. Like Bill Cosby says, we must give our children books but first we must know what books to give them. Books that help them understand our economy, books on technological and scientific and biological advancements being made every day. Books on relationships, not just with each other, but on our foreign neighbors. And certainly books on how to participate in our political system.

Promise, I promise young men and women, and I specifically say again to African American males, because it seems that our country has turned its back on you. And it seems that some areas have even given up hope. I am here today to say I haven't given up on you. And you need to know because I know that you have the talent, you have the intelligence, and now you have the opportunity to make right of this great occasion, and I'm calling on you now to do the right thing.

Don't let all the hard work of your forefathers have done to make this, a great country, go to waste. Young men of African American descent, hear me now. It breaks my heart, and it breaks all of our hearts. This is not the future your forefathers have built for you. This is not the future that we fought for in the '50s and '60s and '70s. What breaks our heart is to see you involved in gangs and selling drugs and killing each other. That breaks our hearts.

We put our lives on the line so that you could enjoy the freedoms that we enjoy today. We put our lives on the line yesterday so that someone—there could be a Barack Obama today. And there could be a Carl Eller today. And there could be other Hall of Famers sitting before you today.

So now I stand here and say to you if the future of America is to be strong, you must be strong. You must hear the cries of our forefathers and pick up the fight that has helped to make this country great and helped make it what it is today.

Know that you are loved and respected and we have high hopes for you—maybe higher than what you imagine. But if this country is to be a winner, you are to be a winner. To be a winner takes two things. Those two things are courage and commitment.

It takes courage to be a winner. If you have courage, you can overcome, you can conquer fear, and you can conquer despair. And you must be committed to your goals and to your cause. And commitment means being bound to a course of action—spiritually, emotionally, and intellectually. These two things separate the winners from the losers. And you must be a winner, not losers.

And you can tell the winners from the losers. Here's how you can tell the winners from the losers. The winner is always part of the answer. The loser is always part of the problem. The winner always has a program. The loser always has an excuse. The winner says, "Let me do it for you." And the loser says, "Uh-uh, it's not my job." The winner sees an answer for every problem and the loser sees a problem in every answer. The winner sees a green near every sand trap; the loser sees two or three sand traps near every green. The winner says, "It may be difficult, but it is possible." And the loser says, "It may be possible, but it's too difficult."

Ladies and gentlemen, young men, young ladies, especially the young men that I'm talking to: Be the winners!

■ ■ ■ ■

Harry Carson
New York Giants Linebacker
Class of 2006

A nine-time Pro Bowl selection, Carson is thought to be the first player who ever doused his head coach with Gatorade.

Presented by His Son, Donald Carson

When my father first asked me to present him, I said, "Sure," without hesitating. But as the day got closer, I didn't know exactly what

I wanted to say. I had so much I wanted to say to you, but they only gave me two minutes to speak, so I kind of wound it down. I thought to myself, I can talk about the fishing trips we went on, me and my brother, many, many fish that we caught, but that would be a lie. We never caught anything. We mainly sat on the boat and caught sunburn. But the time we spent was always great.

The one thing I can talk about my dad is my dad as a father and as a person. Just thinking back, just about a month ago, we went to the National Institutes of Health in Maryland for my six-month checkup with my illness. It was supposed to be a one-day trip. The doctors didn't exactly like the progress I was making and decided undergoing another treatment is something I would need to do as soon as possible.

While sitting there, while the doctors were making their decisions on different things, my dad asked me, "Is there anything from home that you want?" I was like, "No," not even thinking about it. Then I thought, man, my roommate is out of town. I thought to myself, saying it out loud without thinking, "Man, my fish are going to die." I didn't think anything of it.

But later on that afternoon, it was late, around six or something, my dad jumped in the car, drove from Maryland to Savannah, Georgia, just to feed my fish, which didn't really mean that much because they were like $2 fish from Walmart. But I don't know too many people who would do such a thing like that. But my father did. Being the person that he is, that's the type of thing that he does. He goes out of his way to do things for others when necessarily he doesn't have to.

My father always talks to his kids about their needs and wants. So he always says, "Is it a need or is it a want?" He has this thing with hand movements. If it's a want, you really don't need it. Then he'll go into some useless speech we usually don't listen to, it goes in one ear and out the other. But as I grow older, I'm appreciative to my father for his life lessons that he's taught me.

If I ask my father today whether the Hall of Fame is a need or a want, he will probably say it's not a need, because going to nine Pro Bowls, he was voted by his opposition and the players he played against.

That was enough to validate his career. He would say it's a want. He wouldn't say it's a want for him, he would say it's a want for his family, friends, and fans, because the people want it so dearly for him.

Thinking about it, I would say he's right. The Hall of Fame isn't a need or a want for you, Dad. It's something that you so deserve.

Harry Carson

I had the opportunity to play a fantastic game with fantastic people. When I was elected to the Pro Football Hall of Fame, some people asked me, "Why aren't you happy about being elected?" Well, I can't be happy about it until I get one or two things off of my chest, and please indulge me.

As a Hall of Famer, I want to implore the NFL and its union to look at the product that you have up on this stage. These are great individuals. The honor of making it into the Hall of Fame is great, but it was even greater to have the opportunity to play in a league with eighteen thousand individuals. There are some of the best individuals I've ever encountered.

We'd get on the field and we'd fight tooth and nail, we'd try to knock each other out, then we'd walk off the field, pat each other on the rear end, and say, "Congratulations, hang in there." I'm extremely proud to have participated in that game with those eighteen thousand individuals.

I would hope that the leaders of the NFL, the future commissioner, and the player association do a much better job of looking out for those individuals. You got to look out for 'em. If we made the league what it is, you have to take better care of your own. . . .

I'm not a religious person, but I'm a spiritual person. I feel very strongly that my maker put me in this position for a reason, and that is to represent all of those who preceded me and to represent those who will come after me. I'm told that this bust will be around for a good forty thousand years. That's a long time.

I'm looking at my granddaughter here, my nieces, my granddaughter's children and grandchildren to be able to come to Canton, Ohio, to see what their ancestor did and to know there's absolutely nothing beyond their reach.

■ ■ ■ ■

Warren Moon
Houston Oilers, Minnesota Vikings, Seattle Seahawks, and Kansas City Chiefs Quarterback
Class of 2006

In seventeen seasons, Moon passed for 49,325 yards and 291 touchdowns. He was voted to eight straight Pro Bowls, nine overall.

Presented by Agent Leigh Steinberg

In 1978, when Warren Moon was being scouted, a number of NFL personnel strongly suggested to me he would have a better chance for success if he would change his playing position. In certain football circles, there was doubt as to the ability or desirability of an African American to master the high-profile quarterback position with its emphasis on intelligence and leadership. Warren answered that question with steely resolve.

"Never," he said. "I was born to play quarterback. No one's going to stop me from fulfilling my dream."

That moment played a critical role in reshaping NFL attitudes and opening the door for future generations. Warren followed his dream to Canada, where his brilliant play on the field led in 1984 to a three-league twelve-team competition for his services that resulted in Houston making him the highest-paid player in the history of the National Football League.

After seventeen seasons with his dazzling performances on the field—that's eight straight Pro Bowls—his dignified bearing off the field, Warren's steely resolve showed the stuff that dreams are made of. He wore number 1 for a reason.

Here we are, two old Hamilton High grads thirty years later and seventy thousand yards later standing in the shadow of the Hall of Fame. Warren Moon is about to make history as the first African American quarterback in the modern era to enter the Hall of Fame. And because of his courage and perseverance, he won't be the last.

From the Rose Bowl to Edmonton to Houston to Minnesota to Seattle to Kansas City to our office in Newport Beach, I've been honored to walk the road and dream the dream with you.

Warren Moon

Football for me has been a journey. It was a journey that started forty-four years ago for me, playing at Baldwin Hills Community Park in the Pop Warner Association at ten years old.

I played on some teams that were very, very talented, or either we had coaches that just didn't understand personnel. On my first team there, I played with another guy who is a member of the Hall of Fame, James Lofton. We were both on the same team together, James being a defensive end and me being a linebacker. That tells you what kind of talent we had on our team, or that tells you our coaches just didn't know what the heck they were doing.

A lot has been said about me as being the first African American quarterback in the Pro Football Hall of Fame. It's a subject that I'm very uncomfortable about sometimes only because I've always wanted to be judged as just a quarterback. But because I am the first, and because significance does come with that, I accept that. I accept the fact that I am the first. But I also remember all the guys before me who blazed that trail to give me the inspiration and the motivation to keep going forward, like Willie Thrower, the first black quarterback to play in an NFL game; like Marlin Briscoe, who is here today, the first to start in an NFL game; like James Harris, who is here today, the first to lead his teams to the playoffs. Then on into my era with Doug Williams, the first black quarterback to go to the Super Bowl and be Most Valuable Player; like Randall Cunningham, one of the most exciting players during our era; like Vince Evans, who played twenty-plus years of professional football. All of us did what we had to do to make the game a little bit better for the guys coming after us.

I played this game not for just myself, not just for my teammates, but I always had that extra burden when I went on that field that I had a responsibility to play the game for my people. That extra burden I probably didn't need to go out on the field with, because I probably would have been a much better player if I didn't have that burden. But you know what, I carried that burden proudly.

As I looked at young people all along my route as a professional football player, they always told me, "Warren, you got to represent. Warren, you got to represent. Warren, you got to represent." Well, I'm standing here to say that, "I hope I did represent while I played in the National Football League."

I have four of the best kids I think that any father could ever ask for. They are all in college. They're all very polite. They're all very good-looking. I think they're all going to be very successful. But the thing I love about them the most is, as a father, as a professional football player, it takes you away from home a lot. You miss a lot of things. As I moved around the National Football League, my family stayed in Houston. So I missed out on a lot of things in their lives. Those are things that I can never get back.

But I always ask them, "How do you feel about me going here to play?" They always told me, "Dad, just follow your dream." I want to thank you all for letting me follow my dream.

CHAPTER 8

MENTORS

STEVE LARGENT

NOBODY SETS OUT TO BE A MENTOR, BUT FEW JOBS
are more important.

The best mentors are the most patient, the most experienced, the most giving of their time. Often they are not paid for their efforts, not if they are parents or friends. But the payoff can turn out to be greater than anyone imagines. Molding a young life, or really any life, in a way it was not shaped before is reward enough.

Ultimately, mentors know what their pupils don't, at least not right away: Nobody can reach a final destination without first being shown the way.

■　■　■　■

Steve Largent
Seattle Seahawks Wide Receiver
Class of 1995

Largent caught 819 passes for 13,089 yards and one hundred touchdowns. At one point, Largent caught at least one pass in 177 straight games.

Presented by Seahawks Vice President Gary Wright

In 1976, Steve drove along the highway from Houston to Oklahoma City after being cut by the Oilers. It looked like his professional career was over before it had begun. But a magical fourteen-year detour in Seattle has brought him here to Canton, Ohio, where he belongs. Steve Largent has left a legacy not of numbers, records, and honors. Records and honors can be broken, but the spirit and standard he set will always, always live.

Steve Largent

My story, like so many others, is a story of mentors—people who challenged me when I questioned myself, people who believed in me against all the evidence.

My mother, who never missed a game or never missed a practice. In fact, she talked me out of quitting football when I was a sophomore in high school.

My grandfather, who stepped into the gap when my folks were divorced.

My coaches taught me the game of football and the meaning of leadership. When I close my eyes, I can still hear their voices, hear their whistles. They still shape the character of my life.

I was one of those players, as you know, who was labeled early as too small and too slow. I came to depend on people who saw me actually as bigger and faster than I really was. We all need people who believe in us. They expand the boundaries we place on our own lives. In my case, their influence did more than improve my performance in this great game. It filled a hollowness in my own life I could not explain or even understand.

When a child grows up today without a father there is an empty place where someone must stand providing an example of character and confidence. If no one takes that place, a child can live in a shadow all their lives. Their emptiness is often filled with despair, by anger, or even violence.

This commonplace tragedy has become the central problem of our society. It has become an epidemic of secret suffering. But if someone takes that place, a child can escape the shadows. He can find confidence, courage, and conscience. And perhaps even find his way to the Pro Football Hall of Fame.

I have extraordinary respect for the men and women who accept that responsibility and play that role in young lives today. They leave an influence more lasting than any law. The really heroic people are not those who break records. The really heroic people are the ones who can mend a broken spirit. My accomplishment today is a tribute to those people in my life who were willing to do that for me.

■ ■ ■ ■

Art Donovan
Baltimore Colts, New York Yanks, and
Dallas Texans Defensive Tackle
Class of 1968

A vital part of Baltimore's climb to powerhouse status in the 1950s, Donovan was selected to five Pro Bowls.

If I say it's not a pleasure to be here, I'd only be lying. I could go on and thank everybody from the time I started playing football back in grammar school at Mount St. Michaels, but I'd only miss a lot of people. But there are two people here this afternoon that I'd really like to thank.

A fella named Don Kellett, who was really instrumental in me staying in professional football. When I wanted to go home and join the New York City Police Department, he talked me out of it.

There's another fella here who I hit more, I guess, than anybody I've ever hit or anybody will hit in their life. A fella who played opposite of me for nine years, and he and I, in a period of nine years, must have hit each other I'd say one hundred thousand times. A fella that is here today to honor me, I think one of the finest offensive guards that ever played professional football, Alex Sandusky.

■ ■ ■ ■

Jim Brown
Cleveland Browns Fullback
Class of 1971

After being voted to nine consecutive Pro Bowls and leading the NFL in rushing in eight years, Brown retired with 12,312 rushing yards and 756 points.

Presented by Long Island Attorney Ken Molloy

I'm going to reveal to you today a love story. It's a love story that started way back in a little hamlet of Manhasset, New York, on Long Island, which sits among the bays of the Long Island Sound; where the wonderful people of Manhasset fell in love with a young boy at the age of thirteen, Jimmy Brown.

And I'm tickled to know that his children are here. There's Kevin, James, and Kim, and I go back and remember Jimmy at about the same age and his intensity as a young man, his will to win, to succeed, to do whatever was necessary to achieve his goals. And at that young age, his goal was to be the best professional football player in the United States.

He has achieved that pinnacle and I think it important and worthy to note here today, some of the people in little Manhasset who helped Jimmy. . . . You can go down the names, and it's a cross-section of America all the way, and the product of that cross-section of America is the man that we've come to honor today. And I would like, if you will indulge me, to point out two lessons.

It has been said by the philosophers that the world can learn a lesson from every man, and I think there are two lessons that should be learned from the life of Jimmy Brown. One is that all of you people who are in what they call "the power structure" today should look around you. There are young, talented, bright-eyed, bushy-tailed kids who are ready and willing to rise to the heights, and they can do it if you'll look and give them the opportunity.

To you young people is the second lesson, and that is, as Jim has gone through life, he has been a keen observer of society around him and in honesty—and he's an honest person—he found some things he could criticize, some things he could object to. And he did this, but he did it with this honesty and what made it honest and valid was the fact that whenever he criticized, it was based upon the fact that his contribution always exceeded his protests, and I think this is the key to young people.

Jim Brown

My mother is here today and she had a tough struggle when I was a little boy. She had to take care of me all by herself and I never tell her that, so I thought I'd take this time to say thank you because you worked very hard.

And there are a few men here representing the community of Manhasset, Long Island. Now regardless of what you've heard about me, me being outspoken, saying what I want to say, doing things I wanted to do, you probably never heard the great story about the people in Manhasset.

Today we have Kenny Molloy, who I chose to present me here today because Kenny was the leader of that community. But we also have the superintendent of Manhasset schools, Dr. Raymond Collins, who's somewhere out there, and you won't know him, but I know him very well because he was instrumental in my early development. He came to Syracuse and he kept me in school. He did all the things that a superintendent wouldn't do to keep a young man on the right track.

And finally, there's Ed Walsh, who was my high school coach. And if I was a highly religious man, I would think that this man would be a saint because I couldn't imagine him doing anything wrong. And I love him as I love the rest of the people in the community of Manhasset. They are here today and most of all, I want to publicly give them my thanks because they came into my life at a time where I could have gone in many, many directions.

So to all of you, I hope you can remember that. Remember that the arrogant and bad Jim Brown can be humble when he is given true love and when he is able to talk about people that he truly respects.

■　■　■　■

Frank Gifford
New York Giants Halfback
Class of 1977

Gifford starred on both offense and defense, playing in seven Pro Bowls. In 1956, he was the NFL Player of the Year.

Presented by Giants Owner Wellington Mara

For me, for twenty-five years, Frank Gifford has personified the son every father dreams of, the player every coach dreams of, the father any son would cherish. I like the man.

For many of us, he is the author of a book called *Gifford on Courage*, a subject he knows a great deal about. All of us know him now as he's the sports telecaster who insists on letting the event tell the story. In speaking of Frank Gifford in any of these facets of his life, it is necessary to speak in terms of humility, versatility, and excellence. These three characteristics are woven closely together in the pattern of Frank's life.

In any memory of Frank Gifford's, there is one picture that is always present—unwanted and starved—but always there. It is a Frank Gifford, very still, at a field in Yankees Stadium [after Eagles Hall-of-Fame linebacker Chuck Bednarik hit him and stood over him in November 1960]. You thought he might die—you knew he would never play again. But he didn't die, and he played again, and how he played.

When he announced his retirement in March of 1965, my brother, Jack, who was then president of the Giants, said Frank Gifford was one of the greatest players who ever played for the Giants. He had a dignity, tone, and class during our entire operation. Even among stars he was a standout.

Frank Gifford

All five of us—and I think you will have to agree it is quite a unique class coming in—have been pondering what we might say when we came to this moment. Forrest Gregg and I were talking about it a minute ago, and Gale Sayers and I were sitting back in the quiet solitude of a room, and I am sure we each have our own thoughts of why we are here and how we got here. I think we all agree on one thing because I think I know all of these men well enough to know that we are deeply appreciative of the God-given physical ability. But it doesn't start there and it doesn't end there.

All of us are aware as we go through life there are people who have incredible influence on us emotionally and physically. You run a great risk at a time like this—perhaps the greatest moment of my athletic life standing here—you run a great risk of overlooking so many people, but there are a few in my life that played such an important role.

I don't want to use this as a philosophical forum because it is not meant to be that. But I have a couple of deep feelings about the game of football and many of those feelings have been attacked. The game of football over the years has been attacked as so many other great institutions of our country have been attacked. The professional football, college football, street football, it offers a great deal to young people. There are five of us up here today to prove just that. There are over ninety more enshrined in the Hall of Fame that offer you something to strive for.

You don't always get there, but sometimes when you strive hard enough, what we do reach is better than the goal you set. I believe in our society today, and, unfortunately, that too is changing. When you go out on the football field and you are playing the game as best as you can, you don't look around and say, "That man is black," or "that man is white." You just care that it gets done and it gets done the right way. Football in so many ways has so many things to offer a troubled society.

■ ■ ■ ■

Joe Namath
New York Jets and Los Angeles Rams Quarterback
Class of 1985

The first quarterback to pass for more than four thousand yards in a season, in 1967, Namath guaranteed and delivered victory over the Colts in Super Bowl III.

Presented by Beaver Falls (Pennsylvania)
High School Football Coach Larry Bruno

If I had to choose one word to describe the fabulous career of Joe Namath, that word would be confidence.

When Joe played football for Beaver Falls High School, the entire football team believed whatever play Joe called would work. They would make it work because they knew Joe had confidence in them.

A few years later, when Joe was playing professional football for the New York Jets and the Jets were playing in Super Bowl III, Joe made the statement, "I guarantee we will beat the Colts." This was not a cocky or brash statement. The Jets were a seventeen-point underdog, but again when Joe said we could win, his teammates believed they could win, just like in high school. The Jets did win that Super Bowl and pulled off one of the greatest upsets in modern football history.

Incidentally, the quarterback of the Colts that day was Johnny Unitas, Joe's idol in high school. Joe even wore number 19 in high school, and that jersey will be included in the Hall of Fame.

If Joe continues to have the same kind of confidence in his new field of entertainment, maybe someday we will be watching the Academy Awards program and the emcee will say, "The envelope please, and the winner is, ladies and gentlemen, Joe Namath."

Joe Namath

When a boy is in school, age sixteen or seventeen, there are a lot of directions he may go. I was headed in some directions that could have been the wrong directions. Well, my high school coach, Larry Bruno, helped me a heck of a lot, steered me right.

He told me one day in a meeting, told our whole team, he said, "Fellows, if you don't dream about it, it will never happen. But you can't just dream about it, you have to go out and make it happen. You have to work hard."

With that in mind, I dreamt of a high school championship and we won it. We went out and worked for it and got it. At the University of Alabama, where I was lucky to go to school and find a new family, we won the national championship because we were led by Coach Paul "Bear" Bryant. He worked us hard and our goals were high.

Before I left Alabama, Coach Paul "Bear" Bryant gave me this advice: "Look, Joe, you're getting ready to go into pro football. Do you know what kind of people you are going to be working with?" And I said, "No, sir," and he said: "You sure better consider this because it is mighty important. The kind of people you are around, and the kind of people you are working with in this life is mighty important. Take that into consideration."

I was able to go to the New York Jets to play for another great coach. Coach Weeb Ewbank. I'll tell you what, a ballplayer could not have been luckier. Without Coach Ewbank's guidance, I could have fallen flat on my face. But Weeb had a way of handling people, a good way of handling people, both on and off the playing field.

I must have played for four or five other head coaches after Weeb, and I believe Weeb got smarter and smarter with every head coach I played for. I didn't realize how sharp Weeb was until after he retired. Weeb, I want to thank you personally, bud; you kept me together when times were rough. You picked me up and gave me the encouragement I needed to succeed. You gave me the good football sense to get out there and keep playing, and without your help I wouldn't be here.

I get goose bumps when I walk through the Hall of Fame. I see guys in there that I have admired my entire life, at least when I was old enough to start understanding football.

I never dreamt of being in the Professional Football Hall of Fame, and I'm thankful to many people for this great honor.

■　■　■　■

Dwight Stephenson
Miami Dolphins Center
Class of 1998

Recognized as the premier center of his time, Stephenson was selected to five straight Pro Bowls.

Presented by Colts and Dolphins Coach Don Shula

Dwight was one of the hardest workers that I ever coached. He worked out every day in the weight room as if his job were at stake. And he treated every practice session as though he was getting ready to play in the Super Bowl. I found that out early in our first scrimmage after drafting Dwight.

His teammate at Alabama, Don McNeal, was playing the left corner for us on defense and we ran a screen pass. And on this screen pass, McNeal came up to contain the play, and Dwight pulled along the line of scrimmage and he took McNeal on in the flat and knocked him up into the stands and then just stood there and grinned. And that was his teammate.

And I knew what was going to happen to opposing players during Dwight's career.

Dwight Stephenson

I went to the University of Alabama and that's where I had the opportunity to play for the legendary Paul "Bear" Bryant, which at that time was probably the best thing that could have happened for me.

He was a person that was interested in making good people. He didn't want just good football players, but he wanted us to be good people. He would take us out there on the football field and work us, and boy, it didn't seem like he really cared about us. And then he'd walk through the dining room and he'd come up and say, "Dwight, how's your momma doing? Is she still working?" He really showed an interest in football players.

Then I had the opportunity to go to Miami and play for the legendary coach Don Shula. When I went down to Miami, I didn't expect a whole lot out of myself, but I didn't know what would happen. But when you get around Coach Shula, he is like an extension of the University of Alabama. The same things we practiced there, Coach Bryant taught us. And he gave me the opportunity to play there and play professional football for the Dolphins. Coach Shula, I really appreciate you.

■　■　■　■

Tom Landry
Dallas Cowboys Coach
Class of 1990

An innovator on offense and defense, Landry compiled a 270-178-6 record, with twenty consecutive winning seasons.

Presented by Cowboys Quarterback Roger Staubach

Those of you who have watched Coach Landry on the sidelines all those years might have formed an impression of him as impassive or unemotional. The media played that up quite a bit. But the truth is that despite the cool outward appearance, Tom Landry is one of the most sensitive, caring individuals God ever put on this earth. And in a sport as tough as football can be, Tom Landry is as tough as he can be.

Tom's sincere desire to win was right on top of his list, but he also cared for the individual and for the team, and that is what made him a winner. He agonized over tough decisions. You will find that former players believe that Coach Landry made them better individuals. The high tribute we can offer is genuine respect. Tom Landry certainly earned that from the athletes he influenced in his three decades of coaching. He also has earned it off the field in a lifetime of giving and caring.

So there are contrasts that I have tried to put together—the spiritual side of Tom Landry, conservative yet innovative, quiet but generous in giving. He might appear distant, but he is always warm, compassionate, and understanding. Which is the real Tom Landry? They all are. He is actually what he appears to be. There is no pretense in his style, no false images to maintain. His genuine nature and goodwill make him stand out as the individual unique in his time. Tom Landry defines the word *class*.

In one of my weaker moments, I called Tom, "the man in the funny hat." Speaking for football fans across the country, we miss that image on Sunday afternoons. But we are thankful for the memories he has given us, for the grace and dignity he brought to our sport. He has touched all of us in a way few could.

Tom Landry

In my life, I think the one man that made a great difference was my coach in junior high and high school. I only had one coach when I was in junior high and high school. He taught me a lot about football. He taught me fundamentals. He taught me values. He taught me to pay a price to win. He contributed greatly to my success and, really, I am talking about all coaches, all the junior high and senior high coaches of America. What an impact they have on the youth of America—where we need the impact today.

Of course, the last year has been a very interesting one for me. I got fired and I got into the Hall of Fame, all in one year. So you coaches remember that there are always good things at the end of the rainbow, if you stick with it.

■ ■ ■ ■

John Hannah
New England Patriots Guard
Class of 1991

Renowned as the premier guard of his era, Hannah was an All-Pro ten years and played in nine Pro Bowls.

God, I love football. And to be inducted into the Hall of Fame is probably the one fulfillment of a lifelong dream. You just don't know what it means to me.

I remember when I was growing up in Albertsville, Alabama, and Mom and Dad would take us to church, and as soon as church was over, we would fly home to try to see guys like Ray Nitschke, Gale Sayers, Dick Butkus. Man, I would sit there and froth at the mouth and say, "Wonder if I'll ever be good enough to play with those guys."

And I remember even playing in the NFL and I had a coach, Jim Ringo, that had played the game, and I went to him one time and said, "Coach, do you think I was good enough?" Well, what today means to me is, I made the cut. I'm on the team and right now, I have the honor of playing alongside the greatest heroes that ever played football. I also want to believe that this award means in some small way I might have given something back to the game that has given me so much.

I also want to thank a gentleman that couldn't be here today, and that is Coach Paul Bryant. Coach Bryant left for me a lesson of setting lofty goals. And not only that, but to run life's race to reach those goals. The greatest lesson that he left with me was that you have to beat your body. You've got to make it your slave if you ever want to get where you want to go.

I want to thank people like Coach Fairbanks who taught me the importance of organization and surrounding yourself with talent so you could rely on the special gifts of others. He taught me that plans are frustrated without consultation, but with wise counsel they are established.

I want to thank people like Red Miller who was my first offensive line coach in the NFL. He told me there is no better pleasure in life than to enjoy what you are doing because then you give it the best that you've got and, when you look back, you're happy with what you've done.

I want to thank Jim Ringo, who is probably my favorite and best offensive line coach. What he taught me was you can't cling to and rely on the basics, but that you have to push on to reach the full capabilities of the talents you have been given.

I want to thank my dad for one of the greatest lessons any man has ever learned and I hope I will never forget it, and that is to never be satisfied with what you have done; always reach out and forget what lies behind and press on to what lies ahead.

■　■　■　■

Ronnie Lott
San Francisco 49ers, Los Angeles Raiders, and New York Jets Defensive Back
Class of 2000

Lott was voted to ten Pro Bowls. He intercepted sixty-three passes and was named to the NFL's Seventy-fifth Anniversary Team.

I stand a little straighter and a little taller here today because of the greatest giant of all, my loving dad. He taught me to seek success in all facets in my life. He taught me the values of life, the purpose for living. He taught me to have honor and to show respect. Dr. Harry

Edwards once said that people who come to your funeral come not for what you accomplished, but for what you stand for. Dad, you stand as our rock. . . .

I couldn't have made it this far without my teachers and coaches. They were all giants in my life. My high school coach, Bill Christopher, who would make us listen to the General Patton speech. I don't know if you guys have heard the General Patton speech, but I'd lay there every night in the dark thinking about what it's like to be an American and how we don't tolerate losers. It toughened our spirit and strengthened our resolve, and I appreciate it.

And finally, to all the football fans out here, I hope you love this game as much as I do. I've been very fortunate to be around greatness this weekend. One of the things that I found out about greatness is the character. It's amazing when you're around greatness and what you see. I hope you guys all have the opportunity to feel like I've felt this past weekend. Each and every one of these men behind me have given more than just their body and soul; they've given it all to you. I hope you all understand that these men are not just football players, they're great men. They're great people. They love this game.

■　■　■　■

Joe Montana
San Francisco 49ers and
Kansas City Chiefs Quarterback
Class of 2000

Montana was MVP in Super Bowls XVI, XIX, and XXIV. He was voted to eight Pro Bowls and was All-NFL three times.

Presented by 49ers Owner Eddie DeBartolo Jr.

Look at any old picture of Joe Montana right after he's thrown a touchdown pass and you'll see it. Arms raised in the air, that special gleam in his eyes, a grin full of pure joy. This is the spirit that defined him, the spirit that created the champion that he is.

But excellence wasn't an accident for Joe. It was a habit, a singular act of talent and discipline. He was a master, and he was skilled in an art. He was the kind of player who could take his time and finesse his way down the field for a touchdown, or drive ninety yards in ninety seconds without ever perceiving it as an insurmountable obstacle. You can be sure none of his teammates did, either.

Whether fifteen minutes or fifteen seconds remained, Joe always maintained the same level of composure. He was a leader, the hero you always wanted to emulate and a legend to behold. It goes without saying that Joe Montana's athletic abilities were phenomenal, but we all know that, don't we?

Joe Montana

We all started in Pop Warner, and I'm going to name off some of my coaches. Carl Crawley and Cecil Palmer were Pop Warner coaches who taught me the meaning of really not quitting. Because as a kid, most guys want to quit the game. I tried to quit at some point, but between my father and those two gentlemen, they got me back on the field. Wouldn't let me quit in the middle of the season. Taught me not to go ahead and be a quitter, to go in and stay there. And then the next year, thank God, I came back to play again. My high school coach, Jeff Petrucci, taught me most of my fundamentals.

The next few people I think had the most impact on my life, starting with the man who drafted me, Bill Walsh. There are a lot of things that I learned from Bill throughout my career, but I think the one thing that I continue throughout my life is that wish to be perfect. The need for perfection. He pushed me and pushed us, especially the quarterback position which he was so proud of, to want to be perfect. And if you missed perfect, you ended up with great. And that he could handle, nothing else. He taught me to be the same way.

And most important, to my wife and also my best friend, Jennifer. It's not the easiest, living with an athlete. They'll all tell you we seem cool and calm on the outside, but inside, we're a mess. There's a lot happening there and they've got to deal with a lot that people never begin to see. And I love her to death, and I thank her for her support and her sacrifice. She gave up a career so that I could continue mine. As often as I don't say it, I do very much appreciate it.

■　■　■　■

Lynn Swann
Pittsburgh Steelers Wide Receiver
Class of 2001

The MVP of Super Bowl X, Swann was selected to
three Pro Bowls.

Presented by Steelers Wide Receiver John Stallworth

It is a single honor to be here today to present someone that I have the privilege of calling my friend, Lynn Swann.

Desire, character, cohesiveness are the ingredients that go into making a great athlete and truly a good person. Do you have the desire to be great and the willingness to work towards that? Do you have the foundation of good character that allows you to overcome the obstacles in life rather than crumble under the stress? Can you achieve the cohesiveness necessary to be a team player?

During Lynn's life, during his career, he has answered that with a resounding yes. He's answered every doubt that there's ever been about him with a resounding yes.

Lynn Swann

I want to thank my father, Willie Swann. When I first started playing football against my middle brother, Calvin, who was a much better athlete, my father said, "Well, I'm not sure, Lynn, that you're going to be so good."

So when he took me out to buy the football shoes I wanted, the really expensive ones with the stripes to look really cool, my father said, "I don't know, son, I don't know. We shouldn't be investing that much money into your shoes. You may not be wearing them that long. All right?"

And I felt kind of bad. But you know what the important thing was? The important thing was my father was with me and he took me to get those shoes.

What makes a career and what I take with me is certainly a sense of satisfaction of having performed in a big moment. But it's a response and reaction of people who've played the game.

My happiness and greatest joy of my career and whatever I've achieved have come from the words of people like Andre Reed, from Jerry Rice, from the Randy Mosses and Cris Carters, who came up to me at various points in their careers and lives and said, "Lynn Swann, you were the man. I wanted to be like you. I wanted to play the game the way you played it."

When you have that kind of impact and those caliber of players tell you that's what they want to do, then you know in your heart, regardless of whether you stand here or not, you played the very best football a man could possibly play.

CHAPTER 9

LOMBARDI

WILLIE DAVIS AND
EDDIE ROBINSON

VINCE LOMBARDI'S SPIRIT LIVES ON. IN GREEN BAY,
where his name still is attached to a middle school, a cancer clinic,
a family dentistry, a steak house, a gas station, an avenue, and, of
course, the Packers. It lives in NFL history. And his name graces the
Super Bowl trophy.

His imprint also is on the men he coached. They speak about
him as if they still can hear him, as if they never met anybody like

him. Those who don't know him seem to have a certain fascination with him.

To this day, Lombardi is the standard by which any other football coach is measured. His words still are gospel, his records still recounted, his phrases still recalled, his lessons still relived.

■   ■   ■   ■

Willie Davis
Cleveland Browns and
Green Bay Packers Defensive End
Class of 1981

An All-NFL player for five seasons and a Pro Bowl selection for five years, Davis did not miss a game in his twelve-year career. This is a very special occasion because it is the first time my family has ever been together. I am truly proud of this moment because it was through football that I learned how to win and it was through football that I learned how to enjoy the thrill of success and it was also through football that I developed the will to succeed.

Coaches have been a very important part of my life, and I would just like to read a poem of the last speech from Vince Lombardi, a man I truly loved and admired. These words reflect my feelings.

I owe most everything to football, which I have spent the greater part of my life in. I have never lost my respect, my admiration and love, for what I consider a great day. And each Sunday after the battle, your team savors its victory. The other lives in the bitterness of defeat. And many hurts are a small price to pay for having won. And to the loser there is no reason which is adequate enough to the winner, there 100 percent elation, 100 percent fun, 100 percent laughter, and yet the only thing left to the loser is resolution and determination.

Most important of all, to be successful in life demands that each man make a personal commitment to excellence and to victory even though we know deep down that the ultimate victory can never be completely won. Yet that victory must be pursued and it must be wooed with every fiber of our body, with every bit of our might and all of our effort.

And each week, there is a new encounter, each day there is a new challenge. And yet all of the display, and all of the color, and all of the glamour, and all of the excitement, and all of the rewards, and all of the money, these things are only limited in the memory. But the spirit, the will to win, the will to excel, these are the things that will endure and really these are the qualities, larger and more important than any of the events they occasion.

Just as the value of all of our daily efforts are greater, are more enduring really if they create in each one of us a person who grows, a person who understands, one who really lives, one who prevails for a larger and more meaningful victory—not only now but in time and hopefully in eternity.

Indeed, I would say that the quality of each man's life is the full measure of that man's personal commitment to excellence and to victory—whether it be in football, whether it be in business, whether it be in politics or government or what have you. And likewise, too, I think it teaches that work and sacrifice and perseverance and competitive drive and the selflessness, a respect for authority, is the price that each and every one of us must pay to achieve any goal that's worthwhile.

■ ■ ■ ■

Vince Lombardi
Green Bay Packers and
Washington Redskins Head Coach
Class of 1971

In ten years, Lombardi compiled a 105-35-6 coaching record that included five NFL titles and victories in Super Bowls I and II.

Presented by Giants Owner Wellington Mara

A trip to the Hall of Fame is truly an inspiration to a member of the National Football League. To see its exhibits and to stand as it were in the shadows of those great men in whose reflected glory we all ask to be long remembered. It brings a full realization, the debt we owe to them and a resolution that we will never forget it, in our stewardship of this heritage they have given us.

Vince Lombardi did not invent professional football and he did not found the National Football League, but he embellished both of them to a degree never surpassed and seldom, if ever, equaled. He made winners out of his players and losers out of his opponents.

Accepting on Behalf of Vince Lombardi, His Son, Vince Lombardi Jr.

If my father were here today, he would indeed be very pleased, for although there has been much written and said about him, few people realize how strongly my father felt about the National Football League. Few people realize how proud my father was to be a part of the tradition and the image of the National Football League, and few people realize how much my father cherished his association with the players and the coaches and the owners and the other members of the National Football League.

Obviously you do not earn an honor such as this on your own; it takes the help and cooperation of many, many people, and my father was no exception. Because my time is limited, I cannot thank all the people who should share this honor. I sincerely hope that it is enough that they know who they are.

However, I would like to take this occasion to call attention to and to thank one person in particular. That person through love and understanding, more than any other, was responsible for the success my father did enjoy. That person, Marie Lombardi, my mother.

■ ■ ■ ■

Jim Taylor
Green Bay Packers and
New Orleans Saints Fullback
Class of 1976

Taylor rushed for 8,597 yards and scored 558 points. In 1962, he led the league in rushing and scoring with nineteen touchdowns.

Presented by Marie Lombardi,
Wife of Packers Coach Vince Lombardi

About six weeks ago I wasn't sure I could be here because I was in the hospital having a nerve block on my face, and it is a terrible thing because it numbs the one side of your face and your mouth doesn't work too well. And what could be worse for a woman if her mouth doesn't work too well?

It shattered me pretty badly when I knew I just couldn't be here, so I called my son in Seattle and I said, "Vince, you better call Jimmy and tell him I can't go to Canton because I can't speak." He said, "All right, Mother, if that's what you want."

An hour later, I called him back and said, "Vince, don't call Jimmy because a big voice up there said to me, 'You better be in Canton and you better do a good job!'" So here I am, and I better do a good job because he probably would trade me. And I just kind of suspect that I am pinch-hitting for that Italian with that big voice who can't be here.

Now everybody knows of those fine records that Jimmy made in Green Bay, those magnificent five years where he gained over one thousand yards. I know he did because I saw him gain every single one of them. But I have to say today is the day he will take the most pride in because, you see, he is the first, the very first, of the great Packers players of what is known as the great Lombardi era to be taken into the Hall of Fame.

And it occurs to me when I go into the Hall and I see the history of the great National Football League that the years of the '60s were something special. I think it was professional football's finest hour. And the Packers players of the '60s dominated football at its finest hour and it must be a great joy for Jimmy to know that he is the first to reach the top.

As Coach Lombardi used to say, "I don't care anything about gimmicks or tricks on offense. You play this game with power, you do what you do best, and you do it again, again, and again." Jimmy Taylor was that power and he used to say we had thunder and lightning on the Green Bay Packers, and Jimmy Taylor was that thunder.

And I have a tape at home and on that tape, an interview with Howard Cosell, Vince evaluates the players and he says this about Jimmy Taylor and I quote: "Jim Taylor isn't big for a fullback, but when you bump against him it's like bumping against an iron statue. In fact, he likes that feeling. The thing about Jimmy is he really likes people. I don't know anyone on the squad that has a greater need or a greater capacity for friendship and understanding than Jim Taylor."

Vince and Jim did have their misunderstandings, but who didn't? And I saw something I would like to share with you and it's special because it's the only time it happened. When the coach was sick and in the hospital in Washington, many, many Packers players came to see him and one of them was Jim Taylor. And I went in the room with him, and Vince took his hand and he held it for such a long time. And friends, the love and the understanding that went between those two hands, I will never, never forget.

We have a great need in our country today for great heroes. We don't have any heroes, but I believe the men here enshrined in the Hall of Fame are today's heroes.

Jim Taylor

What gave me the opportunity to be the player I was was the teamwork and the unity that was molded into our ball club through Vince Lombardi. There were so many wonderful years and honors and occasions. One certainly can be excited about the people who I was connected with, the ones who gave me an opportunity to play football.

I would like to say just a few words about the late coach, Vince Lombardi. He probably instilled in me the admiration, the dedication, the discipline, the determination as a football player and as a man that I have been connected with.

■ ■ ■ ■

Bart Starr
Green Bay Packers Quarterback
Class of 1977

Starr quarterbacked the Packers to six division titles, five NFL titles, and the first two Super Bowl wins, in which he was Most Valuable Player.

Presented by University of Kentucky Assistant Coach Bill Moseley

Bart sought to be a successful football player in the NFL. He achieved this goal to a degree that had not before been seen. It did not come altogether easy.

Bart Starr was not born a naturally great quarterback. Bart had to work to make himself into an outstanding field general. Bart had the intelligence to become a great quarterback. He used his intelligence to the fullest in his development as a superb leader. He used every available resource to aid him in improving as a successful athlete.

In Bart's high school days, I can very well remember the skinny, freckle-faced kid in a group around his coach. Anytime there was something to be taught, Bart was dead serious, soaking up everything that he could. His eyes were always focused on getting instructions.

You will notice that this strong countenance still exists in the face of this young man. I know that after practice, home on weekends, Bart was in his backyard, drilling and working and trying to grasp the ideas that were taught in practice. This, among other things, is the reason Bart Starr became a great quarterback. He was willing to work and to dedicate himself to being the best.

Bart Starr

Years ago, when General Douglas MacArthur had retired and was living out his life in the Waldorf-Astoria Hotel, a struggling young writer asked for permission to interview the general, which was granted. Although quite nervous, as he entered the room, he was made to feel at ease by the general. His opening question was, "General, when you were commandant at West Point years ago, you were an advocate of athletic competition. Do you still feel as strongly today about the merits of athletic competition as you did then?"

The general replied brilliantly. "Young man, the infinite values of athletic competition have but intensified with the passage of time. It is a vital character builder, for it molds the youth of our country for their future roles as custodians of the Republic. Fathers and mothers who would have their sons become men should have them play the game. For upon the fields of friendly strife are sown the seeds that, upon other fields, on other days, will bear the fruits of victory."

If I may be presumptuous, the inductees behind me here today personify those words.

I made it as a rookie quarterback in Green Bay when the rosters were only thirty-three in number because my wife seated there must have retrieved hundreds of footballs for me that summer. I hung a tire in an A-frame in a field next to her parents' home in Jackson, Mississippi, and worked twice a day, throwing as many as my arm would allow. She retrieved every one of them. Honey, to you I'll always be grateful.

After a few short years in the league, we were privileged to have the legendary Vince Lombardi become our coach and leader. I need not tell you of his exploits and his record of coaching. You've heard them many times over, but I think the things that have been stated today are indicative of what he told us and we learned many valuable lessons. He was an exceptional teacher and an inspirational leader. He taught us the meaning of commitment, unselfishness, purpose, pride, and an unrelenting quest for excellence. Those of us who had the opportunity to play for him came to appreciate even more the spelling of the word TEAM [Together Everyone Achieves More]. You must be willing to subordinate your own desires, egos, and ambitions for the good of the team. Because as that team grows and prospers, so will you as an individual, and what you remember most are your TEAMMATES.

■　■　■　■

Forrest Gregg
Green Bay Packers and
Dallas Cowboys Offensive Tackle
Class of 1977

A nine-time Pro Bowl selection, Gregg played 188 consecutive games. He also played on seven NFL championship teams and three Super Bowl winners.

Presented by Marie Lombardi,
Wife of Packers Coach Vince Lombardi

When I am getting ready to come to Canton, Ohio, for this great weekend, I get so excited; I can't wait to get on the airplane. And I would like to congratulate these inductees and particularly their families who made so many sacrifices to make this great honor possible.

I would like to talk about Forrest Gregg the man. I read somewhere that Vince Lombardi made football players out of men and men out of football players, but not this man. He was probably the finest all-around team player that ever played this game, proof of the fact being that when he was an All-Pro tackle with the Packers, he was perfectly willing to make the supreme sacrifice of switching from tackle to guard when he was needed and to be able to make that switch and then to be voted an All-Pro guard at that position.

Now when Forrest was about thirty years old he decided to maybe look for his future. And he was offered a coaching job at the University of Tennessee, and after a very short time he had second thoughts about it. So the coach and I were down in Puerto Rico on vacation and, needless to say, he was pretty upset about this chain of events.

One night in our room, the phone rang and it was one of the assistant Packers coaches. He said, "Vince, Forrest Gregg wants to come back and play. Do you want him?"

Well, friends, Vince yelled so loud through the phone the room shook, the building shook, and even the grounds shook. He wanted Forrest back so bad and, Forrest, you might have signed the first $1 million contract for the National Football League, he wanted you back that bad. Because how do you replace a Forrest Gregg as a player, as a coach, as a man, and as a dear friend?

And to use the old clichés of honest, integrity, commitment, excellence, dedication—I don't know of any man who these apply to more than Forrest Gregg.

Forrest Gregg

What happened this morning was the most emotional thing that has happened to me in my lifetime. When I was going down the street in that parade, I saw friends that I knew and I saw my family sitting on the side. It made me think back as to how it all started and I don't want to get too deep into this right now, about how it all started, because I'm already pretty emotional about it. But as I look out and see my family, I think how empty it would be, how little it would mean if I did not have them to share it with.

Sometimes in the game of football, not just professional football, but in all football, the families sometimes are left a little bit to the side. But I can tell you this much right now. If it had not been for my wife, Barbara, her love and her encouragement, I would not be standing here right now. My two children, Karen my daughter and Forrest Jr. my son. They have known nothing in their lives but professional football.

I sit and I listen to Marie Lombardi talk about Vince Lombardi, talk about the Green Bay Packers. Marie, I would have given anything in the world to have known that Vince said that on the telephone. I would have asked for a lot more money. Vince Lombardi—I can't talk up here without mentioning his name and think about what he did for me and I know when Bart gets up here, he's going to say the same thing. This man was the maximum, for a lack of a better adjective to describe him, as a football coach. And this lady who sits back here and presented me, we have such a great love for her that it is hard to express right here.

■ ■ ■ ■

Herb Adderley
Green Bay Packers and Dallas Cowboys Cornerback
Class of 1980

Adderley played in four Super Bowls and five Pro Bowls, and intercepted forty-eight passes during his career.

Presented by Packers Defensive End Willie Davis

I remember Herb best for nine years we played on the same side of the field. I saw Herb make some of the greatest plays ever among the defensive team at Green Bay. Along with teammate Dave Robinson, we truly controlled the left side of the Packer defense. He always played well in the big game. His sixty-yard return for a touchdown in Super Bowl II is one of only two touchdowns in thirteen years in the Super Bowl from interceptions.

Herb was committed to being the best cornerback in the NFL, and somehow today, most of us who played and most of us who saw him play realized that he accomplished his commitment. His personal pride and dedication to high standards was a true inspiration to every Green Bay Packer. Herb was a competitor with unusual ability to make the big effort.

Herb Adderley

I would like to take time to thank the two people responsible for my football career. Number one would be my high school coach, Mr. Charles Martin, who is deceased. I can honestly say if it wasn't for Mr. Charles Martin back in Philadelphia in 1955, when I started playing in high school, there is no way I would be here because I thought that I was a basketball player. In fact, I would have bet that I was a basketball player.

But this man saw something in me that I didn't see or realize in myself. He said, "I think you could play football and you can play it well." I said, "Well, I don't know, because I never played football, just around the streets."

You hear Bill Cosby, who is a good friend, you hear him talking about playing touch football and running behind the bus in the alley, and the cans and stuff, and we were involved in that and I didn't play organized football until high school. Mr. Charles Martin—I will always remember him and his spirit will live within me. He helped me get to Michigan State.

I had several offers, scholarship offers, and he asked me, "Listen, I'm setting this up for you, what do you want to do?" So I said I would like to go to Michigan State University and he said, "Why?" And I said, "Well, there is a fellow there that is wearing number 26, Clarence Peaks." I said, "I don't know the man, never seen him except for on television. Never met him, but he is the kind of guy that I would like to be like and I would like to go there and see what happens."

He made a phone call to Duffy Daugherty and two days later I was on a plane to Lansing, Michigan. Clarence Peaks met me at the airport, and from there it was history. I told Clarence that I was going to take this number 26 and take it as far as I can, hopefully to the top. And I would like to say that Clarence Peaks is not here, but I did see him last week, and I did thank him for the inspiration that he gave me. He helped me to be someone.

I have to talk about Coach Vince Lombardi because Vince Lombardi reminds me so much of my high school coach. Those two people had more to do with me playing football and being successful than anybody in the world.

I feel a certain sadness in my heart, but I can feel happy and feel good because the spirit of my high school coach and Vince Lombardi is within me. Coach Lombardi had the nerve to draft me number one in 1961 and that was probably the biggest thrill of my entire career, being drafted number one. And I said I have to repay this man for having enough nerve to draft me number one.

■ ■ ■ ■

Paul Hornung
Green Bay Packers Halfback
Class of 1986

In the 1961 NFL title game, Hornung scored a record nineteen points. He finished his career with 760 points and led the NFL in scoring in three years, including 1960, when he scored a record 176 points.

Presented by Packers Wide Receiver Max McGee

I wouldn't be here today if Vince Lombardi was alive because Vince and Paul had a very great personal relationship as well as football relationship. And Vince would run me off and he would make this presentation.

Vince once made a statement that I think signifies what Paul really is. He said, "When the game is on the line, Paul Hornung is the greatest player I ever saw."

And by gosh, I believe it.

Paul Hornung

I have waited a long time to get here. This weekend I will be able to take with me forever.

It started off in my hometown of Louisville on Thursday and is continuing on, forever. I don't have time to thank all my friends, my former coaches, and my former teammates, but I do want to thank a little lady for encouraging a youngster to play football. She got mad when I came in a little late sometimes and she is here today. This is just as important for my little mother, who raised me all by herself.

And as Max said—Lombardi. He meant a lot to all of us. For Paul Hornung, he probably meant a lot more than he did to the other inductees.

I have always said there are ten inductees in the Hall of Fame from that Green Bay Packer team, but there are only two athletes off that team that would have been in the Hall of Fame if they played for the New Orleans Saints, the New York Giants, the Kansas City Chiefs, any team anywhere. Herb Adderley and Forrest Gregg were those two athletes. They were that good.

But the rest of us, including Nitschke, needed Lombardi. Taylor needed him, Starr needed him, but above all, Hornung needed him. I think he would be a very happy man today.

I saw young Vince two days ago and as the years go by, he is a spitting image. We love Lombardi. It was a special time and a special team. There was a genuine love on that football team and I was glad to be a part of it. . . .

And I want to thank my little wife, Angela, who I married and got me off the streets, thank God. If she ever puts me back on them, I'll kill her. She was Mike McCormack's secretary at the Philadelphia Eagles, and she also knows about football. She knows what it is like to be hired and fired in professional football. She has been a great inspiration to me and she will be until the day I die.

And last, again, I want to thank Vince for the weather.

■　■　■　■

Henry Jordan
Cleveland Browns and
Green Bay Packers Defensive Tackle
Class of 1995

A fixture at defensive tackle during the Packers dynasty, Jordan played in four Pro Bowls, seven NFL title games, and Super Bowls I and II.

Presented by Friend Don Kovach

One of Jordan's many renowned public quips was he played professional football for three reasons: the love of the game, the love of money, and the fear of Vince Lombardi.

His love of football was self-evident. His reference to the love of money was in typical Jordan fashion—a not-so-subtle reference to the fact that all those who have been honored here before, and those that will follow, understand the concept of professionalism. Henry understood that winning wasn't everything, but the only thing. Winning determined the size of your paycheck.

He made it known to his teammates and his coaches that in the field of professional football, not taking care of business affected each team member's pocketbook. Henry would have nothing less than absolute commitment from himself and the other Packer team members. He was the quintessential professional.

His reference to the fear of Vince Lombardi would have been more appropriately phrased as a deep respect for his responsibility as a head coach of a championship team and the manner in which he fulfilled those responsibilities. To be effective he knew that Lombardi needed unflagging respect from his players. Henry gained Lombardi's respect as well.

Few people knew that Henry walked out of preseason camp one year not because of salary but because he was dissatisfied with the way that Lombardi was treating him. He believed that the coach should have known that Henry was the one man on the Packers' squad that knew what was going on in the lives of the various team members and how it affected the team's performance—things that the coach didn't know but which Henry would address on and off the field in his own way.

History tells us that Jordan returned to the camp having won the respect few people have attained. Lombardi treated Jordan differently.

Accepting on Behalf of Henry Jordan,
His Son, Henry Jordan Jr.

My sisters and I have grown up feeling that the men that have played football with my dad are extended uncles to our family, and that if at anytime we needed anything—anything—they would be there. And I know I share these feelings with many Packer children today. This was a top-down philosophy driven home by Coach Lombardi himself.

Coach Lombardi used to say as a player you have only three things to worry about: religion, family, and the Green Bay Packers—not necessarily in that order. I think he came to instill in them that your family and the Packers were one and the same. And that quality of discipline and unity is what made the difference when the chips were down.

Coach Lombardi, thank you for promoting an environment that allowed my dad to maximize and hone his God-given skills and then on Sundays, letting him have the stage to show those gifts to the world.

CHAPTER 10

PERSEVERANCE

GALE SAYERS
AND GEORGE HALAS

LIKE ANY PERSON IN ANY FIELD, EACH HALL-OF-FAME
player faced obstacles that, at times, seemed insurmountable.

Many stumbled, on and off the field. Just as many were thrown for
a loss, in and out of the game. Almost all were bloodied at one point

or another, only to battle on the way Hall-of-Fame players, and the most accomplished of people, do.

Though they beat the odds to get to the NFL, and beat even greater odds to get to the Pro Football Hall of Fame, their stories and their backgrounds in many ways do not seem all that different from anyone else's. Yet somewhere along the way, a parent helped them, a coach guided them, a thought inspired them, and their will drove them to overcome and to succeed. They recognized that, for all the demands placed upon them, they also were provided many strengths.

And at times of crisis, at moments of doubt, they maximized them. They persevered.

■　■　■　■

Gale Sayers
Chicago Bears Running Back
Class of 1977

In his rookie year in 1965, Sayers scored a rookie record twenty-two touchdowns. He led the league in rushing in 1966 and 1969, and was the MVP of three Pro Bowls.

Presented by Bears Coach George Halas

For me and for you, Canton is the birthplace of the National Football League. The date—September 17, 1920—the place Ralph Hay's auto engines agency, seventeen men representing seven clubs who had unheard of dreams for their child. Since that day and until today, July 30, 1977, it has been the most priceless privilege of my professional life to see our dreams come true and to watch our ugly duckling develop into a magnificent eagle.

For this privilege I thank the men of football, men who were and are very special men, who have no equal. Today it is a pleasure to offer my congratulations of the Chicago Bears to Frank Gifford, Forrest Gregg, Bart Starr, and Bill Willis, who join the ranks of those who made our dreams come true.

Now I will tell you publicly that each of you did your job so well that you were the cause of many sleepless nights for me as you helped defeat my beloved Bears. I have caught up now with my sleep and will remember only how pleased I am to share this occasion with you.

Now may I take a few moments to tell you about your fellow enshrine that not only helped make our dreams come true but who also captured my heart, Gale Sayers. Gale Sayers, magic in motion.

The first time I saw Gale Sayers was on film when my assistant had some Kansas University highlights and we watched them over and over again and I was puzzled. I could not believe what I had seen. I knew I was not watching Red Grange. I knew I was not watching George McAfee. I knew I was watching someone special. And I was watching someone I wanted very much with the Bears, but it wasn't easy. Lamar Hunt also had the rights to Gale and that was a pretty tough assignment. But luck was with us.

When I first met Gale, I was impressed with the man. In practice, he went 100 percent. In run plays, he always ran the entire distance to the opposite goal. His teammates admired and respected him because he was always razor sharp physically. Gale recognized that his inherited skills would mean very little without the help of the blockers and he continually expressed his gratitude to them.

If you wish to see perfection as a running back, you had best get a hold of a film of Gale Sayers. He was poetry in motion. His like will never be seen again. Gale Sayers is thirty-four, athletic director of Southern Illinois University. Gale is the youngest player ever to be inducted into the Hall of Fame. With a captured heart and a voice of love, I proudly present for induction into the Hall of Fame, Gale Sayers.

Gale Sayers

God gave me a great gift and I had a lot of help developing for this occasion. Reaching this point, however, is not as important as striving to get here. This is true in all professions and all of life's activities. There are doctors, lawyers, schoolteachers, plumbers, all who strive to do their very best with their abilities.

We hear a lot today about how the American people have lost their dedication to excel. I don't believe that is true. Each of us excels at different things, sometimes in areas that are only a hobby, more often in our life vocation. The most important thing, however, is to strive to do our very best. Nothing is more of a waste than unrealized potential. Sometimes failure to use one's talents to the fullest is often the fault of the individual. Nothing could be more tragic.

I am sure many of you have been to a Special Olympics, and if you have, I am sure you have felt the same exhilaration I have felt in watching young people with disabilities strive as hard as they can in various events. The sense of satisfaction they get from striving is, to them, much more important than where they finish in the competition.

As Robert Browning said, "A man's reach should exceed his grasp." It is aspiring to reach a goal that is important, and if you should reach that goal, set new goals and strive for them.

A longtime basketball coach at the University of Kansas, Dr. Phog Allen, was once asked what was your best team. He responded by saying, "Ask me in twenty-five years and let me see what they have done in their life."

It is not enough to rest on yesterday's triumphs, but to continually strive for new goals and accomplishments. I hope that when we look back twenty-five years from now, we can see this not as a zenith of our accomplishments but as a milestone in a life of striving for excellence, striving for even more distant goals.

■ ■ ■ ■

Emlen Tunnell
New York Giants and Green Bay Packers Safety
Class of 1967

Tunnell intercepted seventy-nine passes and gained more yards on kickoff, punt, and interception returns (924) in 1952 than the NFL's rushing leader.

Presented by Giants Team Chaplain,
Reverend Benedict Dudley

Someone asked me whether or not I ever played the game. I'll be perfectly truthful: Looking back on it now and standing here in the Hall of Fame, I wish I had played football. But I had a very deep religious conviction when I was growing up which kept me from playing the game; I was a very devout coward.

Just about twenty years ago come next spring, I was in the New York Giants' football office, which was then on West Forty-second Street, with a man whom I cherished as the closest friend that I've ever had, who's in the Hall of Fame now and went in with the first inductees, Tim Mara. And I remember that day in the spring when a fella came in the office, said that he had not been drafted by any team in the National Football League, and he wanted to know whether or not he could get a tryout with the New York Giants.

In the beginning, the Maras, Tim and his two sons, Jack and Wellington, probably were not too enthusiastic. Tim didn't know anything about football. Of course, he was a man capable of good judgment, particularly when this young fellow said that he had hitchhiked his way over to New York from Philadelphia. He said that if he didn't get a contract from the Giants, he didn't have any money to go back home again. They gave him a chance and here we are just a little more than nineteen years later.

He did many things. He was a great football player because he had tremendous desire. He had great dedication, and he was willing to pay the price with discipline. I would present him as all of the other gentlemen who have gone in this morning can be presented—not just as a football player but as a wonderful human being with a great big heart for others. In fact, I've never heard him condemn anyone. Somehow or other he has a way of understanding everyone with whom he has ever come into contact with and saying something nice about someone. I wish that I had found perfection of charity in my early years quite as easily and as completely as he has found it.

Emlen Tunnell

I'd like to thank the Mara family that was so nice to give me a chance to play the game that I liked. I guess it goes a little bit beyond like; it's love. And before I get a little choked up here, I'd like to thank the truck driver, wherever he is, that gave me the ride over to New York.

■ ■ ■ ■

Merlin Olsen
Los Angeles Rams Defensive Tackle
Class of 1982

A member of the "Fearsome Foursome," Olsen was named to fourteen consecutive Pro Bowls and the Rams' All-Time Team. My flower is wilting. I have been sitting, searching for a few words, and one of the words that came rather quickly was *improbable.* How very improbable it would be to look back at the course that would bring me here today.

I wanted to be an athlete; that was a desire I carried from a very young age. Unfortunately with feet and hands that didn't quite match the rest of the body, and the ability to fall down on flat sidewalks, I was not very impressive to my coaches. In fact, although my name was on the sign-up sheet usually first or shortly thereafter, I was also one of the first cut from all those teams.

And things got so bad finally in the ninth grade, my junior high school coach pulled me aside and said, "Merlin, why are you doing this to yourself? Why don't you use this energy and apply it to some other field? Go work on the school paper. Find a place to use this energy because our job here at the junior high school is to develop athletes for the high school—and you are never going to be an athlete. Just let it go."

Well, I have to say I didn't always listen to my coaches, and there are some of them back here, and thank goodness I didn't or I would have never had a chance to make it to Canton.

In order to be here, there had to be great commitment not only of physical assets but of mind and emotion. Commitments that often take a very heavy toll on family. I think much of the honor that we share here on the stage today should be handed out to the special members of our family who are here with us.

I don't know how football wives, wives of professional athletes, put up with some of the things that they have to put up with. To be sitting trying to chat with your husband at a restaurant and suddenly an arm goes in front of your face, and your fork is stuck out here, and you realize that someone has just come to get an autograph, not even knowing that you are there. . . .

My mom is a great lady. She came to my first college game, and actually, the first time she saw me play, someone wacked me in the nose and I had a nose bleed that was just buckets of blood pouring down my face before I knew what happened. My father had to grab her as she was coming out of the stands. And I am not sure if she was coming to help me or take on the guy who had hit me.

To know that there were so many people who cared that I was here today, it gives me a feeling that is truly uplifting and special. I love the game of football. I liked playing the game—more than liked playing the game. There was some special magic out on that piece of grass out there on that field. And win or lose when I came off the field, it was always coming down.

I am sure that the thing I miss most about the game is the people, the very special people, and those incredible highs and lows. You can imagine being at the top of the world one minute and down in the cellar the next. Compress that kind of emotion in one brief span and you have the roller coaster life of a professional football player.

But it is a life you come to love, you share with friends, and I don't doubt for a minute that if you could find a time capsule, today's enshrinees would jump in quickly, go back and put on our twenty-year-old bodies, race over and grab the first jersey and helmet we could find, and enjoy—even in this heat—having the chance to once more play the game.

■　■　■　■

Sam Huff
New York Giants and
Washington Redskins Linebacker
Class of 1982

Huff intercepted thirty passes, played in six NFL title games, five Pro Bowls, and was the Redskins' player-coach in 1969.

Presented by Giants Assistant Coach and
Cowboys Head Coach Tom Landry

My first glance of Sam Huff was in 1956, when he reported to our New York Giants training camp in Winooski, Vermont. At that time, he was a six-foot-one, 230-pound offensive and defensive lineman. He looked like a young, baby-faced athlete with a soft-looking body. I was not too impressed when I first saw him.

So it wasn't surprising to see him pack his bags and head for the airport after a few days in training camp. But fortunately, the late Vince Lombardi intercepted him and persuaded him to come back. And I tell you, that was the smartest decision Sam ever made.

I figured then he was probably intelligent enough to play middle linebacker for us. But Sam was a very dedicated player and good student of the game. I never had any trouble with him. Anytime he started to goof off, I gave him two choices—he either straighten up his act or go back to the coal mines of West Virginia.

You know, it's amazing how quick he straightened up.

Sam Huff

Now here is something I would like to share with you about a football player:

You can criticize him, but you can't discourage him. You can defeat his team, but you can't make him quit. You can get him out of a game, but you can't get him out of football. He is your personal representative on the field, your symbol of fair and hard play.

He may not be an All-American, but he is an example of the American way. He is judged not for his race, nor for his social standing, not for his finances, but by the democratic yardstick of how well he blocks, tackles, and sacrifices individual glory for the overall success of his team. He is a hardworking, untiring, determined kid, doing the very best he can for his team.

And when you come out of the stadium, disappointed and feeling upset that your team has lost, he can make you feel mighty ashamed with just two sincerely spoken words—*we tried*.

■　■　■　■

George Musso
Chicago Bears Guard and Tackle
Class of 1982

Musso became the first player to achieve All-NFL status at two positions—tackle in 1935 and guard in 1937.

A lot of you see me walking with a cane and having people help me. I want you to know that this didn't have a thing to do with football.

Twenty years ago I was in a head-on accident in Illinois. I was going to an old-pro meeting in St. Louis, and someone made a mistake and went around a truck and hit one of my old teammates. Bill Butler from Alabama and I were going over to a pro football meeting at a place called the Hill, which is an Italian area over at St. Louis. Well, we never made it.

It put me in the hospital with fifty-four broken bones. Both my legs were broken, my knees, my chest, my back, one ankle, and a break down below the knee. I was unconscious for five weeks and was not expected to live. When I finally awakened, my legs were just hanging there in a state of ropes and wires. I just couldn't believe it. But that didn't stop me. I just made up my mind that wouldn't stop me and within five and a half months, I did get out of there, using walkers and canes. I was out of there and finally went home and took a lot of therapy, and that is why I use the cane.

The first time I met Mr. Halas was in the spring of 1933. I was in Millikin University in Decatur, Illinois, and I had received a letter from the Chicago Bears. In the letter it said that he would like to see me, he would like for me to come up and have a tryout with the Bears. Enclosed was a $5 check with a note that said, "This $5 check will take care of your $3 train fare from Decatur to Chicago on the Wabash, and there will be $2 for incidentals."

Well, that was about the largest bonus I have ever gotten and I think it was hard back in those days for even Halas to mail me the $5 because in 1933, he still owed some of the boys in 1932. I was fortunate to get that $5.

I went on to work twelve years for Mr. Halas and his ball club. One thing about Halas, he was fair, he was honest, he is a man of his word and a great coach and a great businessman. He had all the qualities. He saw way back when—and he told a few of us fellows—that football was going to be larger than baseball. And we are about there now.

I remember back in those years we played the kind of football your Canton Bulldogs played—rough, tough, get out there and play. Played sixty minutes and, of course, Halas wanted to try to make gentlemen out of some of us. You know a lot of them liked to go on the train and go into the other big cities with just shirts and short sleeves, but Mr. Halas put down a rule.

He said, "When we travel, we are going with coats and ties. If we go on trains, we go with coats and ties, when we go into the hotels we have coats and ties." And he was building all the time. He could see this from way back, and he had, of course, in this amount of time, changed some of the rules about college ballplayers not being able to go ahead and to sign until after their class had graduated.

I don't think we would have this today if it wouldn't have been for Mr. Halas, Art Rooney, Tim Mara, Curly Lambeau, and George

Marshall. If Halas hadn't gotten all these fellows together and kept this league going, it wouldn't be here. A lot of them had to go out and borrow money like he did, even Charley Bidwill in Chicago. I think Charley was a good friend of Halas, and a millionaire in Chicago, and I think Halas could talk him out of anything he wanted. I think that was how he kept the Bears going.

Here I am before you and I am going into the Hall of Fame and there is nothing greater in anyone's life than to finally finish in a sport that he has participated in and to go as high as he can go. And I think one thing that I am proud of and honored for is my wife and three daughters and my twelve grandchildren, all sitting out here. My wife, Pauline, we will be married forty-six years in December, and we have gotten along pretty good all these years. Of course, we never argue because when we start, I take a walk and go outside. I spend a lot of time outside.

■　■　■　■

Paul Warfield
Cleveland Browns and
Miami Dolphins Wide Receiver
Class of 1983

An eight-time Pro Bowl player and a key to Cleveland and Miami's offenses, Warfield caught passes worth 8,565 yards and eighty-five touchdowns.

Presented by Warren Harding High School (Ohio)
Coach Gene Slaughter

After spending thirty-three years of my life as a coach, I have come to realize that coaching is nothing more than a series of experiences. But if you are lucky, there will be an experience that will be the ultimate of all those things. Today I have reached my ultimate experience.

Paul Warfield—All-State, All-Ohio, All-American, All-Pro, and the finest player I have ever coached and the most feared receiver of all times—is brought to this dais.

Wherever this young man played he always contributed to the greatest of the game with his unparalleled skill. He brought dignity and respect to, and for, himself, and when the moment had arrived, Paul gave all he had. Paul, your hallmark of faith and dignity, your pride and humility, have made you what you are in this day of turmoil and cynicism. You have all the characteristics that young and old should look up and hold high before America.

Paul Warfield

It is awesome when I reflect back from where I came from. Twenty-five years ago, it is almost ironic that just a few hundred yards from here, over there in that stadium right there, that I really came to the crossroads of my very young career.

I was just a second-year football player at Warren Harding High School, and the previous week of my very first game, I sustained a number of bumps and bruises. I wasn't quite sure that football was worth enduring with all its aggravations, bumps, and bruises, but nevertheless, I was able to get through the following week. And then on a Friday night some twenty-five years ago, a wonderful thing happened to me at Fawcett Stadium. Gene Slaughter called my number numerous times that night and I had a very productive evening.

Suddenly, those bumps and bruises really didn't matter. Suddenly, I knew this was a game I wanted to pursue. I knew that I wanted to stay in football and stay involved.

That was a very valuable lesson that I learned right there at a young age. I learned that there is going to be a little pain and sometimes a little suffering in what we want, and sometimes we have to have the conviction and perseverance to stay with it. Little did I know twenty-five years ago that when I walked out of that stadium, that at a later date, today's date, I would be standing on the platform before you.

Gene Slaughter had a very positive impact on me as a young junior high school student in search of possible football success. Gene Slaughter came to our junior high school in the spring of 1957 and he talked to all of the young athletes who were there. I got the very distinct impression he was talking with me individually, and what he had to say to me that day made me only want to be a part of what he was going to be a part of at Warren Harding High School.

I wanted to please Gene Slaughter. I worked to become the kind of football player and individual that Gene Slaughter wanted his players to become. Gene Slaughter said the kind of things that were important for the community. He told us that we were highly visible. He told us we had to be just as good in the classroom as we were on the field of play. He told us we had an ultimate responsibility to be good citizens of the school and good citizens of the community. It was no small wonder that we were successful on the field and it was no small wonder that my teammates were successful off the field.

Then came the privilege of joining one of the legendary coaches in all of college football, Woody Hayes. It was a tremendous experience for me to play for him for three years at Ohio State University. I learned more than just blocking and passing down there, and Woody Hayes saw it as his mission to develop young men, not just develop players for the NFL.

He stressed the same things that Gene Slaughter stressed. He stressed the fact that we were there at the university first as students, secondly as football players. It is no small wonder that this man would stop two days before the Michigan game and talk to us not about game plans, not about how we were going to compete against Michigan, but talk to us about what we were doing in school, how our families were doing, and whether we were measuring up to those standards. I respected Woody Hayes for that. All of his former players respected him for that. He was a man with great integrity, tremendous honesty, and, above all else, great compassion. Those are qualities you have to look up to.

The lessons I have learned regarding character, sportsmanship, and humility come from the great coaches. They come from family. And they have given me a sense, I believe, of commitment—commitment to dedicate my ability as a player and commitment to striving for excellence.

So I say to many of the young people who are out there in the audience today, it is a great experience to have played in competitive sports and to have played in the NFL. The vital lesson that I have learned, and I think many of the athletes have learned, is no different to lessons that are learned in life itself.

There are day-to-day struggles. There are times in which we fail. There are times in which we must learn to get up off the gutter. Life is not going to be one smooth road. It is not going to be easy, and consequently, if you have that reserve from your experiences you can draw from, the chances are you will meet with success.

■ ■ ■ ■

Larry Csonka
Miami Dolphins and New York Giants Running Back
Class of 1987

The MVP of Super Bowl VIII, Csonka rushed for 8,081 yards and scored sixty-eight touchdowns during a career in which he fumbled only twenty-one times on 1,891 carries.

Presented by Colts and Dolphins Coach Don Shula

I once called him the modern-day Nagurski. What separates Larry from some of the game's other greats is his superior competitive instincts and his love for playing football the old-fashioned way. He was blood and guts, dirt all over him, never leaving the game.

In his career—high school, college, and the pros—he had twelve broken noses. He just recently had it fixed; you will see how handsome he is when he gets up here.

Larry Csonka

Coach Fortner came to the gym to see me in my sophomore year and move me to fullback into my junior year, and he helped me make a very large decision. We all went out for the grass drill on our first day of practice, an August day much like this, and he was yelling at us. At the time, a red convertible went by the practice field and honked its horn. It was a friend of mine, and he had two long-haired blondes in his car and they were waving. At that time, Coach Fortner said, "Fellows, there it is. You can either be here doing this or there doing that. . . . Now hit the dirt!"

Everyone did except me. I had to think about it for a minute. And Fortner, like Shula, didn't hesitate to lose the momentum of the moment. He said, "Down, Csonka!"

Naturally I went down and stayed with it ever after.

■ ■ ■ ■

Len Dawson
Pittsburgh Steelers, Cleveland Browns, Dallas Texans, and Kansas City Chiefs Quarterback
Class of 1987

A four-time AFL passing champion, Dawson threw for 28,711 yards and 239 touchdowns.

Presented by Texans, Chiefs, and Saints Coach Hank Stram

When I think of Lenny, I think of family because I knew him way before I had a family. As my wife, Phyllis, often said, I spent more time with him than I did with our family of six. You know, she was probably right.

When I think of Lenny, I also think of honor, I think of class, I think of style, I think of grace, and I think of dignity.

When I think of Lenny, I think of winning because he played a dominant role in helping us become the winningest team in the history of the American Football League. We won four championships, a Super Bowl, and every big game there was to win.

When I think of Lenny, I think of leadership because he was a natural leader. He was captain of his Alliance football team, Purdue, the Dallas Texans, and the Kansas City Chiefs. He led by example, and the bigger the game, the better he played. He was our man of the moment. Greatness is measured by the test of time and Lenny passed that test with flying colors.

Len Dawson

I have been very, very fortunate. I am the seventh son of a seventh son. And all my life they said, "Hey, that's great—that's good luck."

In 1960–61, I had completed five years in the NFL and that was about the time you started building the Pro Football Hall of Fame. And I am sure if anyone would have asked at that time, "Don't you think Len Dawson might one day be here?" after they got up off the floor from laughing, they would say, "Why should he be? What has he done?"

But I am the seventh son of a seventh son. Things happen to me. A man in Dallas, Texas, by the name of Lamar Hunt had a dream. He wanted to get into professional football in a league called the AFL. And he had the good sense to hire Hank Stram as the coach. Hank Stram knew me at Purdue, as he had recruited me out of Alliance High School to attend Purdue. That was my saving grace.

Because to tell you the truth, I was awful after five years of not playing. The skills that I once had were gone. Had it not been for Hank Stram and knowing me, there would not have been a seventh look for the seventh son of a seventh son.

■　■　■　■

Joe Greene
Pittsburgh Steelers Defensive Tackle
Class of 1987

The NFL Defensive Player of the Year in 1972 and 1974, Greene was a four-time Super Bowl champion and played in ten Pro Bowls.

Presented by Steelers Coach Chuck Noll

As I look at all the enshrinees, there's no question that they have played the game physically. They are quick, they are strong, they do all things well. But the thing I think that sets Joe aside from everybody else is his attitude. It is something you don't do anything to get. It is something that you have; you have it deep down. He had all kinds of attitudes, but probably the best was, he wanted to play the game very badly.

Before his senior year, I was scouting with the Baltimore Colts, and I went through North Texas State, and I had the chance to watch Joe for three years, and the last time I had a chance to talk with him. There was no question, it just came through that this man wanted a professional football career. It was a very important thing to him, and that is a prime ingredient.

Joe Greene

As I reflect, I start thinking about high school, thinking about my high school coaches, Coach Elliott, Coach Moore. See I was the big guy around, but my heart wasn't as big as my body, and I really didn't want to play football. But they made me come out and play football. I want to thank them for not letting me quit when the weather got hot, the sprints hard, the work got devastating. I think it made me a tougher person.

Then there is Mr. [Art] Rooney, the Chief. No one can make you feel more welcome than the Chief—"Have a cigar, my boy!" You know, I still have the first one he gave me when I signed my contract at the Roosevelt Hotel. It may not smoke very good, but it sure does look good. He gave the organization the dignity and the class that it possesses.

And then there is the twelfth man. See you always need the twelfth man. In Pittsburgh, if you are not at the stadium at 1 p.m. on Sunday in the fall, you are at the wrong place. Pittsburgh, they are always there. Without the fans, it is something different. We certainly appreciate and love you for that. And you have impacted my life because you are important.

■　■　■　■

Don Maynard
New York Giants, New York Titans/Jets, and
St. Louis Cardinals Wide Receiver
Class of 1987

Maynard had at least fifty catches and one thousand receiving yards in five different seasons. He finished with 633 receptions for 11,834 yards and eighty-eight touchdowns.

Presented by Jets and Rams Quarterback Joe Namath

I will tell you about two games, and four plays, that stand out in my mind. We happened to be playing the same football team, a very good football team; they still are to this day. They were a tough rival of ours, even though they were all the way out in California—the Oakland Raiders. Nice bunch of guys—very tough football team.

Well, we were backed up on our own one-yard line. But Don had this wonderful knack of being able to go after the football, judging the flight and adjusting his speed. Even though we were on our own one-yard line, I called a "go" pattern, decided to go ahead and give Don a chance to make the play. Well, I just laid it out there with all the confidence in the world for Don being able to come down with the football. He did, for a fifty-one-yard gain, just like that.

He came back to the huddle and I said, "Hey, Don, how you feeling?" He said, "Shoot, Joe, I'm just fine." That's the way he talks, you see. I said, "You think you can do it again?" He said, "Hey, you go ahead and lay it out there. I'll go get it."

Well, he was right. Here we are, on the forty-nine-yard line, and I called the same play and another "go" pattern to Don. I just threw it up in the air, he made the judgment, went up after it, and stepped into the end zone for a touchdown. Two plays, ninety-nine yards. He made the plays.

A little while later we were playing for the AFL championship against a very good Oakland Raiders team. We had just fallen behind 23–20. I'm sitting on the bench, feeling mighty low because old Joe just threw the interception that set up the score. Don comes over to me, leans over, pats me on the shoulder, and said, "Now take it easy, Joe. Don't get down on yourself. Anytime you want it, I can get a step on that man, and you let me have it." Well, boy, he said that with so much confidence, it made me feel much better.

Sure enough we got up to the line of scrimmage, this defensive back climbed up on Don. I called the audible, a maximum protection pass play, dropped back to throw, and laid the ball out there. Don Maynard made one of the greatest catches of all time. And if you see it on film or have seen it on film, you will understand what I'm talking about. He made an over-the-shoulder catch, brought it in one-handed, and was knocked out of bounds on the six-yard line.

We had first and goal for the AFC championship. I figured the Raiders were going to count on a running play at the time, so I was going to outsmart them and call a play-action pass. Well, the Raiders were a little smarter than I figured. I faked an off left tackle run to [Matt] Snell, then I dropped back looking for George Sauer but he was covered, looked for Bill Mathis but he was covered, came back to big boy Pete Lammons but he was covered. And about that time, I saw that big number 13—Maynard—streaking across the back of the end zone.

Boy, I threw that thing as quick as I could, as fast as I could. It was a fastball, down low, and Don slid down there and cradled that ball and we all went on to the Super Bowl.

Don Maynard, he was the man our opponents worried about, the knockout punch, lightning in a bottle, nitro just waiting to explode. He could fly with the grace of a great Thoroughbred and he galloped through the very best football players of the world.

Don Maynard

You know it is really a shame that everyone can't experience the great enjoyment of life I have had here and there, especially from the first grade, where I rode a mule six miles to a school that had a one-room schoolhouse with six rows, and each row was a grade, and you had one teacher.

Yes, it is a long way to Canton, Ohio, even to New York City. I look out here and I see more people out there than in some towns I lived in. I looked up at the first brick building in New York, and it had more bricks than some of the towns that I lived in then.

I came to play and I came to stay.

Football was a game, Country Don was my name.

I made a mark and I became a star, with a lot of help from near and far.

There are good ones and great ones, I played with and against. Thank you, good Lord, for that wonderful chance.

As I played my part many times even late after dark, I don't have to look back as I played it with my heart.

The direction from where I came, resulted in a whole lot of fame.

I played the best and I believe I passed the test. I am glad this is over, I need some rest.

■　■　■　■

Buck Buchanan
Kansas City Chiefs Defensive Tackle
Class of 1990

During thirteen years in which he led the Chiefs to appearances in Super Bowls I and IV, Buchanan did not miss a game.

Presented by Chiefs and Saints Coach Hank Stram

Buck had it all. He had style, he had speed, he had quickness, and he had strength combined with the ability to lead. He was a constant team player who was infused with a great attitude. It didn't take long for Buck to earn front-page success as the premier defensive lineman in the AFL. He was exceptionally strong against the run and had the added dimension of being an excellent up-the-field rusher.

To highlight this point, he batted down sixteen passes at or behind the line of scrimmage in 1967. By this time, Buck had become such a dominant force that my good friend, Al Davis, was compelled to find someone with the kind of size and strength necessary to neutralize Buck. Consequently, the Raiders drafted Gene Upshaw in the opening round of the first AFL-NFL draft in 1967. And this became the most storied one-on-one rivalry in AFL history.

Gene sums up his respect for Buck by saying this: "I was big, but Buck was bigger and stronger. It was hard to believe that someone so big could be so quick. It was like trying to block a goalpost. For the most part, I enjoyed playing against the other guys, but when I played against Buchanan, I couldn't sleep the night before."

And Gene, after watching all those films we watched, it was obvious that you spent more time holding Buck than you did your wife.

Buck Buchanan

I would like this bronze bust to serve as a greater purpose than a testimony to my football career. I sincerely hope this will stand as a symbol of inspiration to all young people where hard work and honest effort can take you. Being consistent in your work and never quitting until you have reached the finish line will bring you the desired results. Today I am thankful I am able to cross the finish line.

To the young people in all walks of life may I say, "Never give up your hopes and dreams of success."

■ ■ ■ ■

Jan Stenerud
Kansas City Chiefs, Green Bay Packers, and Minnesota Vikings Kicker
Class of 1991

The first pure placekicker to enter the Hall of Fame, Stenerud scored 1,699 points on 580 extra points and 373 field goals.
Nearly thirty years ago, I was recruited from Norway to Montana

State on a ski scholarship. One autumn afternoon my junior year in 1964, I did something that would dramatically change my life forever. I attempted to kick a football a couple of times.

To keep in shape for ski season, I would always run the stadium steps at Montana State to get ready for the long, hard ski season. And the football team was always practicing. And this one day, I decided to go down and kick a few footballs. As a youth in Norway, I had played a lot of soccer and I guess I had an urge to try this oval ball. I went down and tried a few using my toes, the way everybody else kicked those days. All of a sudden, I realized if I approached this ball at an angle and hit it with the side of my foot, it was more comfortable for me. I did, and the basketball coach, Roger Craft, had observed me and ran over to the football coach, Jim Sweeney, and informed him that a ski jumper was kicking the hell out of the ball out there.

A couple of weeks later, while I was running the stadium steps, Coach Sweeney summoned me down from the stands. He asked if I could kick off and showed me how to put the ball on the tee. I kicked off five times and two of them went through the goalpost—and that was from the forty-yard line in those days, seventy yards away. I wasn't really sure if I had done okay or not. But I guess I did because Coach Sweeney tried to convince me to go out for spring football the next year, which I did.

It is undeniable that a kicker's position is isolated and that the skills that are necessary to become an outstanding kicker are different from those skills required to play most other positions. It is a job with intense pressure. I always felt if I had two bad games, I would be unemployed.

Let me close by going back to where it started . . . ski jumping. When you get off that ramp and you fly through the air for a moment, you feel as though you have conquered the world as you are soaring high above the ground. Today with these memories, and this honor, I got the same feeling—the feeling that my feet are not touching the ground.

■ ■ ■ ■

Larry Little
San Diego Chargers and Miami Dolphins Guard
Class of 1993

The anchor of the Dolphins' powerful rushing attack in the 1970s, Little was voted to five Pro Bowls and started three Super Bowls.

Presented by Colts and Dolphins Coach Don Shula

No one was more misnamed than Larry Little. He wasn't little; he was a giant in his profession and the first right guard and only the third guard overall to be voted into the Hall of Fame.

He was a local product who made good. Growing up near the shadow of the Orange Bowl, when he finally made it as a player on that field, he cast a shadow of his own that symbolized the desire and determination of the great Dolphin teams. It was an honor to coach a player with heart, intensity, and the will to win.

Larry Little

I remember sitting all those Saturdays and watching these programs or inductions, and visualizing me being up here one day making my Hall-of-Fame speech. It is rewarding for the way I came into the league. It is especially rewarding because I wasn't drafted, receiving a $750 bonus. Just being in the league and getting the opportunity to play was quite an honor, so I didn't care how much money I made. I just wanted to have an opportunity.

Football prepared me for so many things in life—how to deal with the peaks and valleys, the bitter with the sweet, self-motivation, and believing in myself and working with others. When I first went out for football at Booker T. Washington High School in Miami, I was in the ninth grade and only thirteen years old. I know I probably would have been voted the most unlikely to succeed. I was so bad I didn't get equipment until the season started. But I was only a ninth grader.

I had a friend of mine named Joe Walker who was a blind deejay in Atlanta, Georgia, who made a statement at the end of his show every week: "A winner never quits and a quitter never wins," and I took that along with me because I knew I was going to be a winner.

■ ■ ■ ■

Dan Fouts
San Diego Chargers Quarterback
Class of 1993

A six-time Pro Bowl selection, Fouts threw for 43,040 yards and 254 touchdowns. He was the NFL's MVP in 1982.

It has been said that a football career is similar to a roller coaster ride. I have gone from a pro prospect, to a third-round selection, to a rookie quarterback, to a fledgling quarterback, to a struggling quarterback, to a promising signal caller, to All-Pro almost, to All-Pro, to Player of the Year, to potential Hall of Famer, to aging superstar, to ex-quarterback, to certain Hall of Famer, to be elected in the first year of eligibility.

This gold jacket, these steps, this Hall of Fame, and, as a roller coaster ride, it too has been thrilling.

■ ■ ■ ■

Mike Webster
Pittsburgh Steelers and Kansas City Chiefs Center
Class of 1997

During a seventeen-year career, Webster played in 245 games, nine Pro Bowls, and won four Super Bowls.

Presented by Steelers Quarterback Terry Bradshaw

When Mike called and asked me to present him today, I was in shock. Quite honestly, I didn't feel like I deserved this great honor, this great privilege that he has bestowed upon me. I actually said, "Why?" He said, "Who knows me better than you, Blond Bomber?"

So I had to put together some thoughts about Mike Webster, and I got to thinking, when I was a child, I had a dream. Everybody here has dreamed. All of you out here at some point in time in your life sat down and had a dream. And whether or not it came true mattered not. But the fact that you had a purpose in your life and something to get up and try every day was all you needed.

My dream was this: I want to play in the National Football League. So finally, after I had this dream, I said, "What's it going to be like, Terry. What's it going to be like?" I said, "Well, first of all, I got to have me a great offense. I got to have somebody that can run down the field, and when I throw it up in the air, there will be number 88 catching all these passes."

Then I said, "I got one guy on the right. I got to have a receiver on the left to complement that tiny little number 88." So he sent me a guy out of Alabama A&M, John Stallworth, who makes great catches.

Then I said, "If we're going to have all these great people, we got to have somebody to run the football. So give me a fullback out of Penn State, isn't that right?" And if he's going to be a great one, you got to have a nickname. We'll call him the "Italian Stallion." Franco Harris, inducted into the Hall of Fame, was our fullback. He ran the traps.

And I sat back and took a look at my dream and I said, "Ah, this is good!" Now give me a defense that can stop all this offense, and give them a nickname 'cause you win with defense in the NFL. You got to have a nickname—"Steel Curtain." And then the dream was complete. I had a great owner in Art Rooney; I had a great coach in Chuck Noll.

What good is a machine if you ain't got a center? And oh, did I get a center! I just didn't get any old center. No siree, I got the best that's ever played the game, ever put his hands down on a football.

And I said to my dream, "If you're going to give me this guy, make sure he ain't as pretty as me," and he ain't. I said, "Make him six-foot-two, make him 250 pounds out of Tomahawk, Wisconsin."

Drafted in the fifth round, 1974, he was the only center I ever saw the first time that my arms actually were bigger than his. I loved him from the very first moment I put my hands under his butt.

He was the total package. He could get down low and squat under a nose tackle. We didn't have to double-team with him because he was strong, he was quick—quickest hands you ever saw—move right, move left, the man was outstanding. Nobody has ever compared to Mike Webster.

I turned him on to Jimmy Dean Hot Pork Sausage. I taught him how to scramble eggs with whole butter. Taught him what apple butter was on toast, and he sat by me every Sunday morning as I went through my game plan 'cause he knew I couldn't read real well and he helped me every Sunday morning. I showed him what buttermilk tasted like, and he drank a gallon of it every Sunday morning on game day.

I said, "Dream, give me a winner. Give me somebody I can count on. Give me somebody I can talk to. Give me somebody that'll help me in a game, somebody that'll tell me, 'Terry, no, don't run this play.' Somebody to help me with the slide calls." Mike did. Someone to help me with max protection, Mike did. Mike controlled it. Mike ran it. We needed him, we used him, we leaned on him. He was the strength in our offense.

There has never been, or there ever will be, another man as committed, as totally dedicated to making himself the very best that he could possibly be. He was the backbone of our offense, our spine.

There never has been and never will be another Mike Webster—Mike Lewis Webster. I love this man, I always have. He is dear and precious to us all. Ladies and gentlemen, the last time I was here in 1989, I said this: "Just one more time, let me put my hands under Mike Webster's butt! Just one more time! Let me take that snap! Are you ready? Are you ready, Mike?"

Mike Webster

I was no ballerina out there. I wasn't pretentious and I worked hard because I was scared. I was scared I'd fail, honest to God, I was scared I'd fail. And I'm still scared of that. Because that's the motivator that we go through. And the failure I'm talking about is the failure to be the very best that we have been given the talent to be and are accountable for.

But in a lot of ways, ladies and gentlemen, we are the same. We have the same fears, we have the same desires, we have the same temptations. But it is important to be truthful with ourselves so we understand them. And as a football player, you embarrass yourself a lot of times. I mean, over and over and over again. I've embarrassed myself over and over and over again, and I admit it.

But you know what? If I concentrated or tried to concentrate and worked every second, twenty-four hours a day for every moment of my life not to do it, I'd still embarrass myself. And I'd still make mistakes and screw up, but that's okay. And it's okay for other people to do that. And if you do that and if you realize that, then you can make progress. Then you can be willing to go forward and attempt things and learn what life's really all about.

■　■　■　■

Lawrence Taylor
New York Giants Linebacker
Class of 1999

A ten-time Pro Bowl selection, Taylor redefined the position of outside linebacker.

Presented by His Son, Lawrence Taylor Jr.

My father wants the best for me just as his parents wanted the best for him growing up in Williamsburg, Virginia. I would like to say thank you to my father for being there for me and never letting me settle for less.

And even though he might not admit it, I thank Ron Jaworski for making my father what he is because without him, he probably would never have broken that sack record.

Lawrence Taylor

People ask me all the time, "Well, the Hall of Fame—you're in the Hall of Fame. What do you want to leave to other people? What do you want other people to remember? What kind of legacy do you want to leave behind?"

And I thought about that. And it's indeed a great honor to be here. But the thing I want to leave all the people is that, life, like anything else, can knock you down. It can tune you out. You'll have problems every day in your life. But sometimes, sometimes you just got to go play. You just got to go play.

And no matter how many times it knocks you down, no matter how many times you think you can't go forward, no matter how many times things just don't go right, you can't quit. Anybody can quit. Anybody can do that. A Hall of Famer never quits.

A Hall of Famer realizes that the crime is not being knocked down; the crime is not getting up again.

■　■　■　■

Jackie Slater
Los Angeles/St. Louis Rams Offensive Tackle
Class of 2001

A seven-time Pro Bowl selection, Slater blocked for seven differ-ent one-thousand-yard rushers. He played twenty seasons and 259 games.

Presented by Rams Coach John Robinson

After about three or four years in the league, Jackie decided to become a great football player. Becoming great for him was not going to be a sudden flash of brilliance or some unbelievable number of yards. It was down and dirty, play after play after play. His work habits were always good, but suddenly they seemed to become almost fanatical. When all the rest of us were going home, you could see Jackie out there working on that backstep.

Jackie Slater

January 7, 1990, Michael Martinez wrote in the *New York Times:* "There is no glamour down there. It is dirt and grass stains, grunt-ing and grabbing, a sea of arms and feet, and numbers—a pile of bodies. It is everything about football and yet nothing. From autumn till winter, the game is played on the line, a place where the strong and the strong-willed survive. Or where careers are seemingly lost in a blink."

You know, functioning in an environment of organized chaos was a way of life for me for twenty years and I wouldn't have had it any other way. I loved it. . . .

The theme of the Hall of Fame this year is about dreaming. Today is also a confirmation that if you have a dream, you should let no person, place, or thing discourage you from trying to accomplish your dreams.

You see, in 1976, I want to share with you that I left Jackson State University and I went to Skokie, Illinois, to play in what then was the college all-star game, the last one they had. And I was a small school boy and when I got there, I found out that I was third-string left tackle, and third-string left guard, and all the way across the line of scrimmage, I was third string. But I was, first and foremost, step it and fetch it.

"Slater, we need some papers. Can you run down there and get those papers? We're out of pencils, Slater. Can you go and get some pencils for the guys? On the football field, Slater, we need the bags. Could you drag them up here so we can do some drills and hit them?" I made up my mind at that time that I would always do the things that would give me a chance to be a great football player and not a step it and fetch it in the National Football League.

In closing, I would like to simply say these are the words that I pretty much lived by for twenty years. A wise man said, "There's nothing better under the sun for a man to do than to eat, to drink, and to tell himself that his work is good." I like to think my work was good and I would like to thank you for telling me that.

■　■　■　■

John Stallworth
Pittsburgh Steelers Wide Receiver
Class of 2002

Stallworth scored the go-ahead touchdown in Super Bowl XIV on a seventy-three-yard reception. He finished his career with 537 receptions for 8,723 yards and sixty-three touchdowns.

Presented by His Son, John Stallworth Jr.

When I was five years old, I was in the Pittsburgh Steelers locker room, waiting for my dad, and a reporter came up to me and asked me, "Who's your favorite football player of all time?" With all the confidence in the world, I said, "Lynn Swann."

Today, to my dad and to everyone here, I'd like to correct that statement a little bit and say that my favorite player of all time is John Stallworth.

In preparation for this occasion, I was looking through some of my dad's old memorabilia and came across a *Sports Illustrated* issue in which the title of an article read, "The Stalwart"—spelled s-t-a-l-w-a-r-t—"of the Steelers." I had seen that article when I was younger and I remembered thinking, "My gosh, *Sports Illustrated* misspelled Stallworth." Of course they had not misspelled Stallworth. They had used an adjective meaning perseverance, being powerfully built, and being steadfast. And those three adjectives perfectly describe my father.

At the early age of five or six, my father was tested, his perseverance was tested, when he was paralyzed and told by the local physician that he had polio. Of course he didn't, but the doctor had told my father that he could never play football or walk again. But my dad's unquestionable spirit was apparent even at that young age. He was able to shrug off those inauspicious predictions and later become a captain of his high school football team, although in his senior year, they won only one game.

But my dad's dreams did not end there because he was able to go to Alabama A&M, and his dreams began to take flight. But John Stallworth is also a man that is powerfully built. I'm not talking about his physical strength; I'm talking about the strength of his character, his will, and his determination.

My father at Alabama A&M was playing defensive back and running back, positions that he didn't really feel comfortable in, positions that he felt his destiny could not be fulfilled. And at the time, Alabama A&M was not a passing offense, so he went to Coach Lewis Crews and asked to be put in a receiver position. Of course, he was met with a little speculation. But he felt his destiny would be made as a receiver and he was determined to become one.

So he came to practice earlier and he stayed later than all of his other teammates. And after seeing the records for touchdowns scored in a season, passes caught in a season, and leading his team to a conference title, he became All-American.

He had faced the limitations of a situation and soared over the doubts of others with pure determination. Vince Lombardi once said, "There's only one way to succeed in anything and that is to give everything. I firmly believe that any man's finest hour, his greatest fulfillment of all he holds dear, is the moment when he has worked his heart out in a good cause and lies exhausted on the field of battle—victorious."

Today my father is still a stalwart of life. I stand here with the pleasure to be a part of my dad's finest hour and to help him and others look back on the playing field of his life and to say yes, Dad, you are victorious. Ladies and gentlemen, it's my honor to present to you a stalwart of all-time, my dad, John Stallworth.

John Stallworth

Johnny spoke of a time in my childhood where I was paralyzed, and I came away from that time with a deep appreciation of joy of just running, an appreciation of how precious time is and awakening to the importance of relationships.

I had to deal with, at a young age, my own mortality. It was a constant thought for me, and the only way I could get rid of that thought or remove it was to be determined, commit myself to doing something to be remembered. That desire and those newfound appreciations have motivated me throughout my life.

I've learned that in every relationship there are opportunities to learn. I learned from my college teachers and my grade school teachers how effective we can be when we are passionate about our calling. From the folks of my childhood neighborhood, I have learned to persevere in difficult times. From my college coaches at Alabama A&M, I learned how you can still accomplish much with a small budget. From my church family, I've learned how a strong belief in God can see you through to the other side.

I've learned from Donnie Shell how to stay focused when everything around you demands your attention. From Chuck Noll, I've learned the meaning of true leadership. One aspect of that is to deny personal fame and glory for the sake of the team. From Franco Harris, I've learned how you treat people regardless of their status. From Jack Ham, I've learned that greatness doesn't have to promote itself. From L. C. Greenwood, I've learned a certain style, a certain grace. From Jack Lambert, I've learned about an unquenchable competitive nature. From Lynn Swann, how to perform in difficult situations. From Rocky Bleier, commitment; Mel Blount, benevolence; Bradshaw, perseverance; and Joe Greene, leadership style. I've learned from people around me all through my fourteen years in Pittsburgh.

I've learned that first impressions are not always correct. My first day in Pittsburgh was a midwinter night right after the draft. It was cold, the trees were barren, it was snowing, and I didn't bring a big coat from Alabama. I don't think I owned a big coat. And I was going to a team that didn't seem to be terribly interested in throwing the football, the kiss of death for a receiver. My first impression of that situation was this: it's not a good thing.

Eight months later, I arrived at the airport and caravanned into Pittsburgh after our first Super Bowl win. It was cold. The trees were equally as barren. It was snowing. But the difference was the people.

They were lining the highway from the airport all the way to the city, easily a twenty-minute drive. You would have thought it was midsummer. . . .

As you've heard, I've had some wonderful people in my life who have within them a tremendous capacity to do good. And they chose to exercise that capacity for my benefit. Family, friends, neighbors, coaches, and acquaintances and some people I will never know. Thank you for exercising your capacity to do good things for me. We all have that capacity. Some choose to exercise it, some choose not to, and I stand here because of some people that chose to.

I believe firmly that more of us need to exercise that capacity to do good things. Who knows, that recipient of your kindness may motivate a young person to become a Hall-of-Fame receiver, or maybe a truly committed schoolteacher, or maybe a youngster that might want to be a fireman, who may at some point have to make the choice of running into a burning skyscraper. Or maybe just a young lady who grows up to be the neighborhood Kool-Aid mom. Who knows? But this world needs us to try.

At a banquet not too long ago in Alabama, one of the recipients of an award made this statement: "Our talent is God's gift to us, and how we use that talent is our gift back to Him." I pray that God finds my gift back to Him a worthy one.

APPENDIX

ENSHRINEES BY YEAR OF INDUCTION

*Deceased
(Date of enshrinement in parentheses)

1963 CHARTER CLASS
(September 7, 1963)

Sammy Baugh*

Bert Bell*

Joe Carr*

Earl "Dutch" Clark*

Harold "Red" Grange*

George Halas*

Mel Hein*

Wilbur "Pete" Henry*

Robert "Cal" Hubbard*

Don Hutson*

Earl "Curly" Lambeau*

Tim Mara*

George Preston Marshall*

John "Blood" McNally*

Bronko Nagurski*
Ernie Nevers*
Jim Thorpe*

CLASS OF 1964
(September 6, 1964)

Jimmy Conzelman*
Ed Healey*
Clarke Hinkle*
William Roy "Link" Lyman*
Mike Michalske*
Art Rooney*
George Trafton*

CLASS OF 1965
(September 12, 1965)

Guy Chamberlin*
John "Paddy" Driscoll*
Dan Fortmann*
Otto Graham*
Sid Luckman*
Steve Van Buren
Bob Waterfield*

CLASS OF 1966
(September 17, 1966)

Bill Dudley
Joe Guyon*
Arnie Herber*
Walt Kiesling*
George McAfee*

Steve Owen*
Hugh "Shorty" Ray*
Clyde "Bulldog" Turner*

CLASS OF 1967
(August 5, 1967)

Chuck Bednarik
Charles W. Bidwill Sr.*
Paul Brown*
Bobby Layne*
Dan Reeves*
Ken Strong*
Joe Stydahar*
Emlen Tunnell*

CLASS OF 1968
(August 3, 1968)

Cliff Battles*
Art Donovan
Elroy "Crazylegs" Hirsch*
Wayne Millner*
Marion Motley*
Charley Trippi
Alex Wojciechowicz*

CLASS OF 1969
(September 13, 1969)

Albert Glen "Turk" Edwards*
Earle "Greasy" Neale*
Leo Nomellini*
Joe Perry
Ernie Stautner*

CLASS OF 1970
(August 8, 1970)

Jack Christiansen*
Tom Fears*
Hugh McElhenny
Pete Pihos

CLASS OF 1971
(July 31, 1971)

Jim Brown
Bill Hewitt*
Frank "Bruiser" Kinard*
Vince Lombardi*
Andy Robustelli
Y. A. Tittle
Norm Van Brocklin*

CLASS OF 1972
(July 29, 1972)

Lamar Hunt*
Gino Marchetti
Ollie Matson
Clarence "Ace" Parker

CLASS OF 1973
(July 28, 1973)

Raymond Berry
Jim Parker*
Joe Schmidt

CLASS OF 1974
(July 27, 1974)

Tony Canadeo*
Bill George*
Lou Groza*
Dick "Night Train" Lane*

CLASS OF 1975
(August 2, 1975)

Roosevelt Brown*
George Connor*
Dante Lavelli*
Lenny Moore

CLASS OF 1976
(July 24, 1976)

Ray Flaherty*
Len Ford*
Jim Taylor

CLASS OF 1977
(July 30, 1977)

Frank Gifford
Forrest Gregg
Gale Sayers
Bart Starr
Bill Willis*

CLASS OF 1978
(July 29, 1978)

Lance Alworth
Weeb Ewbank*
Alphonse "Tuffy" Leemans*
Ray Nitschke*
Larry Wilson

CLASS OF 1979
(July 28, 1979)

Dick Butkus
Yale Lary
Ron Mix
Johnny Unitas*

CLASS OF 1980
(August 2, 1980)

Herb Adderley
David "Deacon" Jones
Bob Lilly
Jim Otto

CLASS OF 1981
(August 1, 1981)

Morris "Red" Badgro*
George Blanda
Willie Davis
Jim Ringo*

CLASS OF 1982
(August 7, 1982)

Doug Atkins
Sam Huff
George Musso*
Merlin Olsen

CLASS OF 1983
(July 30, 1983)

Bobby Bell
Sid Gillman*
Sonny Jurgensen
Bobby Mitchell
Paul Warfield

CLASS OF 1984
(July 28, 1984)

Willie Brown
Mike McCormack
Charley Taylor
Arnie Weinmeister*

CLASS OF 1985
(August 3, 1985)

Frank Gatski*
Joe Namath
Pete Rozelle*
O. J. Simpson
Roger Staubach

CLASS OF 1986
(August 2, 1986)

Paul Hornung
Ken Houston
Willie Lanier
Fran Tarkenton
Doak Walker*

CLASS OF 1987
(August 8, 1987)

Larry Csonka
Len Dawson
Joe Greene
John Henry Johnson
Jim Langer
Don Maynard
Gene Upshaw*

CLASS OF 1988
(July 30, 1988)

Fred Biletnikoff
Mike Ditka
Jack Ham
Alan Page

CLASS OF 1989
(August 5, 1989)

Mel Blount
Terry Bradshaw

Art Shell
Willie Wood

CLASS OF 1990
(August 4, 1990)

Buck Buchanan*
Bob Griese
Franco Harris
Ted Hendricks
Jack Lambert
Tom Landry*
Bob St. Clair

CLASS OF 1991
(July 27, 1991)

Earl Campbell
John Hannah
Stan Jones
Tex Schramm*
Jan Stenerud

CLASS OF 1992
(August 1, 1992)

Lem Barney
Al Davis
John Mackey
John Riggins

CLASS OF 1993
(July 31, 1993)

Dan Fouts
Larry Little
Chuck Noll
Walter Payton*
Bill Walsh*

CLASS OF 1994
(July 30, 1994)

Tony Dorsett
Bud Grant
Jimmy Johnson
Leroy Kelly
Jackie Smith
Randy White

CLASS OF 1995
(July 29, 1995)

Jim Finks*
Henry Jordan*
Steve Largent
Lee Roy Selmon
Kellen Winslow

CLASS OF 1996
(July 27, 1996)

Lou Creekmur
Dan Dierdorf
Joe Gibbs

Charlie Joiner
Mel Renfro

CLASS OF 1997
(July 26, 1997)

Mike Haynes
Wellington Mara*
Don Shula
Mike Webster*

CLASS OF 1998
(August 1, 1998)

Paul Krause
Tommy McDonald
Anthony Muñoz
Mike Singletary
Dwight Stephenson

CLASS OF 1999
(August 7, 1999)

Eric Dickerson
Tom Mack
Ozzie Newsome
Billy Shaw
Lawrence Taylor

CLASS OF 2000
(July 29, 2000)

Howie Long
Ronnie Lott

Joe Montana

Dan Rooney

Dave Wilcox

CLASS OF 2001
(August 4, 2001)

Nick Buoniconti

Marv Levy

Mike Munchak

Jackie Slater

Lynn Swann

Ron Yary

Jack Youngblood

CLASS OF 2002
(August 3, 2002)

George Allen*

Dave Casper

Dan Hampton

Jim Kelly

John Stallworth

CLASS OF 2003
(August 3, 2003)

Marcus Allen

Elvin Bethea

Joe DeLamielleure

James Lofton

Hank Stram*

CLASS OF 2004

(August 8, 2004)

Bob "Boomer" Brown
Carl Eller
John Elway
Barry Sanders

CLASS OF 2005

(August 7, 2005)

Benny Friedman*
Dan Marino
Fritz Pollard*
Steve Young

CLASS OF 2006

(August 6, 2006)

Troy Aikman
Harry Carson
John Madden
Warren Moon
Reggie White*
Rayfield Wright

CLASS OF 2007

(August 4, 2007)

Gene Hickerson*
Michael Irvin
Bruce Matthews
Charlie Sanders
Thurman Thomas
Roger Wehrli

CLASS OF 2008
(August 2, 2008)

Fred Dean
Darrell Green
Art Monk
Emmitt Thomas
Andre Tippett
Gary Zimmerman

ACKNOWLEDGMENTS

If game balls could be awarded, this is where they would go:

CHRIS SCHILLING, PRO FOOTBALL HALL OF FAME COMMUNICATIONS ASSISTANT
The unsung hero of this book.

JOE HORRIGAN, PRO FOOTBALL HALL OF FAME VICE PRESIDENT OF COMMUNICATIONS AND EVENTS
The kindest and smartest guy in the room provided the guidance and reason and transcripts to make this happen.

STEVE PERRY, PRO FOOTBALL HALL OF FAME PRESIDENT/EXECUTIVE DIRECTOR
Without his approval, this project never would have moved forward.

PETER FIERLE, PRO FOOTBALL HALL OF FAME MANAGER—DIGITAL MEDIA/ COMMUNICATIONS
After serving as my first guide in Canton, Fierle served as a second set of eyes for reading the manuscript.

RYAN REBHOLZ, PRO FOOTBALL HALL OF FAME RESEARCH ASSISTANT
Someone had to double- and triple-check the spelling of all the names and the facts from all these years.

SALEEM CHOUDHRY, PRO FOOTBALL HALL OF FAME RESEARCHER

Bringing the names to life, Choudhry gathered the pictures in this book.

SCOTT WAXMAN, LITERARY AGENT

He believed in me before the book even was born.

MAURO DiPRETA, HARPERCOLLINS VICE PRESIDENT AND EXECUTIVE EDITOR

As good an editor as there is, DiPreta has provided the assist from my first book to my last.

JEN SCHULKIND, HARPERCOLLINS ASSISTANT EDITOR

She did all the unheralded but greatly needed work.

LORI J. LEWIS, HARPERCOLLINS COPY EDITOR

She did an all-pro editing job.

ROGER GOODELL, NFL COMMISSIONER

In the middle of madness, Goodell took the time to write the fore-word he did.

PETE ABITANTE, SPECIAL ASSISTANT TO THE COMMISSIONER

Here's hoping Abitante has room on his shelves for one more book.

GREG AIELLO, NFL SENIOR VICE PRESIDENT TO PUBLIC RELATIONS

A superb editor to go along with all the other duties he performs.

GARY GERTZOG, LEAGUE COUNSEL

Gertzog gave the project a push when it was stalling.

DERRICK CRAWFORD, LEAGUE COUNSEL

When permission for the book was requested, Crawford granted it.

Eric Weinberger, NFL Network Executive Producer
Former boss allowed his reporter to report this book.

NFL Network
My former second family.

Michael Irvin, Hall-of-Fame Wide Receiver
The loquacious one delivered an unrehearsed, from-the-heart speech that awakened me from my sleep that night with the idea to compile the book you now hold in your hands.

Mike Haynes, NFL Player Development
And ace recruiter.

The Class of Football
This book can only be as good as the words of the men enshrined in the Pro Football Hall of Fame.